WRITING AND ORALITY

Writing and Orality

Nationality, Culture, and Nineteenth-Century Scottish Fiction

PENNY FIELDING

CLARENDON PRESS · OXFORD
1996

Oxford University Press, Walton Street, Oxford OX2 6DP
Oxford New York
Athens Auckland Bangkok Bombay
Calcutta Cape Town Dar es Salaam Delhi
Florence Hong Kong Istanbul Karachi
Kuala Lumpur Madras Madrid Melbourne
Mexico City Nairobi Paris Singapore
Taipei Tokyo Toronto
and associated companies in
Berlin Ibadan

Oxford is a trade mark of Oxford University Press

Published in the United States
by Oxford University Press Inc., New York

British Library Cataloguing in Publication Data
Data available

Library of Congress Cataloging in Publication Data
Fielding, Penny.
Writing and orality: nationality, culture, and nineteenth-century
Scottish fiction/Penny Fielding.
Includes bibliographical references.
1. Scottish fiction—19th century—History and criticism.
2. Literature and society—Scotland—History—19th century.
3. National characteristics, Scottish, in literature. 4. Language
and culture—Scotland. 5. Oral tradition—Scotland. 6. Scotland—
In literature. I. Title.
PR8601.F54 1996 823'.8099411—dc20 95-49059
ISBN 0-19-812180-6

1 3 5 7 9 10 8 6 4 2

Typeset by Cambrian Typesetters, Frimley, Surrey
Printed in Great Britain
on acid-free paper by
Bookcraft Ltd.
Midsomer Norton, Avon

For my father
JOHN FIELDING
and in memory of my mother
ELIZABETH FIELDING

Acknowledgements

THIS book was substantially written while I was a lecturer at Trinity College Dublin, where the students of my seminars in nineteenth-century fiction kindly allowed me to turn discussions to the topic of speech and writing more often than was strictly necessary. Their own ideas were of great importance to the course of my thinking. My thanks are also due to the staff of Trinity College Library, the Bodleian Library, and the National Library of Scotland for their help with my research. I owe a great debt of gratitude for the particular suggestions as well as the more pervasive intellectual stimulation of a number of colleagues and friends, and thank Pamela Beasant, Thomas Docherty, Aileen Douglas, Fiona Robertson, and Ian Campbell Ross. In the later stages of writing, Ian Duncan's generous encouragement and advice have been of immense value. My most particular thanks are due to Karina Williamson, for continuing to cast her learned eye over my work, and to John Lyon, for putting ideas into my head.

A part of Chapter 3 appeared in a slightly different form in *Studies in Hogg and his World*, 5 (1994), 70–81, and I am grateful to the editor, Gill Hughes, for permission to reproduce this material.

Contents

Textual Note and Abbreviations

Until the arrival of the Edinburgh Editions of the fiction of Scott, Hogg, and Stevenson (which were only beginning to appear at the time of writing) the selection of texts by these writers remains a problem. In general my policy has been to use modern, edited texts where these are available and early editions where they are not. Where there is no modern edition of Scott's novels I have used Andrew Lang's Border Edition. Essays by Stevenson and Lang originally published separately as magazine articles are cited in their first collected editions.

Abbreviations used throughout the text are as follows:

AB	Andrew Lang, *Adventures Among Books* (London: Longman's, Green and Co., 1905).
BB	Andrew Lang, *Books and Bookmen* (London: Longman's, Green and Co., 1887).
BM	*Blackwood's Edinburgh Magazine.*
Border	Border Edition of the *Waverley Novels*, ed. Andrew Lang (24 vols., London: Charles C. Nimmo, 1898–9).
CM	Andrew Lang, *Custom and Myth* (London: Longman's, Green and Co., 1884).
ER	*Edinburgh Review.*
Life	J. G. Lockhart, *Memoirs of the Life of Sir Walter Scott, Bart.* (7 vols., Edinburgh: Robert Cadell, 1837–8).
MP	R. L. Stevenson, *Memories and Portraits* (London: Chatto and Windus, 1887).
MPW	*The Miscellaneous Prose Works of Sir Walter Scott, Bart.*, ed. J. G. Lockhart (30 vols., Edinburgh: Adam and Charles Black, 1869–71).
NLS	National Library of Scotland.
PM	James Hogg, *The Three Perils of Man: War Women and Witchcraft*, ed. Douglas Gifford, 2nd edn. (Edinburgh: Scottish Academic Press, 1989).
PW	*The Poetical Works of Sir Walter Scott, Bart.* 12 vols., (Edinburgh: Robert Cadell, 1833–4).
QR	*Quarterly Review.*
S	Walter Benjamin, 'The Storyteller: Reflections on the Work of Nicolai Leskov', in *Illuminations*, trans. Harry

Zohn, ed. Hannah Arendt (London: Fontana, 1973).

Stories   James Hogg, *Selected Stories and Sketches*, ed. Douglas S. Mack (Edinburgh: Scottish Academic Press, 1982).

Tales   James Hogg, *Tales of Love and Mystery*, ed. David Groves (Edinburgh: Canongate, 1985).

Introduction: Rites of Speech

TOM LEONARD writes:

> this is thi
> six a clock
> news thi
> man said n
> thi reason
> a talk wia
> BBC accent
> iz coz yi
> widny wahnt
> mi ti talk
> aboot thi
> trooth wia
> voice lik
> wanna yoo
> scruff. . . .[1]

This is a written transcription of speech which phonetically 'misrepresents' the speaking voice of the newsreader who in turn appears to be vocalizing a written text. Speech and writing seem to be in contention, but which comes first? Which takes priority? Does Leonard's written text, which emphasizes the phonetic powers of writing, constitute a second-order sign system striving to reproduce the sound of an original speech? Or is it the imagined speaking voice which subverts the original written text of the newsreader? There are no obvious answers to these questions, but one thing is clear: Leonard's poem is drawing attention to speaking and writing as political phenomena. The 'trooth', which is never revealed to us, is less significant than the social registers in which it is to be uttered. Speech has no unique asocial identity but divides into two registers: the 'BBC accent' which we are supposed to trust, and

---

[1] Tom Leonard, from 'Unrelated Incidents', in *Intimate Voices* (Newcastle upon Tyne: Galloping Dog Press, 1984), 88.

the 'scruff' voice which we are not (although the poem itself subverts this distinction).

Leonard was publishing poems dealing with this modern, politicized orality throughout the 1970s, just as universities were beginning to get used to what has now become the most famous analysis of speech and writing in recent decades, Jacques Derrida's *Of Grammatology*.[2] Since the publication of this work we have rightly become wary of the addiction of Western culture to logocentrism's metaphysics of presence. But increasingly we recognize that Derrida's adjustment of Rousseau's impossible political history of speech and writing by drawing both into a broader field of textuality does not, as Leonard reminds us, resolve all political differences between them.[3] Indeed, it may be that the politicization of the speech/writing opposition, far from nostalgically imagining the return of social coherence and uniformity, is a way of exposing and disrupting conservative assumptions about language.[4] In our own century, the politicization of the oral has become a means of re-examining literary and textual histories. This revaluation of orality has come to identify it not with a self-contained community that represents the whole of the people. Rather, it seeks to draw attention to already marginalized groups whose textual experiences have been suppressed by gender repression, or colonialism, or the capitalism of textual production: 'oral history' invades the territories previously reserved for an official, written variety. In Scotland, such strategies have been particularly useful in reviving the oral texts of women. Catherine Kerrigan's collection of Scottish women poets pays particular attention to the women singers who transmitted ballads to more famous male collectors. Kerrigan comments: 'The ballad is a tale told in verse and, given the predominance of

[2] The ways in which phonetic writing, far from attempting to capture the single meaning of speech, can subvert graphocentric authority are explored by a number of modern Scottish writers including James Kelman and Liz Lochhead.

[3] Jacques Derrida, *Of Grammatology*, trans. Gayatri Chakravorty Spivak (Baltimore and London: Johns Hopkins University Press, 1976).

[4] This has been of particular importance for some post-colonial theorists. Edward Kamau Brathwaite, for example, explores nationalist reassertion of Caribbean traditions of song over the enforcement of a colonializing iambic pentametre, concluding that 'one characteristic of the nation language is its orality' (*The History of the Voice: The Development of Nation Language in Anglophone Caribbean Poetry* (London and Port of Spain: New Beacon Books, 1984), 17).

women in the tradition, it is not surprising to find that many of these works recount a whole range of women's experiences.'[5] As my own book will argue, the association of the oral with women and its consequent demotion as a medium would recur ? throughout the nineteenth century in Scotland.

But even here we should hesitate before reintroducing orality as if it were an endangered species whose peculiar qualities must be preserved, for the identification of those qualities can be extremely problematic. If we associate orality too far with a lost authenticity which has been obscured by the mechanisms of print or indeed of modern Western society in general, we are in danger of limiting the political relevance of the oral by consigning it back to the state of nature where it has resided during much of its theoretical history. Only comparatively recently has the old authority of 'folklore' with its oral purity been replaced by a less innocent and less discrete 'popular culture' in which speech and writing interact. The more we examine the relationship between 'orality' and 'writing', the less stable it seems to be, and the less confident we become in deciding quite what these terms signify.

The Uses of Orality

The theories of orality which deconstruction set out to unmask are founded on the premiss that the oral does not need analysis. Rousseau's nostalgia for a lost primitive orality assumes that his readers will recognize what they cannot have experienced because orality itself is a medium for self-evident truths: 'It was easy for the ancients to make themselves understood by people in public. They could speak all day with no discomfort. Generals could address their troops and be understood, with no exhaustion at all.'[6]

An unwillingness to interrogate orality persists. Even in

---

[5] *An Anthology of Scottish Women Poets*, ed. Catherine Kerrigan (Edinburgh, Edinburgh University Press, 1991), 3. For orality as a means of enabling working-class Scottish historiography see *The People's Past*, ed. Edward J. Cowan (Edinburgh: Polygon, 1991).

[6] Jean-Jacques Rousseau, *Essay on the Origin of Languages*, trans. John H. Moran (New York: Frederick Ungar, 1966), 73.

twentieth-century studies of the writing of the nineteenth century, the oral can seem like a resource on which authors could draw to lend a particular, although usually unspecified, flavour to their work. Interpolated narratives are often said to be redolent of 'oral storytelling', characters speak with the voices of 'an oral world' and sometimes with the prose or ballad rhythms of that world. The difficulty with passing references to orality is that they are not always explained, rather relying on the assumption that the oral is always one thing and the nature of its existence always available to everyone. But the self-evident nature of orality is itself based on a paradox: on the one hand, the oral is something every one knows, it is shared experience, communal knowledge, the wisdom of the people. On the other hand, the oral cannot really be known at all because of its habit of vanishing without record into the past. The oral is oddly positioned between the absolute, and the absolutely conditional: the very concept of a 'saying' is of an unchanging general truth, yet the need to locate the oral in a lost or fading past imbues it with fragility and provisionality.

The oral is never simply one thing and what orality signifies in nineteenth-century writing cannot be understood without considering its uses as an agent in the creation and re-creation of cultural norms and values. The oral is always other: of writing (speech), of culture (the voice of nature), of the modern (a pre-modern past). This phenomenon is particularly marked in the nineteenth century, when some traditional foes of orality—urbanization, manufacturing technology, science—dominated that century's sense of its own value systems. In order that orality can be contained and managed, it is usually located elsewhere than in the temporal centre. Orality, it seems, is something more valuable dead than alive: the phrase 'the death of orality' is sometimes popularly used as if entire populations lost the power of speech with the advent of writing, or the printing press, or mass publishing, or industrialization, or literary modernism. In a familiar mode, the nineteenth-century Scottish ballad collector William Motherwell blames the combined agencies of industrialization and the increase of literacy as the cause of the death of oral transmission: 'the changes which, within this half century, the manners and habits of our peasantry and labouring classes, with whom this song has been cherished, have undergone, are inimical to its further preservation.'[7] Orality is often what we use to give the anxieties of our own culture a shape and a focus; it is what we remove from our perceived present in order to make sense of it. Handily, the often mentioned 'death' of orality is an ever-moving point marking off our own present (whenever that might be) from a lost past. So, throughout the nineteenth and twentieth centuries, the oral has become involved with anxieties about urbanization, changes in social and familial structures, the ascendancy of science as the sole arbiter of reality. In the face of these worries, we construct a rural, pastoral oral, handed down from one member of a close-knit family or community to another, which transmits empirical human truths rather than the abstractions of science. But at the same time as we are bemoaning the loss of an oral past, we are putting orality to another use in order to shore up the values of the present. The idealization of orality turns out to be a strategy in which its assumed 'death' is a means for ignoring its survival in marginalized forms. Western culture has tended until very recently to devalue the oral in its own societies (and particularly in the societies of post-colonial cultures) for the reassurance that books and writing are the real art and the oral composition of songs, stories, and histories is not. In this context, Derrida's most important insight into the uses of orality is not the concept that Western culture is phonocentric, but that it is deeply imbued with the sense of writing as *pharmakon*: simultaneously poison and cure.[8] Writing poisons the well of a pure orality that guarantees moral values and authentic experience, but it is also the only means of transmuting that experience into a form acceptable to a literate and socially 'advanced' readership. Indeed, in order to describe the conditions of Scottish writing it may be necessary to rearrange this pattern and to see writing as in some ways primary to the valuation of language in society, and to propose not two kinds of writing, but two kinds of orality: a 'good' variety, which aspires to the security of writing, and a 'bad' version which does not. In

---

[7] William Motherwell, *Minstrelsy: Ancient and Modern* (Glasgow: John Wylie, 1827), p. cii.

[8] For Derrida's analysis of this figure in Plato's *Phaedrus* see his *Dissemination*, trans. Barbara Johnson (London: Athlone Press, 1981).

the earlier part of this study I investigate how the kind of writing that emerges from this formulation is not identical with the self-evident, instinctively recognized 'good writing' which takes such metaphoric forms as 'the book of nature' or 'the word of God'. Scottish writing can become a good in its own right, not one supplemental to speech or dependent on any meaning it may contain, and can be used to construct ideas about identity and origins.

Speaking and/or Writing

It is difficult to reconcile the oral as a modern enabling force that can reinstate the textual experiences of socially repressed cultures with Derrida's insistence that writing, rather than speech, is the representative form of all language. Ruth Finnegan offers an alternative perspective on the history of the oral which identifies it as neither a lost Utopia nor a state of textuality whose signs are no different from those of writing, but as something socially generated and culturally specific: 'Oral communication looks at first sight unproblematic and "natural". But, like literacy, or indeed, computer technology, its use too rests on social and cultural conventions and on a man-made system of communication—in this case the remarkable system of human speech'.[9]

But if orality is a system, is it a different system from writing? Large claims have been made for the socially and psychologically transforming differences between orality and literacy, perhaps the largest of all from Marshall McLuhan: 'Until WRITING was invented, we lived in acoustic space, where all backward peoples still live: boundless, directionless, horizonless.'[10] Although typically inflated here by McLuhan, this dualism has been a very seductive—and often highly profitable—line of inquiry which I explore further in Chapter 6. Since Walter Ong's important and influential study *Orality and Literacy*, we have become accustomed to the idea that 'writing restructures conscious-

---

[9] Ruth Finnegan, *Literacy and Orality: Studies in the Technology of Communication* (Oxford: Blackwell, 1988), 4.

[10] Marshall McLuhan, *Counterblast* (London: Rapp and Whiting, 1970), 13.

ness'.[11] According to this theory, not only are social developments facilitated but also the consciousness of individuals is
modified first by the advent of writing and then by the
development of print technology. In the present book, while
using many of Ong's insights, I reverse the general pattern of his
inquiry, and look not so much at how speech and writing
determine the course of social history, but the other way round,
a view in which speech and writing are less the agents of change
and more its objects.

Twentieth-century anthropological fieldwork into the socialization of orality and literacy has come a long way since
Lévy-Bruhl's conclusion that the 'primitive mind' was irreconcil-
ably different from the civilized variety owing to its inability to
think in terms of logical abstractions.[12] Modern anthropological studies have stressed the ways in which societies with
strong oral traditions use literacy for particular cultural
purposes and in specific social circumstances.[13] It is not so much
writing itself that is influential as its social forms: letters,
invitations, textbooks, and written instructions of various kinds.
Similarly, it may not be literacy alone which alters societies but
the socializing processes of schooling through which literacy is
attained.[14] Writing is thus different from speech in its social
functions rather than in any inherent qualities it may possess or
in any transcendent psychological transformations it may bring
about. My own inquiry is thus not into any substantive
differences between speech and writing but into the ways they
are figured in the textual productions of a particular society:
nineteenth-century Scotland. Scotland offers a particularly
interesting example of the socialization of speech and writing

[11] Walter J. Ong, *Orality and Literacy: The Technologizing of the Word*
(London and New York: Methuen, 1982), chapter heading for pp. 78–116.
[12] Lucien Lévy-Bruhl, *Primitive Mentality*, trans. Lillian A. Clare (New York:
Macmillan, 1923). See also A. R. Luria's experimental analysis of illiterate people in
Uzbekistan in the 1930s: *Cognitive Development: Its Cultural and Social Founda-
tions*, trans. Martin Lopez-Morillas and Lynn Solotaroff, ed. Michael Cole
(Cambridge, Mass.: Harvard University Press, 1976).
[13] For example, Jack Goody's work on West African societies in *The Interface
Between the Written and the Oral* (Cambridge: Cambridge University Press, 1987);
and, particularly influential on my own work, Ruth Finnegan's study of the Pacific
Rim in her *Literacy and Orality*.
[14] See Sylvia Scribner and Michael Cole, *The Psychology of Literacy* (Cambridge,
Mass.: Harvard University Press, 1981).

because each was so important in Scotland's attempts to form a national identity within Britain.

Scottish Orality

The construction of nineteenth-century Scottish orality has its roots in Scotland's attempts to establish a cohesive sense of British nationhood in the second half of the previous century following the collapse of militaristic Scottish nationalism at Culloden in 1746. Speech and writing are powerful tools in the construction of the nation because each can assist in the homogenization of a populace which might otherwise remain disparate in terms of class and language. The eighteenth century with its proliferation of dictionaries, grammars, and writing schools in Britain as a whole saw the establishing of a dominant linguistic competence taught through writing. In turn, the creation of a written standard through schooling and the opening up to the literate of advancement in administrative professions both serve to reinforce a potent myth of middle-class national identity. This general picture is made sharper by the conditions governing Scotland's aspirations to be British. Those Scots who sought to benefit from the social and financial opportunities of Hanoverian Britain were anxious to shake off the stigma of what was commonly seen as a pre-Union feudal past.[15] Such modernization might be brought about in different ways and these are ways which begin already to complicate the formulation of Scottish orality and literacy.

By the second half of the eighteenth century, Scotland, with its distinctive parish school system and great ancient universities, was consolidating a view of the greater availability of Scottish education over its English counterpart which was to last throughout the nineteenth century and beyond. Within Scotland, literacy itself was seen as a passport to the markets and administrative positions of Imperial Britain, and outwith its borders Scotland was already beginning to advertise itself as an

[15] For the reconstruction of Scottish history as British, see Colin Kidd, *Subverting Scotland's Past: Scottish Whig Historians and the Creation of an Anglo-British Identity, 1689–c.1830* (Cambridge: Cambridge University Press, 1993).

unusually literate nation whose educated population had much
to offer Britain. Literacy transforms the lower classes into good
citizens, but, more than this, into citizens who may also be
useful in running British interests abroad. In 1784 a petition for
the relief of parish schoolmasters characterizes Scots as subjects
whose propensity to obey might readily be transformed into an
ability to command:

The common people of North Britain have long possessed a degree of
education, both in morals and in letters, unknown to any other subjects
of the same rank in the British empire; and hence they have been much
employed, and much approved, in the active departments of life
throughout all Europe. The neighbouring nations are all ready to
confess, that no servants are more faithful, sober, honest, and
industrious; no sailors more hardy and resolute; no soldiers more
patient of discipline, or less licentious; and no citizens who know better
both to command and to obey.[16]

For the professional classes the rewards were even greater. The
literacy offered by the parish schools was the foundation for an
education which could lead to opportunities for advancement in
the distinctively Scottish institutions of the university, the
church, and the law. However, the equation of literacy with a
particularly Scottish Britishness could not obliterate anxieties
about Scotland's pre-Union history simply by offering an
alternative point of origin in 1707. Scotland's modern condition
needed to be authenticated by its pre-modern past, yet it was
this very past, devalued by unenlightened feudalism, which
threatened Scotland's modernity in British eyes. Rather than
simply abandoning such a past, Scots like James Macpherson
mythologized it into a romance that could be a more appropriate
precursor for British Scotland.

　　Both the celebrity of the Ossian poems and the arguments
over their provenance characterize the oral as at once a
troublesome site of contested authenticity and a figure of
national origin. Ossianic romance made Scotland famous by
offering a mythic oral source of sensibility, heroism, and poetry
which fed into European Romanticism. But the myth of Ossian
is not as natural or as universal as it might at first appear.

---

[16] 'Memorial for the Parish-schoolmasters in Scotland', *Scots Magazine*, 46
(1784), 1–4 (p. 4).

Macpherson's Celts are as civilized as they are primitive. Admirably warlike, they are also given to holding 'democratical meetings' and, in short, evincing the imperial and civil values of eighteenth-century Britain.[17] In Macpherson's Celtic revival, the voice of the oral past is not Rousseau's pre-social cry of nature but the discourse of an already complex social structure, as Hugh Blair noticed: 'Bards continued to flourish; not as a set of strolling songsters . . . but as an order of men highly respected in the state, and supported by a publick establishment.'[18] Bards, supposedly the bearers of primitive orality, were not in fact the primary voice of nature but embodied the desire of most eighteenth-century poets to be publicly acclaimed and materially supported.

In fact, when the romance of orality is constructed by a dominant ideology it begins to look suspiciously like writing. Northrop Frye makes a distinction between 'naive' romance, expressed in oral and folkloric forms, and its 'sentimental' counterpart, a literary reclamation of those forms.[19] In addition, Jack Goody makes the relevant comment that 'The "myth" is developed in writing while folktales continue to have an oral half-life around the winter hearth'.[20] Despite its marketable orality eighteenth-century Scotland remained a deeply graphocentric society which promoted the sentimental romance at the expense of the naïve. The actual oral tradition in the Highlands was actively discouraged and modern Gaels maligned for their low standards of literacy. It was only when it was rescued by Macpherson's written myth-making that Celtic orality could be redeemed.

[17] This is discussed by Leith Davies, ' "Origins of the Specious": James Macpherson's Ossian and the Forging of the British Empire', *The Eighteenth Century: Theory and Interpretation*, 34 (1993), 132–50. See also David Hill Radcliffe, 'Ossian and the Genus of Culture', *Studies in Romanticism*, 31 (1992), 213–32.

[18] Hugh Blair, *A Critical Dissertation on the Poems of Ossian, the Son of Fingal* (London: T. Becket and P. A. De Hondt, 1763), 13.

[19] Northrop Frye, *The Secular Scripture: A Study of the Structure of the Romance* (Cambridge, Mass.: Harvard University Press, 1976). I am indebted to Ian Duncan's analysis of Frye in *Modern Romance and Transformations of the Novel: The Gothic, Scott, Dickens* (Cambridge: Cambridge University Press, 1992), 6–9. Frye's categorization of romance is also profitably explored, in connection with Scott's *Waverley*, by Judith Wilt in *Secret Leaves: The Novels of Walter Scott* (Chicago: University of Chicago Press, 1985), 18–37.

[20] Goody, *The Interface Between the Written and the Oral*, p. xv.

It is not surprising that Hugh Blair, occupant of the specially created chair of Rhetoric and Belles Lettres at Edinburgh University from 1762 to 1783, should have been such an enthusiastic advocate of the genuineness and value of Macpherson's 'discoveries', as rhetoric, the pinnacle of Scottish literacy, is underpinned by the same constructions of the oral. Robert Crawford describes both the Ossianic texts and Blair's *Lectures on Rhetoric and Belles Lettres* as 'a skilled effort at cultural translation, turning Scottish material of an unacceptable kind into a form acceptable to a new British audience'.[21] Again like the productions of Ossian, rhetoric stands uneasily between two kinds of orality. One of these it is designed to repress and the other it strenuously promotes. The impetus behind the growth of rhetoric as a subject in Scottish universities was a desire to 'correct' Scottish speech—speech being much more likely than writing to betray Scottishness—by making it more English. Yet courses of rhetoric did not dwell on the suppression of an unacceptable orality. Rather, they replaced it with a much more elevated version of the oral—one which could obliterate regional diversity altogether by replacing it with a universal origin.

Rhetoric was an attempt to embody a very broad history of the evolution of language from 'cries of passion', through Greek and Roman orations and histories, leading to modern public speaking in the institutions of church, university and state, and finally improving the study of 'polite' literature. Rhetoric was a history of the voice, taught through speech and authenticated by phonocentric values: language is 'the expression of our ideas by certain sounds, which are used as the signs of those ideas', and is communicated by means of the warmth and feeling of the speaker's expression.[22] This history, however, takes an unexpected turn. In his account of 'The Rise and Progress of Language' in the seventh lecture, Blair sites the universal origin of all speech in natural cries and goes on to pursue the Rousseauist path of associating speech and face-to-face

---

[21] Robert Crawford, *Devolving English Literature* (Oxford: Clarendon Press, 1992), 36.

[22] Hugh Blair, *Lectures on Rhetoric and Belles Lettres* (2 vols., London: W. Strahan and T. Cadell, 1783), i. 98.

communication with political freedom. Yet rather than identifying this freedom in a lost Eden of speech, he happily relocates it
in the commercial values of eighteenth-century Britain: 'Under
arbitrary governments . . . the art of speaking cannot be such an
instrument of ambition, business, and power, as it is in more
democratical states.'[23] Rhetoric then, like Ossianic literature,
authenticates a Scottish state of nature by supplanting an
undesirable feudal past with the orality of 'democratical
states'—an orality which in fact celebrates the civic and
commercial values of eighteenth-century Britain. The valuing of
Scottish orality is already bound up with a set of political
aspirations.

Orality and Ownership

For all his championing of the oral, Blair was eventually obliged
to submit to the greater financial security of the written.
Twenty-four years after he had started to deliver them orally, he
published his *Lectures* because his students had been circulating
unofficial versions among themselves and some of these had
even been 'exposed to public sale'.[24] This episode draws
attention to a phenomenon which was to characterize the way
orality was represented in the late eighteenth and early
nineteenth centuries. Rather than submitting to rumours of its
death, the oral continued to interact with the written, seizing on
chances to market itself. The collaboration of orality with
popular writing—present throughout the eighteenth century in
broadside tales, ballads, and pamphlets—becomes increasingly
important in the next century, as this book will show. Around
the turn of the century, the relationship between orality and
writing focused on questions of texts as property and the social
and financial benefits at stake. As ballad-collecting became
increasingly popular, questions of the origins of orality were
coextensive with questions about its ownership. In his detailed
study of concepts of literary property in the formation of

[23] Blair, *Lectures on Rhetoric and Belles Lettres*, ii. 9.   [24] Ibid., i, p. iii.

Romantic poetry, Peter Murphy identifies an 'older world', influenced by the oral, in which

the written voice is less individualized, more easily conventional, but accusations of theft . . . are rare because such incidents do not appear to qualify as theft. In the modern world the written self may appear to be more capricious and free, but that self is sutured ever closer to the bodily self, since its career generates profits that the bodily self wants, and which culture becomes ever more capable of overseeing and collecting.[25]

Murphy argues that poets like Hogg and Burns exploit a literary market for 'rustic' authenticity and that this gives rise to tensions between the social ambitions associated with print and the apparent spontaneity of the oral. We can also see these tensions at work in the prose fiction of the period. In Hogg's *The Three Perils of Man*, Colley Carrol, variously referred to in the novel as 'the poet' and 'the minstrel', becomes distressed when he cannot reproduce a rendition of his own work. Colley announces that he is going to sing a song which is, on the one hand, common property; he assumes everyone will know it or at least will 'have heard our maidens chaunt it'. On the other hand, this song is also the poet's own personal property; Colley insists that it 'happens to be mine'. The establishing of this authority depends upon the text's becoming fixed, with a stable existence before any particular telling; that is, the text's being written down. Yet because he has decided to perform the song orally, and cannot remember it particularly well, Colley runs into difficulties and confusion: 'I made the thing, and it is impossible I can forget it—I can't comprehend—'.[26] He will settle for neither a literary market nor an oral tradition, insisting on the correct rendition of 'his' song, yet also reaching out for the assistance of the hearers and repeatedly asking his uncomprehending audience if he is getting the verses right.

Colley's anxiety draws attention not only to economic issues of copyright, but also to questions about narration and ownership. At a time when collectors of ballads and tales, notably Scott, were substantially modifying the texts which they

---

[25] Peter T. Murphy, *Poetry as an Occupation and an Art in Britain, 1760–1830* (Cambridge: Cambridge University Press, 1993), 134.
[26] PM 287, and 290.

advertised as a national resource, it becomes important to establish whether a story is common property, or whether its status changes with its transition to print. In Murphy's phrase, can a story be 'stolen' by a collector? This question with its narratological implications for storytelling are explored further in Chapters 2 and 3, but to begin to answer it we need recourse to a theory of storytelling. Narratology offers us a distinction between the deep unchanging structure of a story and the infinite modifications of the discourses of its narrations. It does not, as Wlad Godzich points out, lead us to a reconciliation between the two, however much we might want one. In the case of history, for example, the desire to be able to discriminate between different historical accounts is pushed out of focus by the recognition that history is itself determined by its narration. Godzich leads us instead to Walter Benjamin's essay 'The Storyteller', a text on which I shall draw throughout this book. Benjamin proposes the idea of storytelling as the communication of experience which can be shared between narrator and audience; he does not make a distinction between that lived experience and the experience of its narration. There is no opposition between a detachable story and a narration generated from it. Godzich sums this up very well: 'While the lived experience of the storyteller was, as Benjamin saw, the condition of his or her authority, the efficacy of the telling lay in the fact that it articulated learnable modes of endowing experience with meaningfulness.'[27]

Benjamin starts off his essay with the comment that the practice of storytelling is dying out and becoming replaced with a culture of information. Although he gives as one example the effects of the 1914–18 war in which the experience of the 'tiny fragile human body' is overwritten by mechanical warfare and cannot afterwards be communicated, he refuses to see the decline of storytelling as a symptom of modernity. In place of this Benjamin takes a broader historical perspective which resists the idea of the sudden death of orality. On the one hand, Benjamin sees shifts in textual practice as symptomatic of our lack of familiarity with storytelling: 'The novelist has isolated

[27] Wlad Godzich, *The Culture of Literacy* (Cambridge, Mass.: Harvard University Press, 1994), 102.

himself. The birthplace of the novel is the solitary individual, who is no longer able to express himself by giving examples of his most important concerns.'[28] Yet Benjamin does not thereby pronounce the absolute death of storytelling—his essay is after all about the storytelling writer Nikolai Leskov and he cites other examples: Hauff, Poe, and Stevenson. There are many other such instances in nineteenth-century fiction. Peter Brooks has identified in the works of Maupassant 'an urban literature, self-consciously a commodity in a marketplace, which nonetheless returns again and again to fictive situations of oral communication'.[29] It is just this condition that we find in nineteenth-century Scottish literature, in which a sense of the difficulties of entering into the oral word is counterbalanced by the possibilities of modifying oral transmission for print circulation. Francis Hart has aptly commented that 'the unusual strength of an oral storytelling tradition in Scottish culture must have been both an obstacle and a challenge to the formal development of the novel' and this book analyses such challenges with special emphasis in Chapter 4.[30]

Rites of Speech

In trying to explain the oral I come up myself against the problem of its complex and elusive existence. Although the speech/writing opposition is fundamental to Western culture's belief in itself, such an opposition is not a very stable one, and, despite its importance to a whole range of concerns, it is certainly not very consistent in its appearances in each of them. Orality is a concept that enters a great number of fields, and nineteenth-century Scottish fiction follows it into most of them, opening up questions about history, folklore, anthropology, and psychology, as well as about narrative theory and linguistics. The sum of these parts I have attempted to represent

---

[28] S 84, 87.
[29] Peter Brooks, 'The Tale vs. The Novel', in *Why the Novel Matters: A Postmodern Perplex*, ed. Mark Spilka and Caroline McCracken-Flesher (1977; repr. Bloomington and Indianapolis: Indiana University Press, 1990), 303–10.
[30] Francis Russell Hart, *The Scottish Novel: From Smollett to Spark* (Cambridge, Mass.: Harvard University Press, 1978), 2.

in the idea of rites of speech, a figure which may usefully bring together the strands of these introductory remarks.

The rites of speech are the ways in which a society uses orality to organize its cultural and aesthetic experiences. That is to say, the oral is identified both with a way of telling stories (in the most general sense of the word), and with particular kinds of narrator and audience, organized according to gender and class, as well as underpinning aesthetic judgements. Scotland in the nineteenth century was a country in which the oral remained a prominent tool in this cultural management, but equally, it was a society in which the evaluation of the oral passed through some rapid changes: changes in education and patterns of literacy which led to a revaluation of the oral and its bifurcation. The social pressures exerted on speech and writing render them unable to sustain any straightforward binary opposition. Rather, they fall into an unstable duality each part of which is continually dividing into authentic and debased versions of itself.

Speech itself comes into being as an identifiable cultural phenomenon only when it becomes established as something different from writing, and when writing becomes a position from which to discuss and to characterize the oral. Thus the rites of speech are, in a self-consciously literary society like nineteenth-century Scotland, also the writing of speech. Writing is the dominant order which administers the ways orality is apportioned into its good and bad varieties, and attempts the control of the result. And so the rites of speech are also the rights of speech, raising political questions about the self-determination of classes in a period much concerned about the definition of civic life. In the negotiations of the relative positions of literacy and orality, speech behaves as writing's object, requiring it constantly to find new means of describing the oral. Because it can never be signified by a single definition, orality is constantly passing from one social signification to another, a currency in which differing social evaluations can be invested. The varying uses to which the oral is put under changing historical conditions are surveyed in Chapters 1 and 5, introducing the two parts of the book which is divided approximately according to the two halves of the century.

For a culture which retains vestiges of an oral past, the phrase

'rites of speech' is imbued with an additional meaning. Kristeva
has written of the rite as 'an abreaction of the pre-sign
impact . . . It is thus that one can underpin anthropologists'
definitions, according to which rites are *acts* rather than
symbols. In other words, rites would not be limited to their
signifying dimension, they would also have a material, active,
translinguistic, magical impact.'[31] In Scottish literature of the
period, the association of some kinds of language with a magical
collapsing of sign and signifier into each other, as in spells or
ritual utterances, is a frequent occurrence. This will be a
recurring theme throughout this book, and is given particular
attention in Chapters 2 and 3, where I explore the ways in which
'magic language'—active rather than descriptive—could be a
potent metaphor for the Scottish writer.

Speech is also a rite which complicates the requirements of
symbolism in another sense. The last quarter of the nineteenth
century saw the emergence of the sign as an object of scientific
scrutiny first in the anthropological obsession with the totem as
a sign of social groupings, and then with the beginnings of
psychoanalysis. The earlier associations of the oral with the
primitive in accounts of the origins and progress of language or
in heroic romance now take on new significances in Scotland
whose interest in anthropology leads into Freudian psychoanalysis. In fact, it is notable how many of the sources Freud
draws on in *Totem and Taboo*—McLennan, Frazer, and Lang—
were Scots. If the speech/writing opposition is recast in the terms
of psychoanalysis, the visual sign (writing or the phallus)
becomes associated with the creation of the conscious while the
oral is repressed into the unconscious and is unable to bear
the same symbolic function as writing. Adapting Walter Ong's
comment that 'writing restructures consciousness', we might
conclude that writing as visual language is what structures
consciousness in the first place. But here again the social
pressures on orality cannot sustain a stable binary construction.
Throughout the second half of this book, I explore how
Stevenson creates a new kind of oral romance as orality becomes
once again bifurcated, this time into a 'healthy' version suitable

---

[31] Julia Kristeva, *Powers of Horror: An Essay on Abjection*, trans. Leon S.
Roudiez (New York: Columbia University Press, 1982), 73–4.

for adventure stories, and its repressed Other, the territory of the unconscious which lurks beneath the 'novel of incident'.

Finally, this unstable orality that refuses to act as the Other against which writing defines itself reminds us that the association of the visible with signification presupposes a patriarchal norm for writing which has been much challenged in twentieth-century feminist theory. Margaret Homans has written of the predicament of the woman writer in a culture where women are associated not with the symbolic but with the literal: 'women writers and their women characters dramatize at once the way in which the relation of women as women to symbolic language is continually in jeopardy and the hope that the father's law might cease to be the exclusive language of literary culture.'[32] In Chapters 5 and 8 I explore the work of a Scottish woman writer, Margaret Oliphant, who takes the traditionally debased mode of the female oral, and constructs a new, and experimentally feminist, orality for the later nineteenth century as the rites of speech start to become rites of passage.

[32] Margaret Homans, *Bearing the Word: Language and Female Experience in Nineteenth-Century Women's Writing* (Chicago and London: University of Chicago Press, 1986), 33.

I

'Mere Reading': Literacy and Orality 1800–1850

W H E N, in *Wuthering Heights*, Lockwood defends himself from Cathy's terrifyingly oral ghost by piling up books against the broken window, he is enacting an episode of special importance to the construction of social morality in the nineteenth century. The book was a weapon in the fight against a whole set of perils which came to be linked with an orality that was irrational, violent, socially disruptive, female. When the second Cathy teaches Hareton Earnshaw to read she redeems his (and retrospectively her own mother's) socially unacceptable habit of throwing books away and makes him worthy of inheriting the middle-class, domestic sphere which, it is hinted, Wuthering Heights is to become. Like Brontë's nineteenth-century Yorkshire, Lowland Scotland's transition to an industrialized society seized upon the book as the sign of social acceptability.[1] Indeed in Scotland, in which literacy was carefully guarded as a measure of national importance, the significance of the books in *Wuthering Heights* are thrown into even sharper focus.

Scotland's construction of a national identity in the nineteenth century is inextricably bound up in the means of its own transmission. Before we can begin to unravel the complex narratives that make up the stories of a country that was constantly redefining its own internal borders and divisions, its relationship with England, its place within Britain and in Europe, we need to give some attention to the forms out of which such narratives were constructed. More particularly, it is important to understand how the control of these forms—at their most fundamental level of speech and writing—is governed

[1] Northern England and Lowland Scotland are often taken as a geographical unit in studies of literacy and education in this period. See R. A. Houston, *Scottish Literacy and the Scottish Identity: Illiteracy and Society in Scotland and Northern England, 1600–1800* (Cambridge: Cambridge University Press, 1985).

by the ideological construction of their value. Scottish culture famously offers two great achievements or assets: first, an unusually (within Europe) early success in popular literacy and sophisticated, intellectually pioneering universities; and secondly, the preservation of an oral tradition in the ballads especially of the Borders and the North-East and even the persistence of a Gaelic oral tradition. Yet the coexistence of these two cultural strands is always subject to more divisive historical circumstances which attempt to establish clear differences between speech and writing.

In nineteenth-century Scotland, orality and literacy pass through a complex and often paradoxical set of relationships in which they are each used in turn both as scapegoats for perceived social problems, and as ways of curing or at least staving off threats to what was to become a dominant Victorian ideology. In the perspective of nineteenth-century Scottish culture, orality and literacy have no stable identities, yet they continually and provocatively recur as notional states which can act as the bearers of a number of different ideological assumptions. Throughout the nineteenth century, Scotland continued to see both orality and literacy as important elements of its own social identity, but exactly what each signified was much less decided; literacy became a currency through which social criteria could be measured, but whose values were in a state of continual adjustment and revision.

Compared with the crisis of literacy in the early nineteenth century, the eighteenth century seemed, and was certainly looked back on as, a period of comparative stability in which speech and writing could coexist, interact, and make themselves available as means of expression across society. The work of Burns, probably the best-known eighteenth-century Scottish writer within and outwith Scotland, happily enacts the interchanges between speech and writing on which much eighteenth-century popular culture depends as it resists any attempt to apportion orality and literacy into what R. A. Houston has called 'separate cultural compartments'.[2]

---

[2] Houston, *Scottish Literacy*, 199. Houston's chapter on 'Oral Culture and Literate Culture', pp. 193–210, sets out popular uses of speech and writing in greater detail. See also Patricia Anderson, *The Printed Image and the Transformation of Popular Culture 1790–1860* (Oxford: Clarendon Press, 1991).

Burns's poems both drew on oral sources and fed back into them, using print as a provisional, rather than a finite resting point for texts.[3] The oral and the written had been juxtaposed and intermingled in popular culture throughout the eighteenth century in Britain. David Vincent characterizes a common state of affairs:

Just as a purchased item of clothing would extend rather than displace an existing wardrobe, so a ballad or chapbook would feed into rather than expel the established repertoire of songs and verses. The labouring poor could not afford the luxury of counterposing the oral and the written in the way of subsequent folklorists.[4]

Yet this earlier period was not without its own anxieties about the role of spoken language in the establishing of a Scottish identity. The importance of rhetoric in the universities was underpinned by an awareness that speaking, rather than writing, was more likely to betray an unwanted provincialism. Opinions such as John Home's that 'Eloquence in the Art of speaking is more necessary for a Scotchman than any body else as he lies under some disadvantages which Art must remove'[5] lead to the notorious attempts of prominent eighteenth-century Scots to purge their language of Scotticisms, which were more easily suppressed in writing than in speech. On the other hand, once free from its socially stigmatizing qualities, an idealized orality was a powerful mark of subjectivity: 'spoken Language

---

[3] On this phenomenon see John Strawhorn, 'Burns and the Bardie Clan', *Scottish Literary Journal*, 8/2 (1981), 5–23; and Mary Ellen Brown, *Burns and Tradition* (Urbana and Chicago: University of Illinois Press, 1984).

[4] David Vincent, *Literacy and Popular Culture, England 1750–1914* (Cambridge: Cambridge University Press, 1989), 198. The transitions between oral and written forms are also discussed in Ruth Finnegan's *Oral Poetry: Its Nature, Significance and Social Context*, 2nd edn. (1977; repr. Bloomington and Indianapolis: Indiana University Press, 1992), 160–8.

[5] Quoted in Richard B. Sher, *Church and University in the Scottish Enlightenment: The Moderate Literati of Edinburgh* (Edinburgh: Edinburgh University Press, 1985), 108. On the suppression of Scotticisms see David Daiches, *Literature and Gentility in Scotland* (Edinburgh: Edinburgh University Press, 1982); and James G. Basker, 'Scotticisms and the Problem of Cultural Identity in Eighteenth-Century Britain', in *Sociability and Society in Eighteenth-Century Scotland*, ed. John Dwyer and Richard B. Sher (Edinburgh: Mercat Press, 1993), 81–95. For the continuing use of Scots in nineteenth-century fiction see Emma Letley's comprehensive *From John Galt to Douglas Brown: Nineteenth-Century Fiction and Scots Language* (Edinburgh: Scottish Academic Press, 1988).

has a great superiority over written Language, in point of energy or force. The voice of the living Speaker, makes an impression on the mind much stronger than can be made by the perusal of any Writing.'[6]

Thus as Scotland continued to negotiate a place in the Union during the eighteenth century, we witness the growth of a phenomenon which was strongly to characterize the nineteenth: the bifurcation of orality into an acclaimed ideal and a disparaged social condition. The representations of the oral along these lines will be the subject of my next chapter; here I want to explore further the status of literacy in nineteenth-century Scotland. By the end of the previous century, literacy was becoming recognized, in England as well as in Scotland, as a way of establishing national character. Southey, writing in a *Quarterly Review* of 1811, argues that having won recognition as a military power, England should introduce a national system of education in order to 'make our prosperity at home keep pace with our reputation abroad'. Throughout the nineteenth century, the education debates in England were, at least in some respects, to look to Scotland as a model, and here Southey claims that 'A national establishment of parochial schools has rendered Scotland the most orderly and moral country in Europe: before that establishment was instituted, it was well nigh the most barbarous. Why should not this blessing be extended to England?'[7]

The political and social disruptions that occurred in Britain as a whole in this period were felt particularly acutely in Scotland as, to many Scots, both radical politics and industrialization constituted alarming challenges to the image of a largely rural and socially stable country. Comments that the Scots were an unusually morally sound and socially well-behaved people began to be interspersed with darker warnings that they had better stay that way. Southey's approval was qualified in another article by an implicit suggestion of what might be at stake if the Scots were to lose the civilizing influences of

---

[6] Hugh Blair, *Lectures on Rhetoric and Belles Lettres* (2 vols., London: W. Strahan and T. Cadell, 1783), i. 136.

[7] [Robert Southey], review of 'Bell and Lancaster's Systems of Education', *QR* 6 (1811), 264–304 (pp. 304 and 302).

education and religion. Ireland could always be pressed into service as Scotland's *doppelgänger*: a sinister double reflecting the savagery underneath Scotland's civilization. Twelve years after the Irish rebellion of 1798 Southey comments: 'Let those who doubt the efficacy of education and religion look at what Scotland is, and recollect what it was two centuries ago. At present the Scotch are beyond all doubt, a peaceable, orderly, and moral nation; two centuries ago they were as turbulent, ferocious, and brutal as the wild Irish are now.'[8]

Even more discomforting for Scottish educationalists was the suspicion that wild Irishness lay within their own borders. The attempts of the Society in Scotland for Propagating Christian Knowledge to educate the largely oral Highland population had been directed against the Gaelic language, or, as it was frequently called, 'Irish'. The image of 'savage', illiterate Highlanders helped to reinforce the connection between orality and immorality as the SSPCK pursued their goal of teaching through the English language in order to 'wear out' Gaelic.

At a time when literacy was the mark of social respectability, the oral was undergoing some changes in the way it was configured in writing of the period. Anxiety about the behaviour of a 'peasant' culture led to a splitting of the image of the oral into a romanticized and idealized form and a demotion of the status of popular orality to a concept to be called 'illiteracy'. The importance of literacy to Scottish society was felt particularly keenly by evangelical social reformers for whom education was a means of ordering social behaviour. Notable among these evangelical philanthropists and instigators of popular education were Henry Duncan, Thomas Chalmers, Thomas Dick, and George Miller. Between them, these men attempted to control the circulation of reading matter: they founded local libraries, edited popular magazines, and published books, both of natural

---

[8] [Robert Southey], review of 'Landt's Description of the Feroe Islands', *QR* 4 (1810), 333–42 (p. 342). For representations of Gaelic in the valuation of orality and literacy in this period, see Lucinda Cole and Richard G. Swartz, ' "Why Should I Wish for Words?": Literacy, Articulation, and the Borders of Literary Culture', in *At the Limits of Romanticism: Essays in Cultural, Feminist, and Materialist Criticism*, ed. Mary A. Favret and Nicola J. Watson (Bloomington and Indianapolis: Indiana University Press, 1994), 143–69.

theology and of fiction, with the aim of ensuring a stable and moral working class.[9]

Illiteracy was a menacing presence in society, and persons formerly and uncontroversially associated with orality were now tainted with the social dangers of illiteracy, the latter being now thought of as being as much a social state as one having anything to do with the condition of being able to read or write. Particularly notorious among such social groupings were ballad-singers and ballad-sellers; even David Stow, a progressive Glasgow educationalist who advocated the use of oral inter-change between teachers and schoolchildren, recognized the low status of ballad-singers. In his review of those Glaswegians most in need of education, he identifies as the very bottom class 'ballad-singers, sand and match sellers, thieves and pickpockets'.[10] Children and their mothers, traditionally seen in terms of storytelling and oral exchange, were also suspect, as, increasingly, were servants who might threaten the literary education of young people by corrupting them with oral tales. In the improving literature of the early nineteenth century, such dangerously corrupt servants were becoming more common than the loyal, feudal, though often conspicuously antiquated, servants of Scott's fiction.

In one way of configuring these social tensions, books become a bastion of class stability, fending off the dangerous forces of orality. The representative role of the book, together with its supporting cast of servants and families, is clearly present in a little cautionary tale published in George Miller's *Monthly Monitor and Philanthropic Museum* of March 1815. The *Monthly Monitor* was subtitled as a 'cheap repository for hints, suggestions, facts, and discoveries, interesting to humanity; and for papers of every description, having a tendency to prevent the commissions of crimes, counteract the baneful effects of

[9] See J. V. Smith's highly informative 'Manners, Morals and Mentalities: Reflections of the Popular Enlightenment of Early Nineteenth-Century Scotland', in *Scottish Culture and Scottish Education 1800–1980*, ed. Walter M. Humes and Hamish M. Paterson (Edinburgh: John Donald, 1983), 25–54.

[10] David Stow, *Moral Training* (1834). Quoted in Laurance James Saunders, *Scottish Democracy 1815–1840: The Social and Intellectual Background* (Edinburgh and London: Oliver and Boyd, 1950), 279.

pernicious sentiments and bad example; encourage a spirit of industry, economy, and frugality among the middling and laborious classes', and it duly sets up an opposition between illiteracy as tantamount to 'the commissions of crimes', and literacy as representing the 'spirit of industry'. The third number, for March 1815, features a story which is to expose 'errors in the education of the lower orders, a fatal cause of corruption and misery to the higher'. The entire social structure, maintains the argument, depends on the correct behaviour of those notorious bearers of a dangerous orality: servants, and especially female servants:

Not only are children in a great degree modelled by the domestics of their parents, but in every stage of early life the influence of attendants may lead to important consequences. The education of the humblest plebeian materially affects the patrician orders, since the poor peasant's offspring act as menials to the farmer, or tradesman, whose sons and daughters imbibe, from the homely drudge, the notions and habits that govern them as members of a splendid establishment.[11]

The story is a parable about good reading and its sinister opposite. Mr Wilkins, in order to pursue his employment as steward to Squire Ellingford, habitually leaves his first wife in charge of the farm, household, and children. The first Mrs Wilkins is a model of the moral behaviour thought appropriate to support the family's domestic economic structure: 'As a wife, her affectionate mildness and judicious firmness, moderated the angry passions of her husband; and the presiding spirit of order, diligence, neatness, and oeconomy, ensured his comfort and prosperity', and she passes on to her family these 'principles of piety, rectitude, and contented industry' (p. 122). After the death of his first wife, Mr Wilkins marries Kitty Hobson who proceeds to spend his money without evincing much of the spirit of contented industry. In an attempt to stem this lamentable financial/moral decline, Mr Wilkins resorts to a stagey demonstration of the bookcase as the symbol of the

---

[11] 'Errors in the Education of the Lower Orders, a Fatal Cause of Corruption and Misery to the Higher', *Monthly Monitor and Philanthropic Museum*, 1 (1815), 121–30 (p. 121). The story is signed 'Th. N. R.'. Further references appear in the text.

only way in which their union can be deemed successful: 'Mr. Wilkins opened a well-filled book-case. "You have a key for this repository, Kitty," says he, "and I have another" ' (p. 125). The symbolic force of the bookcase for which the married couple both have keys is then constructed by Mr Wilkins as epitomizing all the virtues which the reader already knows his first wife to have possessed:

When I was from home, and the little folks asleep, if my wife perceived her spirits flag, she doubled her diligence to finish her needle work or bustling, and then she soothed, or cheered her mind, with one of these ever-ready companions. When some of the boys, or girls, were old enough to sit up at work, she read to them; and to this hour they own the benefits derived from early laying up a store of beneficial information. (p. 125)

Wilkins encourages Kitty to instruct her own daughter, Cecilia, but Kitty refuses and Cecilia receives only 'a smattering of shewy acquirements' (p. 126). She is sent to live with the widow of the squire at the hall where 'the young squire and his companions, with many bachelors of maturer age, were inmates' (p. 126). Here she is 'disgraced' and then spirited off to London. After her father's death, Cecilia is employed as a maid but corrupts the family of Lady Maria B. by arranging 'a criminal engagement' for Lady B. and 'unhappy wedlock' for Lady B.'s nieces (p. 128). She then embarks upon the familiar parabolic life of dissolution and sexual disgrace reserved for transgressing women in both eighteenth- and nineteenth-century texts, leading to prostitution, and eventually death, 'a prey to the most loathsome disease'. On her death-bed she confesses all to Lord K.:

Oh! Lord K. it is in the interest of the greatest in the land to see that the meanest has good instruction in youth, and good books to keep up those impressions through life. Some harmless entertainment for the moments they spend in idle or bad discourse, or reading obscene ballads and wicked stories, might save their betters from much grief and disgrace. (p. 129)

The death-bed spectacle, a dramatic focal-point inviting comparison with the earlier bookcase scene, draws together and emblematizes the elements of the story, and reinforces a series of associations that leads servants from exposure to 'obscene ballads' to the inevitable degraded, syphilitic end. It is notable in this story that it is the book *itself* that is held up—particularly in Wilkins's grand gesture to the bookcase—as a barricade against such dissolution. Certain kinds of books had been seen as dangerous for women throughout the eighteenth century, but in the face of changing attitudes to illiteracy almost any kind of book comes to be seen as better than nothing. This does not mean that books did cease to be policed for their moral contents, but rather that attitudes to texts were contained within an overarching structure that set literacy against illiteracy.

The campaign against illiteracy had a retrospective influence on the characterization of orality, which, unless it escaped the corrupting touch of illiteracy by being sentimentalized, was identified as a subversive social force. This latter phenomenon finds its way into a number of Scott's novels during his long, complex, and often ambivalent relationship with the oral. Scott frequently returns to the connections made between orality and illegitimacy. A number of characters are audibly identified with orality, being marked out by it at their first appearance within novels: Meg Merrilies, Madge Wildfire, and Effie Deans are all heard singing ballads before they are seen in their respective novels, and Norna in *The Pirate* engages in long performances of 'ancient Northern poetry'.[12] The oral is an uncertain territory in the Waverley Novels. It is the source of unofficial power and an important repository of personal and historical memory, yet it either remains on the margins of, or is sacrificed to, a more dominant authority. Characters associated with orality move in and out of novels, exercising powers often outside the law yet usually ending up dead, or exiled from a social order which cannot contain them. The oral, as the territory of the irrational and the illegitimate, is frequently associated with the dangerously female. Oral women question the assumption that the oral is natural; they are either 'unnatural' (Meg and Madge are described as unusually tall and with masculine features), or too natural (Effie is an illegitimate mother). Such women threaten the social law and the laws of family relationships: Effie is suspected of infanticide, Madge Wildfire is implicated

---

[12] *The Pirate*, Border, 86.

in infanticide, and Norna suspects herself of involuntary parricide.[13]

Effie's first appearance in *The Heart of Midlothian* marks a confrontation between the authority of the book—here itself under question—and the challenge of the oral: her first words are from a ballad, but she is at once silenced by Jeanie on the grounds that 'our father's coming out of the byre',[14] a reminder of David Deans's intransigent insistence on biblical authority. Effie strikes back:

'And Dominie Butler—Does he come to see our father, that's so taen wi' his Latin words?' said Effie, delighted to find that, by carrying the war into the enemy's country, she could divert the threatened attack upon herself, and with the petulance of youth she pursued her triumph over her prudent elder sister. She looked at her with a sly air, in which there was something like irony, as she chanted, in a low but marked tone, a scrap of an old Scotch song. (p. 99)

The sibling rivalry is underpinned by a confrontation between the world of books occupied by 'Dominie' Reuben Butler and David Deans, and a 'sly', articulation of the oral which survives in a repressed but subversive form.

Guy Mannering similarly explores the opposition between the book as an absolute cultural symbol and the dangerous realm of orality. In his second novel, Scott, always interested in the social status of physical texts, exposes the legalistic and social authority with which they can become invested. The main representative of the oral in the novel is Meg Merrilies, another of Scott's female characters whose power is both drawn from and limited by orality. Meg is conspicuously illiterate—she points out 'I canna write myself'[15]—yet on her memory depends the whole unravelling of the plot, and the consequent restoration of the Bertrams' social and political interests, as she reveals

---

[13] For Madge Wildfire as an oral woman and other power structures within the novel, see Carol Anderson, 'The Power of Naming: Language, Identity and Betrayal in *The Heart of Midlothian*', in *Scott in Carnival*, ed. J. H. Alexander and David Hewitt (Aberdeen: Association for Scottish Literary Studies, 1993), 189–201. On Meg Merrilies's orality in *Guy Mannering* as an 'oral counter-sublime', see Jan B. Gordon, ' "Liquidating the Sublime": Gossip in Scott's Novels', in *At the Limits of Romanticism*, ed. Favret and Watson, 246–68.

[14] *The Heart of Midlothian*, ed. Claire Lamont (Oxford: Oxford University Press, 1982), 98.

[15] *Guy Mannering*, Border, 467. Further references appear in the text.

the identity of the missing heir, Harry Bertram. Put in another way, the novel, itself a written text, cannot function without her. Her orality represents an alternative power which cannot be confined in writing. Significantly, the reader is shown Mannering 'in vain attempting to make himself master of the exact words of her song' (p. 36), yet Meg, the exponent of a female oral power, cannot quite be 'mastered' by the masculine-sounding Mannering. However, what cannot be mastered can nevertheless be written out and the orality with which Meg is associated is opposed by the representatives of literacy: Dominie Sampson and Mr Pleydell. Both Sampson and Pleydell are closely associated with books, indeed so close is Sampson's identification with them that it is not long before he is described *as* a book: Mannering 'could have recourse to the Dominie as to a dictionary' (p. 339). Pleydell, similarly, is seen in his natural habitat in a library 'surrounded with books' which he describes as 'my tools of trade' (p. 361). Sampson and Pleydell, the denizens of libraries, share an investment in the authority of literacy, against which Meg's power is pitched.

Meg is conspicuously outside the law, as gypsies are 'almost infamous in the eye of the law, scarce capable of bearing evidence' (p. 541). She is also, in Sampson's view, outside moral and social codes being, according to him, 'Harlot, thief, witch and gypsy'. Despite Meg's importance in the restoration of a social order, she remains on its margins, whereas both Sampson and the sign of his authority are absorbed into the Bertram inheritance as his library and Sampson's adjoining apartment are conspicuously inscribed into the plans for the new New Place of Ellangowan. Having gone to extreme lengths to give her unofficial evidence, Meg is killed, but not without resorting to what is, for her, the desperate measure of writing, using an amanuensis to write a letter setting up the final recognition scene and the bookish Sampson to deliver it. Meg's opposition to the order of literacy ends as she is transformed at her death into a loyal servant, whereas Sampson, for all his decayed appearance, is absorbed into the New Place.[16]

---

[16] The stages leading up to this writing out of Meg's voice are traced by Ian Duncan, *Modern Romance and Transformations of the Novel: The Gothic, Scott, Dickens* (Cambridge: Cambridge University Press, 1992), 111–35.

Scott's oral women are both representative of a dying traditional rural society, and touched by a newer attitude to the oral which had its main focus in the towns and cities during the rapid urbanization and industrialization of the Lowlands in the nineteenth century. The demographic changes that accompanied the industrialization of Lowland Scotland had an enormous effect on the education system.[17] With the population shift to the city, the parochial system, with a school funded by local taxation in each parish, became less representative of Scottish education. The burgh schools in the towns and cities, ostensibly the equivalent of the parochial schools, were generally under the control not of the Church but of town councils which were unable to provide—or unwilling to finance—education for all.

The urbanization of Lowland Scotland was felt to challenge directly the traditional moral values of Scottish education; George Lewis wrote in his influential pamphlet *Scotland a Half-Educated Nation*: 'we look in vain, in the large towns of Scotland, for those kindly feelings between all classes, which arose in the parish schools of Scotland, and were cherished in her parish churches, sweetening the intercourse, and strengthening the bands, of society.'[18] And to Scotland's admirers, like J. S. Mill, the enviable qualities of Scottish education were becoming eroded by population expansion in the towns:

To know what our schools may do, we have but to think of what our Scottish Parochial Schools have formerly done. The progress of wealth and population has outgrown the machinery of these schools, and, in the towns especially, they no longer produce their full fruits: but what do not the peasantry of Scotland owe to them?[19]

---

[17] For the complicated relationship between literacy and industrialization in Britain see Jenny Cook-Gumperz, 'Literacy and Schooling: An Unchanging Equation?', in *The Social Construction of Literacy*, ed. Jenny Cook-Gumperz (London: Cambridge University Press, 1986), 16–44.

[18] [George Lewis], *Scotland A Half-Educated Nation Both in the Quantity and Quality of her Educational Institutions* (Glasgow: William Collins, 1834), 43. For the representative value of Lewis's pamphlet in Scottish society, see Donald J. Witherington, ' "Scotland a Half-Educated Nation" in 1834? Reliable Critique or Persuasive Polemic?', *Scottish Culture and Scottish Education*, ed. Humes and Paterson, 55–74.

[19] [J. S. Mill], 'The Claims of Labour: An Essay on the Duties of Employers to the Employed', *ER* 81 (1845), 498–525 (p. 511).

Scottish educationalists began to construct a Golden Age in which popular orality had been contained with a rural parish structure overseen by the local landowner (who was obliged to contribute financially to parish education) and the clergy. Urban orality, however, was a much more threatening concept which, perhaps because it was seen as being so difficult to contain, was also harder to define. The full title of Henry Duncan's *The Young South Country Weaver, or A Journey to Glasgow: A Tale for the Radicals* sums up significant elements in the history and construction of urban orality. Following the collapse of weaving prices, the social structures centred on the weaving trade began to break up, many rural-based hand-loom weavers sought employment in the cities, and the system of training in weaving-shops was abandoned. In its place, the more casual employment of younger girls and boys further curtailed the provision of education to the population as a whole.[20] Scottish cities, with their burgeoning and increasingly uneducated inhabitants, were thus seen as extremely dangerous places in the early decades of the nineteenth century when the British government was particularly nervous about any kind of radicalism and about Jacobinism in particular. Duncan's story is a cautionary tale for weavers who had a history of radical action in the early years of the nineteenth century culminating in the strike of 1812 which was broken by the arrest, trial, and imprisonment of the leaders of the strike committee the following February. It was during this strike that 'combination', the gathering of workers for political protest and thus the site of a radical orality, was criminalized in Scottish Law.[21]

In Duncan's tale, the professionally named William Webster leaves Dumfriesshire for Glasgow, taking with him a talismanic Bible donated by the local minister who hopes that 'the poisonous plant of infidelity cannot take deep root in the soil of Scotland'.[22] Such proves not to be the case, as William quickly encounters all kinds of dissent in his uncle's home in Glasgow.

---

[20] See Saunders, *Scottish Democracy 1815–1840*, 270.

[21] See T. C. Smout, *A History of the Scottish People 1560–1830* (London: Collins, 1969), 420–30.

[22] Henry Duncan, *The Young South Country Weaver; or, A Journey to Glasgow: A Tale for the Radicals*, 2nd edn. (Edinburgh: Waugh and Innes, 1821), 11. Further references appear in the text.

The uncle, a radical, complains about the state of the country but William counters with a speech in praise of the merits of literacy:

And then as to our parish schools! Where will ye find ony thing like them in a' the world? Masters paid by law for instructing the poor!— So that the blessing which our good auld king wished for all his subjects, has long been granted to the lowlands o' Scotland,—that there should-na be ane in the land that couldna *read his Bible*. My father is a loyal subject, and his heart aye warms when he thinks o' this wish, sae worthy o' a king, and sae like what he expected from George III. (p. 29)

It may be surprising to discover that the 'good auld king' here referred to turns out to be George III, a monarch not greatly noted for his contributions to the advancement of literacy. In fact, the speaker is reaching back towards a pre-Union state of Scottish literacy with its close association with Bible reading, and perhaps also towards another 'good auld king', James VI and I, who authorized an English translation of the Bible.[23] The effect is to recast both the former independence of Scotland as a nation and the current independence of its education system as the grounds for a *British* state. Literacy is seen as an admirable political conformity, leaving orality to be constructed as a correspondingly dangerous radicalism. William next experiences a political meeting in which the universities' promotion of oral skills has been supplanted by a much more sinister working-class version of rhetoric. Women and children, traditional purveyors of oral exchange, are seen by William as the natural sources of uncontrollable outbreaks of orality: 'Women and bairns are aye the best at a mob' (p. 48). Disorderly scenes ensue; the orator's 'natural effrontery' reminds the narrator of 'the French Revolutionary assembly' (p. 69) and, Frankenstein-like, the speaker is unable to control the mob which he has worked up. (In an earlier work, *The Cottage Fireside*, Duncan had been careful to distinguish an acceptable orality from this dangerous oratory; the local minister speaks 'not like a professed orator, who had in his closet studied what would

[23] For Bible reading in Scottish education, see Houston, *Scottish Literacy and the Scottish Identity*, and *The Bible in Scottish Life and Literature*, ed. David F. Wright (Edinbugh: Saint Andrew Press, 1988).

produce the most brilliant effect, but like a father instructing his children'.[24]) The narrator sums up the political situation, lamenting the decline in the standards of education established by 'our Scottish ancestors' and making it quite clear that Scotland is in danger of being seduced into radicalism, sedition, and treason:

It is heartbreaking, however, to think how much the enlightened precautions of these wise and good men have of late been neglected by their degenerate descendants. Had their system been adhered to, there can be no reasonable doubt, that, whatever might have been the discontents, the seditions, and the impieties, of the lower classes in the *sister* kingdom, Scotland would not have been disgraced by becoming a party to the encouragement of blasphemous publications, and to those scenes of turbulence and treason, which have for the first time rendered it questionable, whether the superior education of her inhabitants be a blessing or a curse. (pp. 61–2)

Duncan's attack on radicalism in *The Young South Country Weaver* introduces a complication into the promotion of literacy as a political good. For commentators like Henry Duncan the most alarming feature of working-class orality was that it was not really orality at all, but a mixture of oral and written texts. Yet by the nineteenth century, levels of tolerance for the coexistence of orality and literacy had become low; the intermingling of spoken and written forms was seen not as a peaceful coexistence but as the corrupt use by a class associated with the stigma of orality of the power afforded by literacy to produce, as in *The Young South Country Weaver*, 'blasphemous publications'. Because many of these texts emanated from popular presses and were in loose-leaf form, they circulated quickly and were ephemeral, giving their textual life a resemblance to oral circulation, and the oral began to take on the characteristics of a corrupting force. Meg's amanuensis in *Guy Mannering* visibly enacts the degradation of writing by the 'illiterate' classes by producing, according to Pleydell, 'a vile, greasy scrawl' (p. 503). The encroachment of illiteracy upon an idealized literacy was a considerable problem for a country that

---

[24] Henry Duncan, *The Cottage Fireside; or, The Parish Schoolmaster*, 6th edn. (Edinburgh: William Oliphant, 1862), 41.

invested so much in literacy and it challenged Scotland's self-confidence in the democracy of its education system. Indirectly, the fear of radical politics in early nineteenth-century Scotland was due not so much to the failure of education in literacy as to its successes. A literate class will use that literacy for self-determination; those 'who have been to school or who have educated themselves are able to demystify authoritarian regimes and gain access to the information upon which the effective exercise of their newly won rights depends',[25] thus laying claim to a rather different kind of democracy than the generalized meritocracy of Scottish education that was steadily mythologized throughout the nineteenth century.[26]

In order for literacy to remain in the province of middle-class order and stability, popular literacy was generally thought of as '*illiteracy*'. Writing becomes illiteracy partly for its political content, but also because of its exposure to the dangerous scenes of popular orality. The use of handbills and broadsheets for political agitation is a case in point: notices urging action and promising support were circulated during the political riots of the 1790s and the food riots of the early nineteenth century, Duncan's Dumfriesshire being the site of a concentration of popular unrest.[27] In fact, much of this distrust of the wrong kind of writing stemmed from fears of revolution in the early nineteenth century and the advancement of literacy had been a key argument for Tom Paine, who was widely read in Scotland: Duncan's Jacobin radicals get their opinions from 'the vile stink of Thomas Paine's abominations' (p. 92). Duncan saw himself in a tradition of anti-Jacobin writers like Hannah More, whose task was to preserve an ordered and loyal peasantry from the Revolutionary Menace; the *Tales of the Scottish Peasantry*, a collection of moral parables put together by Duncan, are 'written chiefly by a society of clergymen in Dumfries-shire, in

---

[25] Vincent, *Literacy and Popular Culture*, 228.

[26] See R. D. Anderson, *Education and Opportunity in Victorian Scotland* (Oxford: Clarendon Press, 1983), esp. 1–26.

[27] For the general use of written texts for political agitation in Britain, see Vincent, *Literacy and Popular Culture*, 236–41; for the use of handbills in riots in Scotland see Kenneth J. Logue, *Popular Disturbances in Scotland 1780–1815* (Edinburgh: John Donald, 1979), 136, 203–6.

imitation of those excellent productions, the Moral Tales of Mrs. Hannah More'.[28]

As a way of combating illiterate writing, the educationalists ventured into enemy territory, pursuing a policy of containment carried out by means of a process of colonization in which popular forms could be appropriated and controlled by being imitated. Miller's *Monthly Monitor and Philanthropic Museum*, for example, was a self-conscious attempt to reproduce gossip in a morally improving form by publishing lists of fatal accidents, murders, executions, deaths through drinking, and other 'imprudences', as well as recording charitable bequests. However, although the site of orality could to some extent be sanctioned by the presence of the book, the process was not reversible: writing was in danger of corruption when encroached upon by the territory of the oral. Illiterate writing was a kind of writing that could at any time betray the corrupting influence of the touch of orality; a contributor to the *Edinburgh Magazine and Literary Miscellany* describes the writing of perceived radical authors in the terms of a familiar attack upon oral rhetoric, accusing it of being deceptive and manipulative:

Now, such authors as Voltaire, and Volney, and Paine, are extremely dangerous to the happiness of all half-educated persons, writing, as they do, in a plain, simple style, when they sneer and play off their wit; and, in a gaudy and turgid manner, when they wish to conceal their poisonous dogmas and mysteries.[29]

Speech—because of its intimate relationship with the concept of audience—is often seen as dependent on its own physical context and this very association with context was enough to make orality suspect in the eyes of the evangelical educationalists. As traditional sites of oral exchange—taverns, fairs, open-air meetings, and public gatherings—fell out of favour among the moral arbiters of the early nineteenth century, they became supplanted in the texts of Duncan and Miller by more readily controllable localities. In one of Duncan's collection of *Tales of*

[28] Henry Duncan *et al.*, *Tales of the Scottish Peasantry* (Edinburgh: William Oliphant, n.d.), p. v.
[29] 'On the influence of the diffusion of knowledge upon the happiness of the lower ranks of society', *Edinburgh Magazine and Literary Miscellany*, 4 (1819), 121–9 (p. 126).

the *Scottish Peasantry*, 'The Honest Farmer', Admiral Murray banishes all 'petty alehouses' from his estate and in their place establishes 'a friendly society and parish library'.[30] Alternatively, the setting might remain the same but its ideological significance become altered and purified by the presence of the book. This was the case with the growing emphasis on the hearth as a site for private reading rather than for oral storytelling, the Victorian domestic ideology which sanctified the hearth as a restorative space of moral purity.[31] In another of the *Tales of the Scottish Peasantry*, the Bible, as book *par excellence*, is used as a moral corrective within the family sphere: the heroine of 'Jane Morton' tries to counter her family's 'evil habits' by reading 'such passages of holy writ as seemed to strike her most forcibly against the sinful habit of self-indulgence'.[32] (Not surprisingly, William Webster's uncle's 'domestic habits' in his den of radical iniquity are described as 'objectionable' (p. 44) by the narrator of *The Young South Country Weaver*.)

It seemed to some observers that literacy, far from being a political asset to the state, was working to undermine it. In 1819 a letter claiming to be from 'A Village Politician' near Paisley appeared in the *Edinburgh Magazine and Literary Miscellany* to expose the feared results of the education of the working class and the expansion of what the writer refers to as 'illiterate scurrility': 'They become keen politicians, and read with avidity every pamphlet and paper which will feed their heart-burnings, and inflame their discontent. In our own country, this is flagrantly notorious, from the increasing sale of anti-ministerial papers; and every sort of foul garbage is greedily swallowed . . .'[33]

Increasingly, attempts were made to contain the oral qualities of popular literature: its rapid and ephemeral circulation. Thomas Dick wrote to the *Monthly Magazine or British*

---

[30] *Tales of the Scottish Peasantry*, 237.

[31] For hearth-side reading and the Scottish family see J. V. Smith, 'Manners, Morals and Mentalities', 32–4. For Victorian developments on the home as the site of privacy and middle-class domesticity beset by spying servants, see Anthea Trodd, *Domestic Crime in the Victorian Novel* (London: Macmillan, 1989). Trodd's book identifies the fireside as bourgeois locality as a specifically mid-Victorian development, but the phenomenon is also apparent in early texts in Scotland.

[32] *Tales of the Scottish Peasantry*, 75–6.

[33] 'On the influence of the diffusion of knowledge upon the happiness of the lower ranks of society', 125.

Register, insisting that working people be admitted to 'the temple of science', and he argues for the opening up of scientific and literary societies.[34] A pseudonymous reply described the founding of the Greenock library:

Two or three gentlemen of that town had found in many of their friends in each sex, a general complaint against 'the trash in circulating libraries,' and a wish for such an establishment as a general subscription library, proposing that they would immediately transfer their subscriptions from the common libraries of each town, and even increase them, provided they could get books of real knowledge and utility to read, which should also be the property of the subscribers.[35]

By setting up a controlling system in the image of the very thing it was to control, the popular education movement problematized the definition of literacy and its functions. Dominie Sampson's bookishness in *Guy Mannering* raises a question about literacy which became increasingly urgent: what is it for? Despite his staunch opposition to the threats of illiteracy, Sampson is invested by Scott with a curious pointlessness: 'this sort of living catalogue and animated automaton had all the advantages of a literary dumb-waiter' (p. 339). Sampson's association with books dehumanizes him, turning him into a conduit for a literacy whose value as a skill in itself is not defined. Not only this, but such value as literacy *does* represent is in the possession, not of Sampson himself, but of his employer, leaving Sampson as a 'dumb-waiter': an idealized servant, silent and therefore free from servants' corrupting orality, and under the control of a literacy which does not benefit him directly. Increasingly, literacy was seen as a pure good in itself, needing no further explanation as a mark of social acceptability, yet this very lack of explanation was to render it of dubious value to the literate person.

The Glasgow educationalist David Stow worried about the perception that literacy was simply a good in itself, which he

---

[34] Letter signed T. Dick, *Monthly Magazine; or, British Register*, 37 (1814), 219–21. This volume also provided a forum for readers to write recommending books for servants: see pp. 37, 225, 401, and 510 (this last calls others' lists too 'methodistical' and includes *The Vicar of Wakefield*, *History of Remarkable Shipwrecks* and, sadistically, Langton's *Account of Servants who have been executed at Tyburn*).

[35] *Monthly Magazine; or, British Register*, 37 (1814), 503.

discusses under the heading: 'Prejudice in favour of Mere Reading'.[36] Stow complains that although all parents want literacy for their children, they are too easily satisfied: 'Give them it, and no complaints will be heard although not a word will be understood of what they do read.'[37] The evangelical educationalists felt the insubstantiality of 'mere reading' as a framework for Scottish society, and cast around for clear objects of reading which would secure moral improvement. To this end, Thomas Dick tirelessly promoted popular science as a corrective to his fears of a pointlessly educated Scotland:

There is, perhaps, no country in the world where the body of the people are better educated and more intelligent than in North Britain; yet we need not go far either in the city or the country, to be convinced, that the most absurd and superstitious notions, and the grossest ignorance respecting many important subjects intimately connected with human happiness, still prevail among the majority of the population.[38]

The identification of a 'Prejudice in favour of Mere Reading' exposes the problems facing any one who entered into the discourse of literacy in nineteenth-century Scotland. In Duncan's *Young South Country Weaver*, the identification of reading with political conformity glosses over the problem that the ideology of literacy had become increasingly aimless. The Calvinist promotion of literacy in Scotland had fostered a belief in the connection between reading and the determining powers of the individual intellect. To J. S. Mill, this remained one of Scotland's greatest achievements:

For two centuries, the Scottish peasant, compared with the same class in other situations, has been a reflecting, an observing, and therefore naturally a self-governing, a moral and a successful human being— because he has been a reading and discussing one and this he owes above all other causes to the parish schools.[39]

Yet in the social and political climate of early nineteenth-century Scotland, neither the evangelical educationalists nor the

[36] David Stow, *The Training System* (New Edition, Glasgow: Blackie and Sons, 1840), 78–80.   [37] Ibid. 78.
[38] Thomas Dick, *On the Improvement of Society by the Diffusion of Knowledge* (Edinburgh: Waugh and Innes, 1833), 8.
[39] [Mill], 'The Claims of Labour', 511.

anti-Jacobins could support such a view. A common complaint underlined the unwillingness to confront the implications of literacy by claiming that a dissolute working class had perverted the Calvinist project by using literacy to read texts other than the Bible. David Stow felt that the Bible itself was becoming increasingly talismanic and advocated a scene of discussion between teacher and pupil in religious education, yet frequently reading could only be advanced as a good if its values were not open to interrogation. Looked at in a more generalized perspective, the emptiness of literacy as a sign of value was underpinned by the sense that its relationship with industrialization had excluded the interests of Scotland. Not only did the demographic changes brought about by the Industrial Revolution hinder the provision of education, but also literacy itself had failed to guarantee Scotland's economic prosperity. In the first decades of the nineteenth century it had still seemed possible that Scotland's success with literacy might be concomitant with economic prosperity. In 1819 it could be suggested that 'Nor is there any instance, any where, of such progress in wealth, industry, and refinement, as has been exhibited in Scotland within the last forty years ... I have myself no doubt that our singular prosperity is to be attributed to our superior education.'[40]

George Lewis's pamphlet of 1834, *Scotland A Half-Educated Nation*, continued the tendency to see education as Scotland's best claim to national importance, but now only in the insubstantial forms of institutions: 'In all but our parochial churches and parochial schools, we have lost our nationality. In these alone we survive as a nation—stand apart from and superior to England.'[41] If this is the case, then education has become 'mere reading', an empty good in itself leading to neither the moral, nor the social, nor the economic values to which it had been linked.

By mid-century, then, the democratic ideal of Scottish mass literacy was under threat from a number of different directions. In the decades following the Disruption of the Church of

[40] 'On the Modern Education of the Middling Classes', *Edinburgh Magazine and Literary Miscellany*, 4 (1819), 314–18.
[41] [Lewis], *Scotland A Half-Educated Nation*, 75.

Scotland in 1843, the system of church-financed parish schools was, in T. C. Smout's succinct phrase, 'a mess'.[42] As families moved from the Highlands or immigrated from Ireland to the Lowland towns an increasingly large proportion of children were Catholic and had few schools of their own; and the tendency for the children of the poor to seek work at an earlier age further whittled away the effects of education. The perceived failure of Scottish education to guarantee national prosperity (although it did create an unusually literate emigrant body)[43] had a hand in the abandoning of a single, subsidized education programme. Those who could afford to educate their children were by now seeking a more élitist and less distinctively Scottish education. H. M. Paterson sums up the situation which developed throughout the second half of the nineteenth century as new schools arose to meet the growing demand for secondary education among the middle classes:

The increasing tension between solidarity and division was manifest in all the institutions of Scotland's social structure. It was clearly to be seen in the schools with the rise of a largely separate system designed to cater for the bourgeoisie—the increasing numbers of academies, high schools, propriety boarding or 'public' schools and other institutions for the children of an affluent middle class bear witness to this. They arose in response to the demands of an anglicised and expanding bourgeoisie who wished to save the expense of sending their children to schools south of the border.[44]

Even the ideal of the humanizing influence of democratic education was now under threat. In 1834 George Lewis had written that 'the habit of school-going', as encouraged by the church, was the best plan 'to counteract the evils of the factory system'.[45] Whether or not this was the case was never proved, as the habit of school-going among employees was extremely

[42] T. C. Smout, *A Century of the Scottish People, 1830–1950* (London: Collins, 1986), 215. See also pp. 209–33.

[43] See Harvey J. Graff, *The Literacy Myth: Literacy and Social Structure in the Nineteenth-Century City* (New York and London: Academic Press, 1979). Graff quotes statistics which suggest that, among Scots, 'a higher proportion of immigrants to Canada were literate than in the remaining population' (pp. 67–8).

[44] H. M. Paterson, 'Incubus and Ideology: The Development of Secondary Schooling in Scotland, 1900–1939', in *Scottish Culture and Scottish Education*, ed. Humes and Paterson, 197–215 (p. 201).

[45] [Lewis], *Scotland A Half-Educated Nation*, 81.

variable, and the educated factory owners were buying in cheap, uneducated labour. In 1850, an article by the English school inspector Henry Moseley appeared in the *Edinburgh Review* which had come to be regarded as an important forum for debates about Scottish as well as English education. Moseley denies not only the efficacy, but also the advisability of universal education in an industrial society: 'Nothing can be more erroneous than to look upon the advancement of knowledge as a means towards fusing and levelling the classes, or than to qualify as an innovation whatever is done to elevate the social condition of the labouring man.'[46]

Moseley concludes that the unequal struggle to establish equality of education should be abandoned as the middle class will always outstrip its inferior, and the best that can be hoped is that, 'Whilst knowledge is diffusing among the middle classes all the elements of moral and physical well-being in unparalleled abundance',[47] some of this enlightenment will rub off on lower classes. James Hogg, who had first-hand experience of farm labouring, had already warned of new divisions in the work-place: 'the gradual advance of the *aristocracy* of farming . . . has placed such a distance between servants and masters, that in fact they have no communication whatever, and very little interest in common',[48] and now, in Moseley's article, the democratic ideal is already turning into mythology, as the passing of a Golden Age of class stability is mourned:

The farm labourer no longer sits at the same board and partakes of the same substantial fare with the farmer; the master-artificer of the olden time, now become a manufacturer, has forsworn the society of his journeymen; and the trader, advanced to be a merchant, is seen no more living under the same roof with his shopmen and apprentices.[49]

By the mid-nineteenth century the oral was joining the

---

[46] [Henry Moseley], 'Church and State Education', *ER* 92 (1850), 94–136 (p. 95).   [47] Ibid. 98.
[48] James Hogg, 'On the Changes in the Habits, Amusements, and Condition of the Scottish Peasantry', *Quarterly Journal of Agriculture*, 3 (1831–2), 256–63 (p. 263). For an analysis of this phenomenon, see David Vincent, 'The Decline of the Oral Tradition in Popular Culture', in *Popular Culture and Custom in Nineteenth-Century England*, ed. Robert D. Storch (London and Canberra: Croom Helm, 1982), 20–47.
[49] [Moseley], 'Church and State Education', 97.

pastoral in a sentimentalized past where it could more safely be contained. By confining it in the past it was possible again to reassert orality as a better mode than the corrupting influence of popular literature; teaching people to read could now no longer be regarded as the best way of practising democracy while ensuring moral stability. The always unstable scales by which speech and writing are valued tipped once again in favour of an orality sanctioned by its acquisition of an idealized past. Yet this seemingly transcendent oral remained precariously poised and vulnerable to the corrupting influences of its socially debased forms. The strange doublings and splittings-off of speech and writing prove inescapable.

2

Grammar and Glamour: Writing and Authority

As Scottish writers sought to establish national identities for their work in the nineteenth century, they frequently attempted to negotiate Scotland's dual claims for repositioning in an assumed 'British' norm, and drew on Scotland's status both as a source of orality and as an unusually literate society. To promote both orality and literacy afforded Scots a good opportunity to move their own national characteristics into the British centre, not by eradicating Scottishness, but by making Scottish concerns typical of interests common to the whole of British culture, a culture increasingly concerned with the advancement of literacy and in which a version of orality, manifested in ballads, oral epics, and their imitations, was becoming fashionable. But there is a problem with speech and writing in this cultural context: they tend to get locked into binary oppositions which frustrate their evaluation. To put it more simply: speech and writing can exist neither separately nor together. Value remains necessary as orality and literacy both constitute valuable assets, but because of the way they become culturally locked together, to value one results in the devaluation of the other.

Thus it seemed in the interests of Scotland's self-definition and self-promotion (that is, as defined and promoted by its literary figures) to advance both orality and literacy as distinct Scottish achievements. Both were to be valued, yet one cannot be valued without the implicit devaluation of the other. Of course, keeping speech and writing separate at all is continually frustrated by their actual behaviour in a very mixed culture. Yet they had to be made distinct so that they could be valued as cultural assets; if speech is seen to be integrated with writing then it ceases to guarantee the purity of origins for which it was to be valued. While differences between speech and writing do frequently present themselves, these are usually contingent upon circumstance. However, to admit such a position would be to minimize their separate existences and the problem can only be overcome by positing essential differences between them. Attitudes to speech and writing in this context are interesting not so much because they underscore the futility of imagining artificially invented characteristics when in fact there is no difference at all between spoken and written texts, but because such assumptions reveal much about the social conditions under which they are made.

There are at least two ways of dealing with the problematic evaluation of speech and writing which were available to Scottish writers. One is to subvert the distinction by revealing how contingent it is on local contexts (a frequent characteristic of Hogg's writing). The other is to promote an artificial distinction by abstracting an ideal state from a real one. The ideal can then be passed off as an absolute in contradistinction to the murky convolutions of social relativity. This process is at work in changing attitudes to orality in eighteenth- and early nineteenth-century Britain as a whole, and raises particular problems in Scott's editorial work on the *Minstrelsy of the Scottish Border*.

Minstrelsy of the Scottish Border: *The Paradox of Orality*

Scott's *Minstrelsy* represented a chance to promote oral literature but it is also a site in which contradictory uses of orality come into conflict. Orality in late eighteenth-century Britain was undergoing a process of cultural purification in which an ideal was being extracted from the real. Percy and Ritson made ballad literature popular among a fashionable readership, yet, at the same time, actual orality was systematically demoted as the production of socially inferior classes. Spoken tradition was seen as dangerous and literacy was promoted as the province of a more rational morality than that provided by the folktale, and thus the education of middle-class children had to be protected from the corrupting influence of storytelling servants.[1] Orality

---

[1] See Gary Kelly, 'The Limits of Genre and the Institution of Literature: Romanticism between Fact and Fiction', in *Romantic Revolutions: Criticism and*

was acceptable only when purged of its degraded social status by means of the sanction of writing. This situation was particularly marked in Scotland with its tendency, when considering orality as a social phenomenon, to associate it with Scots and Gaelic, both of which were increasingly considered unsuitable languages for representing the progress of Scottish society.

Thus a concept of an orality which is something believed to have an asocial existence and which is admirable, can be set against a concept of 'illiteracy' which is socially determined and to be effaced. In order for orality to be valued, it has to be kept well clear of social realities, and indeed it was. This led to the familiar Romantic idea that orality signalled the expression of natural feeling: Rousseau's phonocentric paradise. Adam Ferguson, for example, traces the beginnings of poetry to the pure language of just such a pre-heteroglossic Eden:

In rude ages men are not separated by distinctions of rank or profession. They live in one manner, and speak one dialect. The bard is not to chuse his expression among the singular accents of different conditions. . . . The name of every object, and of every sentiment, is fixed; and if his conception has the dignity of nature, his expression will have a purity which does not depend on his choice.[2]

Of course orality cannot really exist in an asocial space. Like the idea of 'nature' itself, orality was always being pressed into the service of some political end or other, most famously Burke's use of the oral to advance arguments against petitions for a written constitution. Burke's arguments equate orality with an instinctive recognition of right (later exposed by Tom Paine as metaphysical and ideal)[3] and Burke's annexing of apparently

---

Theory, ed. Kenneth R. Johnson *et al.* (Bloomington and Indianapolis: Indiana University Press, 1990), 158–75.

[2] Adam Ferguson, *An Essay on the History of Civil Society*, ed. Duncan Forbes (Edinburgh: Edinburgh University Press, 1966), 174.

[3] 'A constitution is not a thing in name only, but in fact. It has not an ideal but a real existence; and wherever it cannot be produced in a visible form, there is none' (Tom Paine, *Rights of Man*, ed. Henry Collins (Harmondsworth: Penguin, 1984), 71). For Romantic theories of writing see W. J. T. Mitchell, 'Visible Language: Blake's Wond'rous Art of Writing', in *Romanticism and Contemporary Criticism*, ed. Morris Eaves and Michael Fischer (Ithaca and London: Cornell University Press, 1986), 46–95; and James Chandler, *Wordsworth's Second Nature: A Study of the Poetry and Politics* (Chicago and London: University of Chicago Press, 1984).

empirical truth to his cause parallels the association of oral poetry with a 'pure' or natural feeling which expresses fundamental states of human nature. Again, orality exists in a contingent relationship with writing (here concomitantly devalued as one element of the equation must be in such oppositions) but is passed off as something essential. Scott himself was not averse to exploiting the authoritative persona of the bard for openly political ends. His response to British fears of post-Revolutionary France is the poem 'The Bard's Incantation (Written under the threat of invasion in the autumn of 1804)' in which 'Minstrels and bards of other days' are invited to defend Albion from a Revolutionary 'Spectre with his Bloody Hand'.[4] The Bard's voice is, almost literally, the voice of nature as it mingles with the groaning oak, the stormy breeze, and the waves on the lake to proclaim 'the joys of Liberty'. The purity of the voice from an oral past promises concomitant freedom in the form of anti-Jacobin politics.

The 'orality' that arises out of 'illiteracy', then, is really an unacknowledged construct of a graphocentric society, and this is true of Scotland, which was promoting a version of orality which was in the hands—or the pens—of highly self-consciously literary figures. As Scott passed ballads through the editorial process of his *Minstrelsy of the Scottish Border*, his methods rested not only upon the 'improvement' of individual ballad texts, but also upon the refinement of orality itself. When he came to deal with ballad material which had grown up on the borders of an oral culture, he found it in its usual assortment of spoken and written forms and usages. His earliest exposure to this kind of material, according to his own memoir, was both in the form of his grandmother's oral tales of 'old Border depredations', and in his reading of Allan Ramsay's versions of popular songs for a polite readership, the *Tea-Table Miscellany*.[5] The process of seeking out ballads for inclusion in the

[4] *PW* viii. 357–60.
[5] *Life*, i. 18. For the genesis, inception, and additional volumes of the *Minstrelsy* see also W. E. Wilson, 'The Making of the "Minstrelsy": Scott and Shortreed in Liddesdale', *Cornhill Magazine*, 73 (1932), 266–83; Edgar Johnson, *Sir Walter Scott: The Great Unknown* (2 vols., London: Hamish Hamilton, 1970), i. 172–207; W. F. H. Nicolaisen, 'Scott and the Folk Tradition', in *Sir Walter Scott: The Long-Forgotten Melody*, ed. Alan Bold (London: Vision, 1983), 127–42.

Minstrelsy involved an even more complex mixture of sources—some from oral recitation, some from manuscripts, some from printed versions, with Scott, or his assistants, contributing freely to most of them. Yet despite this inevitable blurring of the oral and the literary, the creative process of the *Minstrelsy*, as it is represented by those who had to do with it, enacts the uneasy splitting-off of the written from the spoken. *Minstrelsy of the Scottish Border* was designed to show off a Scottish National Asset and the story of its inception attracted images of the separate existence of literacy and orality.

Contemporary accounts divide the work's evolution into two competing images, one appearing to epitomize orality and the other literacy. The first of these is of Scott roaming through Liddesdale and Ettrick Forest in search of oral recitations of ballads. In his account of one of these 'raids', Hogg includes an anecdote which emphasizes the seemingly unbridgeable gulf between an oral recitation and a written record. In Hogg's story, his mother, Margaret Laidlaw, makes her now famous remark about her songs: 'They war made for singing, an' no for reading; and they're nouther right spelled nor right setten down.' According to this view, the writing down of the oral is also its destruction; Scott's transcription of Margaret Laidlaw's songs means that he has 'spoilt them a'thegither'.[6]

Other of Scott's friends offered a different account of the *Minstrelsy*'s genesis, and one which emphasizes the literary nature of the undertaking. Lockhart describes the meeting of two of Scott's chief associates and assistants in the preparation of the edition: Richard Heber and John Leyden. This meeting takes place in the symbolic source of what was to become the Author of Waverley industry, the bookshop of Archibald Constable, 'in after life one of the most eminent of British publishers'. Lockhart relates Heber's first encounter with Leyden:

Frequenting the place accordingly, he observed with some curiosity the barbarous aspect and gestures of another daily visitant, who came not

---

[6] James Hogg, *'Memoir of Author's Life' and 'Familiar Anecdotes of Sir Walter Scott'*, ed. Douglas S. Mack (Edinburgh and London: Scottish Academic Press, 1972), 62. Hogg writes that Scott was not persuaded by Mrs Hogg's view and 'answered by a hearty laugh'.

to purchase evidently, but to pore over the more recondite articles of the collection—often balanced for hours on a ladder with a folio in his hand, like Dominie Sampson. The English virtuoso was on the look-out for any books or MSS. that might be of use to the editor of the projected 'Minstrelsy'.[7]

Although this account is radically different from the idea of the oral origins of the *Minstrelsy*, it, like the episode told by Hogg, also reveals traces of the way the oral and the literate are pulled apart. Like Mrs Hogg's comments, Lockhart's story emphasizes the dissimilarity of oral and literary media. The items associated with orality are the 'more recondite articles of the collection' which have to be sought among the apparently indigenous residents of a bookshop.

Though Scott later complained about the coolness of the collection's reception south of the Border, he could not have been unaware that, already in 1802, England offered a good market both for the idea of ballads and for a version of literary Scottishness. The success of Ossian, though not unanimously approved by the Scots, had, in Scott's view, recentred Scotland not only within Britain but also throughout Europe:

while we are compelled to renounce the pleasing idea, 'that Fingal lived, and that Ossian sung,' our national vanity may be equally flattered by the fact that, a remote, and almost a barbarous corner of Scotland, produced, in the 18th century, a bard, capable not only of making an enthusiastic impression on every mind susceptible of poetical beauty, but of giving a new tone to poetry throughout all Europe.[8]

Despite anti-Scottish prejudice in England throughout the second half of the eighteenth century, and the attempts of the Scottish literati to purge their language of Scotticisms, a kind of Scottishness had become marketable by the end of the century.[9] With the representation of bards or minstrels becoming a way of figuring the poet, England's neighbouring countries

[7] *Life*, i. 323.

[8] Walter Scott, 'Laing's Edition of Macpherson', *ER* 6 (1805), 429–62 (p. 462).

[9] For anti-Scottish feeling and the reception of Ossian see Richard B. Sher, 'Percy, Shaw and the Ferguson "Cheat": National Prejudice in the Ossian Wars', in *Ossian Revisited*, ed. Howard Gaskill (Edinburgh: Edinburgh University Press, 1991), 207–45. For attitudes to Ossian in general see Fiona Stafford, *The Sublime Savage: A Study of James Macpherson and the Poems of Ossian* (Edinburgh: Edinburgh University Press, 1988), 163–78.

were invited to adopt the voice of a British culture. During the eighteenth century, writers from both sides of the Border were becoming bardic, most famously Gray ('The Bard', 1757) and Beattie ('The Minstrel', 1771), and ballad imitations were increasingly popular. Bards were not only Scottish (or Welsh or Irish) but British, like the speaker of Scott's 'Incantation' who identifies a common enemy in the French.

The popularity of bards and the success of Burns are symptoms of a complicated and problematic state of affairs for the Scottish writer. The promotion of the ballad as a generally fashionable form threatened the specificity of Scottish ballads. Bardic poets, despite their potentially active political position on England's borders, are useful precisely because they suppress that position in favour of 'natural genius'.[10] In Ferguson's pre-social state, everyone speaks a natural language in which the name of every object is fixed and there can be no concept of dialect. For universality of feeling to be present in the ballads, linguistic variation has to be somehow contained, but this was not always seen to be very easy. Faced with the difficulty of reconciling the natural with the Scottish, arguments about the role of dialect can uncover anxieties about the relationship between poetry and national identity. There is an interesting example of this in one of the *Noctes Ambrosianae*, the series of conversations composed largely by John Wilson, Lockhart, and William Maginn, which featured in *Blackwood's Edinburgh Magazine* between 1822 and 1835.

De Quincey (billed as the 'English Opium-Eater') arrives for dinner in the company of 'Christopher North' (Wilson), 'The Shepherd' (James Hogg), and a few others. The conversation, which starts with a discussion of Burns, turns on the exclusivity of Scottish poetry. The Opium-Eater scorns Scottish pride in the Scots language as a 'national delusion, born of prejudice, ignorance, and bigotry' in which the Scots believe that 'all their various dialects' are impenetrable to the English. The Shepherd duly gives him a Scots vocabulary test, but the Opium-Eater ('smiling graciously') strikes back with a description of one of Hogg's own poems as an example of the universality of Scottish

[10] For a discussion of the complex position of Burns as 'Scotch Bard' see Robert Crawford, *Devolving English Literature* (Oxford: Clarendon Press, 1992), 88–110.

verse. Scottishness is identified as just a good example of the pre-social, natural state:

'Tis a ballad breathing the sweetest, simplest, wildest spirit of Scottish traditionary song—music, as of some antique instrument long-lost, but found at last in the Forest among the decayed roots of trees, and touched, indeed, as by an instinct, by the only man who could reawaken its sleeping chords—the Ettrick Shepherd.[11]

The Shepherd is flattered into compromise on this occasion, and such compromises had to be negotiated elsewhere. With a potential British readership waiting to be tapped, the *Minstrelsy of the Scottish Border* offered Scott a good opportunity for moving Scottish interests to the British centre, providing it could be handled carefully. In the field of primitive poetry, Scotland could, paradoxically, offer access to universal states while maintaining its own national identity. In Romantic Britain, all origins are good, but some are better than others; states of society in their rude originality guarantee the purity of natural feeling, but Scotland in its rude originality seemed particularly natural. Scott's second introduction to the *Minstrelsy*, the 'Remarks on Popular Poetry' written in 1830, intended to describe the general character of popular poetry and to be 'literary' where the earlier introduction was 'historical', hovers round this incongruity.

Scott opens with a discussion of the 'natural tendency' of primitive races to produce rude poetry which 'must have one general character in all nations'.[12] Soon, however, he has returned to the historical field with a discussion of the various Celtic races and the influence of the Anglo-Saxons in Scotland. The general appeal to the Romanticized Celtic Bard is being gradually shaded into a promotion of a peculiarly Scottish genius. All the Celtic races, he remarks, are 'passionately addicted to music' and 'all three bear marks of general resemblance to each other'. But the addiction of the Scots to music is especially passionate, their culture 'in particular, is

---

[11] *The Tavern Sages: Selections from the 'Noctes Ambrosianae'*, ed. J. H. Alexander (Aberdeen: Association for Scottish Literary Studies, 1992), 87. This conversation originally appeared in *Blackwood's* in April 1830.

[12] *PW* i. 6. *Minstrelsy of the Scottish Border* occupies the first 4 volumes of this edition and further references appear in the text.

early noticed and extolled by ancient authors' (i. 28–9). Scott further wonders why some nations' primitive poetry attains a greater degree of excellence than others and infers: 'This must depend in some measure, no doubt, on the temper and manners of the people, or their proximity to those spirit-stirring events which are naturally selected as the subject of poetry, and on the more comprehensive or energetic character of the language spoken by the tribe' (i. 11–12). Again, Scott dexterously combines the pre-social universality of orality with specifics of Scottish society, which, as usual, manages to be more natural than any other. Poetry, something which Scott believes to be common to all nations, arises 'naturally' from the particular events of Scottish history.

In terms of nationalist politics, then, the *Minstrelsy* seemed to offer Scott the perfect opportunity to be both British and Scottish at the same time, and he locates the edition at this point, a true Border position emphasizing contiguity as well as distinctness. His work is to frame and delineate the Scottishness of his subject, as that Scottishness becomes conversely absorbed into a greater British identity:

In the Notes and occasional Dissertations, it has been my object to throw together . . . a variety of remarks, regarding popular super-stitions, and legendary history, which if not now collected, must soon have been totally forgotten. By such efforts, feeble as they are, I may contribute somewhat to the history of my native country; the peculiar features of whose manners and character are daily melting and dissolving into those of her sister and ally. (i. 237–8)

What is notable here, however, is that it is not the ballads themselves that are to contribute to Scotland's national history, but the editor's notes and dissertations. Throughout the edition Scott is concerned to show off the ballads, yet he displays a marked reluctance to let them speak for themselves. Ballads cannot constitute history, which is the job of the educated historian; their banishment to a realm which is both part of history yet unreliable as history throws up some of the activities of orality and its paradoxes.[13]

---

[13] For Scott and ballad history, see Peter T. Murphy, *Poetry as an Occupation and an Art in Britain, 1760–1830* (Cambridge: Cambridge University Press, 1993), 136–83.

When Scott gives his attention to the texts of the ballads, their transmission and their life in the voices of oral reciters, the oral paradox is one between the idealized and the social. In its idealized form orality allows access to the purity of origins, either the natural feeling of all humanity, or the birth of a nation which is part of the former yet distinctive in itself. But in its socialized identity (passed off as an essential quality), it signifies impurity. Orality will destroy its own value because it cannot preserve its own insights. Worse still, it inevitably embarks on a process of corruption. Scott constantly complains about the difficulty of preserving the vision of nature that oral poetry can supply. He wishes that there were more early manuscripts, as writing is seen as essentially better than speech in preserving things. He places himself in the strange position of regretting that his access to oral poetry is so frequently from oral tradition as he laments the loss of an early printed source: 'Could this collection have been found, it would probably have thrown much light on the present publication; but the editor has been obliged to draw his materials chiefly from oral tradition' (i. 223).

Scott is inclined to pass off his disappointment with speech by blaming its characteristics which are in most situations inferior to those of writing. In fact, he often does not see the superior nature of writing as situational at all but absolute. Yet these judgements about writing often cover anxieties about the social status of orality. In 1828 he prefaced the second series of the 'Tales of a Grandfather' with an account, strongly influenced by Adam Ferguson, of the 'Progress of Civilization in Society'. Here, he describes the introduction of writing into civilization:

But it is evident that society, when its advance is dependent upon oral tradition alone, must be liable to many interruptions. The imagination of the speaker, and the dulness or want of comprehension of the hearer, may lead to many errors: and it is generally found that knowledge makes but very slow progress until the art of writing is discovered, by which a fixed, accurate, and substantial form can be given to the wisdom of past ages. When this noble art is attained, there is a sure foundation laid for the preservation and increase of knowledge. The record is removed from the inaccurate recollection of the aged, and placed in a safe, tangible, and imperishable form, which may be subjected to the inspection of various persons, until the sense is completely explained and comprehended, with the least possible chance of doubt or uncertainty.[14]

Scott's assumption is that writing is essentially better than speech, that its inherent characteristics represent a form superior for the desirable task of preserving meaning. Writing is described as 'a fixed, accurate and substantial form', 'safe, tangible and imperishable form'. These essential characteristics make it naturally good at containing within itself things which readers can fully extract when 'the sense is completely ... comprehended'. However, there is a noticeable slippage from the critique of speech to a criticism of speakers; the typical bearer of orality suffers from dullness and is slow to understand. The 'aged' are not seen as bearers of wisdom but, in a period of growing industrialization, are relegated to the realm of non-productivity. This is the pattern that emerges, though more tentatively, in the introductions to the *Minstrelsy*. Scott's frequent consternation over the corruption of texts shades into a larger social anxiety about the moral corruption of the transmitters of those texts.

The paradox of orality is that it guarantees both the purity of origins and the impurity of transmission. Speech appears to give access to moments in which 'the rude minstrel has melted in natural pathos' (i. 219), but, unlike writing, it cannot preserve those moments. The oral past becomes the unattainable other, cut off from the literate present by its own failure to sustain itself, or rather by the ignorance of speakers who have to wait for the invention of writing before their natural feeling can be comprehended. The only consolation for the literary editor is that the ignorance of speakers will sometimes accidently preserve phonetically words which the speaker does not understand. The editor is then able to explain the true meanings of these words because of his superior grasp of logocentrism:

---

[14] *Tales of a Grandfather* (MPW xxiii. 230). Interestingly, this is the kind of view of writing held by Samuel Johnson in the Macpherson affair. Boswell records him saying: 'If the poems were really translated, they were certainly first written down. Let Mr. Macpherson deposit the MS in one of the colleges at Aberdeen where there are people who can judge, and if the professors certify the authenticity, then there will be an end of the controversy' (James Boswell, *The Journal of a Tour to the Hebrides*, ed. Frederick A. Pottle and Charles H. Bennet (London: Heinemann, 1963), 67).

The minstrel who endeavoured to recite with fidelity the words of the author, might indeed fall into errors of sound and sense, and substitute corruptions for words which he did not understand. But the ingenuity of a skilful critic could often, in that case, revive and restore the original meaning; while the corrupted words became, in such cases, a warrant for the authenticity of the whole poem. (i. 21)

Scott passes off his complaints about orality as having to do with the essential characteristics of spoken transmission, while simultaneously hinting that it is really an element of society associated with the oral that is at fault. Again, he regrets the lack of written material and explains that 'it is the nature of popular poetry, as of popular applause, perpetually to shift with the objects of the time; and it is the frail chance of recovering some old manuscript, which alone can gratify our curiosity regarding the earlier efforts of the Border Muse' (i. 222).

The search for origins, the moment of inspiration effected by the Muse, can only be satisfied by writing because of the inherent characteristics, the 'nature', of oral poetry. An ideal of speech may give access to primary inspiration, but it is writing alone that has the essential characteristics to guard that moment of inspiration. However, such essential judgements are in fact founded on social ones. Scott sounds dismissive of the value of an oral community: 'popular' applause starts to shade into 'vulgar'. Because the ballads can never be written down in time, they are consigned to a series of transmitters dogged not only by the inadequacies of speech, but by their own 'ignorance' and 'indolence' and 'crudity'. These flaws make poetry 'slovenly' and its transmitters are engaged in 'degrading and vulgarising' it. Although Scott is discussing poetry which is supposed to be 'rugged' in the first place, it seems as if the discourse of that middle-class ideology of the written word which attempted to suppress lower-class orality has crept into his evaluation. Things get even more extreme when, in a survey of why ballads become corrupted, Scott points to their uncouth audience: minstrels are to be considered 'practising their profession in scenes of vulgar mirth and debauchery, humbling their art to please the ears of drunken clowns, and living with the dissipation natural to men whose precarious subsistence is, according to the ordinary phrase, from hand to mouth only' (i. 59). Speech becomes corrupted by its context: 'the ears of drunken clowns'.

The effect of judgements like these is to reinforce the suspicion that whereas ballads can inspire an interest in national history they are not themselves historical in any sense identifiable to Scott. Performers are cut off from their own history which they are unable to understand even as they reproduce it phonetically. Indeed, phonetic reproduction as the aim of a reciter reduces him or her to the status of a mindless mimic, and such a view does not permit the evolution of the text. Samuel Johnson had believed that oral communities cannot change: 'In nations, where there is hardly the use of letters, what is once out of sight is lost for ever. They think but little, and of their few thoughts, none are wasted on the past.'[15] Scott writes in 'Tales of a Grandfather' that 'knowledge makes but very slow progress until the art of writing is discovered'. The oral is locked into an idealized past of non-change, in contrast to the progress of the present; oral historians are separated from their own stories and a wedge is driven between the idea of history and that of performance. The concept of performance threatens the imagined integrity of the impossible stasis of the non-historical realm in which the oral is confined.

But orality can resist change only in its idealized form. The real form, as Scott continually points out, changes too much as it pursues the course of degeneration. And this very course, however inadequate, offers the Scottish ballad editor some means of identifying a continuity of national history. Recognizing the point at which Scotland's 'manners and character are daily melting and dissolving into those of her sister and ally', Scott also sets his project at a time in which gradual change is present, yet nearly over. The ever available position of orality as something always about to end is locally fixed by Scott to enact this fragile continuity: 'till a very late period, the pipers, of whom there was one attached to each Border town of note, and whose office was often hereditary, were the great depositories of oral, and particularly of poetical, tradition' (i. 224–5).

However, although the Border pipers offer the possibility of a continuous tradition sited in popular usage, Scott is reluctant to

---

[15] Samuel Johnson, *A Journey to the Western Islands of Scotland*, ed. Mary Lascelles (New Haven and London: Yale University Press, 1971), 65.

accept this as a way of determining what ballads are for. The
dominance of a discrete past over the fragile continuity offered
by the ballads is underpinned by a narratology which judges
them by their ability to recount events. Scott therefore concludes
that the stories narrated have an existence independent of any
individual telling. An unreliable narrator, he regrets, is apt 'to
substitute large portions from some other tale, altogether
distinct from that which he has commenced' (i. 228) and ballads
are seen as 'narrating real events' (i. 229). To separate the story
from the performance pushes Scott towards a position in which
language is more representational than creative, towards, in
fact, an anxiety of history which demands documentary
accuracy from historical record. Despite his recognition of
pipers as bearers of oral continuity, Scott cannot acknowledge
the implications of such a continuity: that the ballad narrations
are themselves history and not a record of the past. Scott thus
sets great store by memory, which he characterizes in a
particular way: the best kind of memory is photographic rather
than cumulative, not the historical palimpsest of oral memory,
but the imagined documentary accuracy of writing.

Like orality itself, the idea of authorship can be paradoxical in
Romantic conceptions of the ballad. On the one hand, the lack
of known authors seems inherently democratic, redolent of
Ferguson's primitive age before social divisions occurred.
Furthermore, the evolution of ballads can be located in the kind
of communal tradition articulated by Tilottama Rajan: 'What
stands behind the ballad is not an authorizing figure whose
credentials we can trust, but "tradition": something amorphous,
indicating survival but not in any classical sense, because what is
transmitted through the generations is partly hearsay, superstition, legend.'[16]

Yet arising out of this indeterminacy another view of
authorship could be constructed. The absence of a known
author clears a space for the construction of an idealized author-
figure who answers the wider Romantic desire for poetry to be
an expression of unique creativity. Although, as Rajan points

---

[16] Tilottama Rajan, *The Supplement of Reading: Figures of Understanding in
Romantic Theory and Practice* (Ithaca and London: Cornell University Press, 1990),
138.

out, the difficulty of ascribing ballads to authors 'poses a challenge to the myth of the author as a locus for a fixed meaning',[17] the absent author paradoxically opens up a space into which an abstracted concept of individual authority can be projected. In the matter of 'rude genius' it is negotiable which word qualifies which, and if the early poet-figure could be seen as possessing more genius than rudeness he could become an acceptable model for the modern writer, guaranteeing both the purity of origins and the purity of polite literature, conveniently uncorrupted by actual orality.

In the *Minstrelsy* Scott is initially hesitant about the poet-figures behind the ballads. In the 1802 introduction, he does not venture into the thorny debate as to the social origins of ballads, declining to decide 'Whether they were originally the composition of minstrels, professing the joint arts of poetry and music; or whether they were the occasional effusions of some self-taught bard' (i. 224), but in the later essay he is more outspoken. The ballad author here speaks with the voice of nature but he is a 'highly gifted individual' occupying a privileged position in his society (as in *The Lay of the Last Minstrel*, which 'was not framed for village churls, | But for high dames and mighty earls').[18] Thus the ballad becomes dissociated from the social classes largely responsible for its actual association: 'But the progress of the art is far more dependent on the rise of some highly-gifted individual, possessing in a preeminent and uncommon degree the powers demanded, whose talents influence the taste of a whole nation, and entail on their posterity and language a character almost indelibly sacred' (i. 12).

The need to display the collection as a National Asset pushes Scott towards a view of authorship which in fact eliminates the ballads' transmitters. The relationship between the ballads and the readers of the *Minstrelsy* is predicated on similar but chronologically separate models. The 'posterity' on whom the sacred national tastes are to be bestowed is not the non-individuated (and apparently not very gifted) bearers of ballad tradition, but the literati of Enlightenment Edinburgh.

The *Minstrelsy of the Scottish Border* reveals anxieties about orality and authorship, and the paradoxes to which they give

----

[17] Ibid. 142.   [18] *PW* vi. 47.

rise, provoked by the need to display primitive poetry in the light of national history. But Scott's own career in authorship offered him another way of exploring its authority. The novel was itself at a turning-point in its history, beginning to be viewed as a genre which could rise above the impurities of vulgar romance. The ambiguities of Scott's part in this development are worked out in a novel originally billed as 'A Romance' (later one of the 'Historical Romances'): *The Monastery*.

The Monastery: *The Authority of Books*

The Monastery deals with the physicality of the written word, and the various means whereby it can acquire authority. Most of its action takes place in the sixteenth century, but the introductory matter deals with the transmission of the text in the early nineteenth century (the novel was published in 1820). Between these two periods, and within the sixteenth-century setting itself, interesting correspondences emerge concerning the functions of written texts.

Around the Author of Waverley circulated views that he had single-handedly rescued the novel from its questionable position as a female genre, tainted by romance and popular culture. In her recent *The Achievement of Literary Authority*, Ina Ferris looks at the ways in which 'The Waverley Novels moved the novel out of the subliterary margins of the culture into the literary hierarchy'. The Author of Waverley was a figure associated with this transition of the novel as a genre from 'literary outsider to literary insider'.[19] The designation 'Author of Waverley' denotes the conjunction of the authority of the single-author text (as opposed to the anonymity or multiple authorship of the oral/ephemeral traditions) with the new-found authoritative status of the novel. As the Author of Waverley, Scott was able to use his own anonymity to bind himself even more closely with a recognizable series of texts all by the same author. However, as Ferris observes, the Author of Waverley is

[19] Ina Ferris, *The Achievement of Literary Authority: Gender, History and the Waverley Novels* (Ithaca and London: Cornell University Press, 1991), 1–2.

not necessarily the same person as the author of *Waverley*.[20] The phrase rather opens up a series of possible positions which offer the novelist the opportunity of interrogating his own status and its related authority. After all, as long as Scott maintained his anonymity, anyone might be the Author of Waverley and indeed other candidates were suggested from time to time.

Scott takes full advantage of the paradoxical position of being the Author of Waverley, a figure signifying both the personal and public ownership of the novels, and the prefaces to the novels constitute a debate about their sources, authorship and readership between the Author and his various frame narrators. I want now to look at one of the most interesting of these debates, a head-on confrontation between the Author and Captain Clutterbuck, an encounter which figures most prominently in *The Monastery* but, as it cannot be decided in that novel, spills over into *The Fortunes of Nigel* where it is no more conclusive. *The Monastery*'s preface is of particular importance here because, like the novel as a whole, it concerns itself with the authority which can be claimed by printed books. In *The Monastery*, the Author of Waverley deconstructs that authority which, in other eyes, he was in the process of conferring upon the status of the novel. In *Minstrelsy of the Scottish Border*, the plurivocity of the ballads was encased in and contained by the opinions of the editor, usurping the ballads' potential role as National History. But in *The Monastery*, the opposite is true: the authoring of the story told within the novel is a matter for some friendly negotiation between interested parties and turns out to be irresolvable.

The Monastery is set during the Reformation and purports to be 'compiled from authentic materials of that period, but written in the taste and language of the present day'.[21] In an elaborate 'introductory epistle' by Captain Clutterbuck, the Captain is visited by a mysterious Benedictine monk. The Benedictine is in search of a manuscript, written by his uncle, which he believes to be buried in the ruins of the local

---

[20] See also Jane Millgate, *Scott's Last Edition: A Study in Publishing History* (Edinburgh: Edinburgh University Press, 1987), esp. 108–18, for the identities and positions of the Author of Waverley in relation to the novels' publication.

[21] *The Monastery*, Border, p. lxx. Further references appear in the text.

monastery. The manuscript is duly retrieved and handed to Captain Clutterbuck for publication as a 'present to the British public' (p. lxix) of 1820. But before the public can receive this gift, other matters concerning authorship have to be decided: Clutterbuck next 'sends' the manuscript to the Author of Waverley with the suggestion that he 'will review, or rather revise and correct, the enclosed packet, and prepare it for the press, by such alterations, additions, and curtailments, as you think necessary' (p. lxxii). The manuscript is then to be published with both Captain Clutterbuck and the Author of Waverley named on the title-page. The Author replies in an answering letter that no such partnership will occur on the grounds that Captain Clutterbuck is a fictional character who owes his existence to the Author in the first place. But the last word goes to the Captain, who supplies footnotes to the second Introductory Epistle, commenting on the likely intentions of the 'ingenious author' (p. lxxvii).

All this sets in motion a play between the absolute authority of authors and a much more provisional situation. The figure of the Author that emerges from the two introductory letters seems at first all-powerful: he has the final say regarding the state of the text, he can nullify objections from his characters with the stroke of a pen. He points out that 'my landlady never presented me with any manuscript save her cursed bill' (p. lxxx), thereby deeming himself the absolute origin of his own text (and perversely ignoring the fact that some of his early novels had been published as 'Tales of My Landlord'). He also describes himself as the economic owner of the novel, reminding his readers of the self-consciously literate and literary culture of the early nineteenth century. Scott, a partner in his own printing house, was well aware of the commercial considerations that governed the transmission of his novels to the public; in the publishing world of the 1820s, authorship and ownership were things to be negotiated and established. Captain Clutterbuck sends the material to 'The Author of Waverley' at John Ballantyne's address—the Author is to receive the story not primarily as an author, but as a publisher. The Author then returns a jokey letter to Captain Clutterbuck in which Scott debates as to whose name should appear on the title-page. This is all done in legalistic terms: 'As I give you no title to employ or use the firm of the copartnery we are about to form, I will announce my property in my title-page, and put my own mark on my own chattels, which the attorney tells me it will be a crime to counterfeit' (p. lxxxiii).

All these claims, however, are undermined in the comedy of the prefaces' unpacking of the possible meanings of the designation 'Author of Waverley', a phrase which, while seeming to point to a real author, refuses to fix upon any individual.[22] The Author draws attention to an incident in October 1819, during the writing of *The Monastery*, which offers a very different reading of the status of authors. Advertisements appeared in the London *Morning Chronicle* for a new series of *Tales of My Landlord* (a generic title under which a number of Scott's early novels were published) coming from the pen of Jedediah Cleishbotham, another of Scott's frame narrators who had been 'responsible' for several of his early works. Scott's business associates were immediately alarmed at the possible economic consequences of such a publication. Archibald Constable complains of the advertisements, fearing a plot to divert attention from *Ivanhoe*, of which much was hoped.[23] On 28 October the newspaper published a rejoinder from John Ballantyne, asserting that he is 'morally assured' that the spurious fourth series will not appear, and warning that the copyright to the series title remained with Constable.[24] The anonymous advertiser (in fact one William Fearman) struck back against threats of legal action by challenging the very notion of the author of the novels: 'If,

---

[22] For issues of authorship and anonymity, see Patricia S. Gaston, *Prefacing the Waverley Prefaces: A Reading of Sir Walter Scott's Prefaces to the Waverley Novels* (New York: Peter Lang, 1991) which contains valuable discussions of *The Monastery*'s preface.

[23] NLS MS 23234, p. 72. Constable, unusually, was not the primary publisher of *The Monastery* (that honour having gone to the London partners Longmans with whom relations were strained) and tended to suspect *anything*, including genuine advertisements for *The Monastery* and that novel's progress, as a plot 'to injure *Ivanhoe* and its publishers' (p. 76; see also pp. 78, 81, and 84). Constable similarly suspected Longmans of being behind the bogus advertisements (p. 81). See Jane Millgate, 'Making it New: Scott, Constable, Ballantyne, and the Publication of *Ivanhoe*', *Studies in English Literature 1500–1900*, 34 (1994), 795–811.

[24] *Morning Chronicle*, 28 Oct. 1819. According to Constable, John Ballantyne consulted Scott before sending his letter to the editor (NLS MS 23234, p. 75).

by the Author, you mean Jedediah Cleishbotham', ran his next advertisement, 'That Jedediah will prosecute Jedediah, because Jedediah's stores have furnished a Fourth Series, is as little to be believed as feared.'[25] This seems to have been a fairly accurate summary of the case; Constable, furious, took advice about the matter and had to admit: 'I doubt if we can do anything as to this. Mr. M'Dougal thinks we cannot without the author's name, and that, of course, is *impossible*.'[26] Paradoxically, the 'Author of Waverley' cannot be the author of *Waverley* unless he has another name as well.

The legal situation enacts, outside the novel, a loosening of authorities which is also played out within *The Monastery*, as Scott recognizes Fearman's challenge to the unitary authority of authorship. The Author of Waverley's answer to Captain Clutterbuck's letter is a complex speculation about authorship, fictionality, and economic interest. Clutterbuck himself exists in a jokingly paradoxical position. On the one hand, he is realized by receiving a letter, in reply to his own, from a 'real' author, yet that reply is largely concerned with informing Clutterbuck that it is to 'The Author of Waverley' that he owes his existence. The story of the discovery of the manuscript is a fiction invented by the Author who, in writing to Captain Clutterbuck, is effectively addressing himself, thereby virtually deconstructing himself out of existence. In the Author's writing to an openly invented character, the whole concept of authorship turns out to have been a fictive construction all along. In this context, Scott is rather less severe on the Fearman affair than he might at first seem from the evidence of *The Monastery*. The Author is at first sorry to note that Jedediah 'has misbehaved himself so far as to desert his original patron, and set up for himself' (p. lxxxiii). It seems, then, that fictional narrators do indeed have a free intertextual existence and are at liberty to wander from one text to another. But the Author adds in a footnote:

I am since more correctly informed, that Mr. Cleishbotham died some months since at Gandercleugh, and that the person assuming his name is an impostor. The real Jedediah made a most Christian and edifying end ... Hard that the speculators in print and paper will not allow a good man to rest quiet in his grave! (p. lxxxiii)

[25] *Morning Chronicle*, 30 Oct. 1819.   [26] NLS MS 23234, p. 80.

The Author thus neatly sidesteps the question of who 'owns' Jedediah, a person who, falling into the same category as Captain Clutterbuck, can hardly be said to be 'real'. Disingenuously, Scott, who has already aligned the Author of Waverley with his other fictional narrators, identifies the real enemy as 'the speculators in print* and paper' despite being himself implicated in these nefarious practices. Fiona Robertson points out that 'the frames of the first editions become highly conscious of readers and markets for fiction'[27] and *The Monastery* is no exception. The Author ends his epistle in a way that links the commercial business of publishing to the utopian realm of the imagination. Referring to John Ballantyne's involvement in the Fearman affair he informs Captain Clutterbuck:

I shall soon introduce you to my jocund friend, Mr. John Ballantyne of Trinity-Grove, whom you will find warm from his match at single-stick with a brother Publisher. Peace to their differences! It is a wrathful trade, and the *irritabile genus* comprehends the bookselling as well as the book-writing species. (pp. lxxxiv–lxxxv)

The term 'publisher' slides, as it often did in the early nineteenth century, into the term 'bookseller' with its concomitant stress on economic realities. John Ballantyne is described among the publishers of *The Monastery* on the title-page of the first edition as 'Bookseller to the King'.[28] The term 'trade' embraces the linked professions of writing and selling books, but John is a bookseller with royal connections—at every stage in the prefatory material, the authority of the book slips in and out of focus as its social and economic contingencies are revealed and then covered over. The physical presence of the manuscript suggests an economic materiality suppressed by the 'land of Utopia' (p. lxxx) inhabited by Scott's characters, the real becoming comically dispersed in the ideal.

The prefaces, then, draw on, and play with, Scott's transitional position in the social development of the novel. As greater

---

[27] Fiona Robertson, *Legitimate Histories: Scott, Gothic, and the Authorities of Fiction* (Oxford: Clarendon Press, 1994), 132. In addition to some comments on *The Monastery* pertinent to my discussion here, Robertson offers a particularly searching account of the development of the frame narrative throughout Scott's literary career.

[28] John Ballantyne's role in the publication of *The Monastery* was in fact closer to that of literary agent.

authority became invested in the name 'Author of Waverley' so the Author himself interrogates that authority until its sources are no longer visible. The story which unfolds from the Benedictine's manuscript has a great deal in common with the Clutterbuck sections. Just as that manuscript circulates from hand to hand, so the sixteenth-century story concerns a written text whose perambulations are even more extraordinary. This book is a translation of the Bible into English—a heretical text to the representatives of the Catholic Church who feature in the novel.

As *The Monastery* drops back into the sixteenth-century story, it looks more closely at illiteracy without masking it with an idealized 'orality', and interrogates some of the class prejudices in favour of literacy which remain implicit in the *Minstrelsy*. The novel thus sheds interesting light on the debates about orality and literacy in the eighteenth and nineteenth centuries, in which speech or writing could be extracted from a confused field and given an idealized existence to support the distribution of authority. *The Monastery* throws the authority of writing into relief by focusing on a society in transition between illiteracy and literacy. However, the clarity that such an opposition should afford is blurred by the uncertain relationship between the sixteenth-century setting and the novel's nineteenth-century context. What looks at first like the transition from an élitist, pre-modern system of limited literacy to the celebrated democratizing influence of education in modern Scotland is undercut by the novel's strange ending in which it is suggested that Halbert Glendinning's burgeoning career as self-made lad of parts may be less than fully successful. Rather than providing a foil for the success of Scottish literacy, it may be that the Reformation setting provides a means for the novel to investigate—albeit uncertainly—some of the flaws in the Scottish myth of education.

The Monastery explores literacy by seeing it in connection with questions about legitimacy. In the story, this has to do with an anxiety about birth, an authority which cannot be challenged if it is located in something as inherent as blood, but which, if it is not, is open to all sorts of political questions. The interrogation of seemingly inherent value is very pertinent to assumptions about education in the nineteenth century, in which belief in the pure good of literacy was being challenged by the social changes in an increasingly industrialized and urbanized Scotland. As commentators reacted to these demographic changes they increasingly reiterated Adam Smith's view that education was making the Scots a more law-abiding people than the English. Literacy was seen as a check on the unlawful propensities of a population no longer under control and the connection was made between illegality and illegitimacy of birth. The general view of literacy, of course, was not that it was designed to transform the frighteningly immoral working class into a manageable labour force, but that it was a good in and of itself and of real benefit to any individual. In order for literacy to be offered to individuals as a pure good, they had first to be convinced of 'illiteracy' as a pure evil, artificially bifurcating Scottish culture.

Returning to *The Monastery*, we can see how these questions are addressed in the relationship between literacy and legitimacy in the sixteenth century. Literacy in *The Monastery* is the province of two main groups: the educated aristocracy and the Church. Each of the Glendinning brothers, Edward and Halbert, eventually allies himself with one of these, but they both find their acquisition of the status of literacy to be very troubled. The monastery cuts its vassals off from the written word, using tactics not dissimilar to the attempts of the nineteenth-century popular education movement to promulgate literacy. The Church uses literacy as a political tool to control the illiterate, and does so by fostering views about the absolute authority of writing. In *The Monastery*, orality is associated not only with nature but also with preliterate ways of thinking about nature; in the minds of some of the characters, writing takes on an absolute power which the monks then annex. Reading, in the novel, takes on the characteristics of nineteenth-century 'mere reading', with its slippage from Bible reading as a means of understanding, to any reading as a social activity, and a way of controlling political power. When Alice of Avenel reads sections of the Bible in English to the family at Glendearg, they hear it in superstitious reverence 'whether it was fully understood or no' (p. 35). These listeners are characterized in the same way as the ignorant transmitters of ballads in the *Minstrelsy of the Scottish Border*, who uncomprehendingly mimic texts phonetically. The monks are able to use the illiterate characters' primitive views about language to maintain power. These characters see words as substantial things with the intrinsic power to reward or destroy those who come into contact with them. The narrator draws attention to the popular belief that the act of pronouncing the name of something can work as a kind of spell: 'it was deemed highly imprudent to speak of the fairies either by their title of *good neighbours* or by any other, especially when about to pass the places which they were supposed to haunt' (p. 26). This seems particularly true of words that look like substantial things, and which can have no referential function for the illiterate: words such as 'books'.

Scott is drawing on a view of language which is said to pertain to partially literate cultures in which writing can be seen as the instrument of power. Walter Ong remarks that 'Some societies of limited literacy have regarded writing as dangerous to the unwary reader, demanding a guru-like figure to mediate between reader and text.'[29] In Scots, the association of writing with magic is preserved, as 'grammar', or book-learning, became 'glamour', or magical power. When orality and literacy come together, anyone offering to adopt a mediating role has to be treated with some scepticism. The editor of the *Minstrelsy* performed such an operation in reverse: in seeming to mediate between oral texts and a literate readership Scott manœuvred himself into a position which kept orality and literacy firmly apart.

In *The Monastery*, only those who can read Latin can be allowed access to the written word, but the monks' position as intermediaries is dubious. Meg Merrilies, in *Guy Mannering*, is deeply suspicious of the power of Latin grammar as glamour. Subjected by Dominie Sampson to a 'volley' of Latin (or, as she refers to it, 'French gibberish, that would make a dog sick'), Meg strikes back: ' "Is the carl daft," she said, "wi' his glamour?" '[30] In *The Monastery*, however, the efficacy of grammar as glamour is not so easily dismissed. The supposedly superstitious belief in the power of writing is appropriated by

---

[29] Walter J. Ong, *Orality and Literacy: The Technologizing of the Word* (London and New York: Methuen, 1982), 93.
[30] *Guy Mannering*, Border, 467.

the Catholic Church to bolster up its own authority, harried by the English and under threat from the Reformed Church in Scotland. The monks dictate that the English Bible is 'by the order of the Holy Catholic Church, unfit to be in the hands of any lay person', and representatives of the monastery duly attempt to confiscate the book. The monks acknowledge that the book indeed represents 'the Holy Scripture' and therefore that its contents survive the transition from one language to another. No clear reason for the confiscation is given by Father Philip, other than that the very reading of the English words will have fatal consequences:

I tell thee, Elspeth, *the Word slayeth*—that is, the text alone, read with unskilled eye and unhallowed lips, is like those strong medicines which sick men take by the advice of the learned. Such patients recover and thrive; while those dealing in them at their own hand, shall perish by their own deed. (p. 51)

This threat, which to the reader is clearly a political ruse for keeping the considerable power of language in the control of the Church, sounds like a witch-doctor's curse. The effect will be similar to the awful consequences of looking at the book of Michael Scott the Warlock in Hogg's *Three Perils of Man*: 'If any one of you were to look but on one character of this book, his brain would be seared to a cinder, his eyes would fly out of their sockets'.[31] It is the words themselves, and not anything to which they might be used to refer, that have the power of life and death: 'the Word—the mere Word, slayeth' (p. 52). The phrase echoes the biblical one 'the letter killeth, but the spirit giveth life' (2 Corinthians 3:6), a phonocentric sentiment drawn on, as Derrida documents, by many religions. In this case, however, the written letter does not endanger the 'natural' or living word, but defends it; it is the reader, not the word, who is in danger of being slain. In other words, this is an independent writing which does not act on speech, and is not a supplement to speech. It is also different from what Derrida represents as

---

[31] *PM* 335. Michael Scott's book, and indeed the Warlock himself, also put in an appearance, with impressive magical effects, in *The Lay of the Last Minstrel*. Scott mentions the same magic book in *The Monastery* when Clutterbuck alludes to 'Michael Scott's lamp and book of magic power' (p. lxv).

Western culture's idea of 'good writing', a writing that is 'immediately united to the voice and to breath'.[32] Derrida cites the Bible, the written yet living word of God, as the epitome of such writing in Western culture, but the Bible/Black Book of *The Monastery* does not seem quite to fit this pattern as it constitutes a writing that does not derive its identity from speech. On the contrary, the social conditions of Scottish literacy construct a writing that depends on its *not* being orality—indeed a writing which, far from being supplementary to speech, can stand as a linguistic origin. Scott had already provided an instance of the class pressures which push writing into this position. In *The Antiquary*, Jonathan Oldbuck and Sir Arthur Wardour may argue as to whether or not 'Pictish' is a Celtic or Gothic language, but they are agreed on one thing: the advisability of having one's genealogical origins underscored by writing. Oldbuck boasts his descent from 'the painful and industrious typographer, Wolfbrand Oldenbuck', while Wardour, not to be outdone, retorts, 'I have the pleasure to inform you that the name of my ancestor, Gamelyn de Guardover, Miles, is written fairly with his own hand in the earliest copy of the Ragman-roll.'[33] Now in *The Monastery* Scott investigates in greater detail the status of writing as origin by linking it with other ideas about human origins.

The Church's distribution of power through the control of literacy is mirrored in the relationship between literacy and status in the secular world. In the novel's sixteenth-century society, literacy is equated with another power deemed to represent natural authority: birth. The discussion of literacy and its authority is coextensive with a debate about legitimacy. Literacy in the secular world is designated as a high-status activity: Mary Avenel's 'rank and expectations entitled her to be taught the arts of reading and writing' (pp. 132–3). However, the ownership of such status is a very problematic affair in the novel. *The Monastery* is a novel obsessed with illegitimacy either of birth or of succession. Even the most casual enquiry of a minor character is immediately taken to concern legitimacy:

---

[32] Jacques Derrida, *Of Grammatology*, trans. Gayatri Chakravorty Spivak (Baltimore and London: Johns Hopkins University Press, 1976), 17.

[33] *The Antiquary*, Border, 76–7.

Stawarth Bolton's question to Elspeth Glendinning about the paternity of her fair- and dark-haired sons meets with 'a blush of displeasure' (p. 18). The child of Julian Avenel and Catherine Graeme is born out of wedlock, and attention is frequently drawn to the sufferings of Catherine on this score. Many of the principal characters—Piercie Shafton, Murray, Halbert—are worried about their own legitimacy of birth, of status, or of the power they hold.

Because of these anxieties, natural power, like the natural magic of the book, comes into question; when authority ceases to be seen as inherent it is more difficult to establish. The Earl of Murray's very status as the 'natural' child of James V shows how precarious the natural can be: his authority, as the narrator points out, is tarnished by the 'stain of illegitimacy' (p. 492). His parentage—aristocratic but illegitimate—is the source both of his power and of the compromising of that power. The naturalness of blood can only be fully authoritative when supported by the social sanction of the marriage ceremony. *The Monastery*'s daringly illegitimate conclusion could not be sustained into its sequel where a novelistic marriage-plot smooths things over. In a brazen revision of the plot of *The Monastery* at the end of *The Abbot*, Julian and Catherine are said to have been married (by Father Philip) all along, but it is alleged that Julian, having changed his mind, persuaded Catherine 'to believe that the ceremony had been performed by one not in holy orders, and having no authority to that effect'.[34]

The Abbot is a move even further away from the essential or magical power practised in *The Monastery*. In *The Abbot*, the state of being married has to be negotiated and established by the appropriate authorities. Roland's new-found legitimacy has to be verified by a surprisingly large number of documents sanctioned by the legal authority of writing: Father Philip's attestation, the marriage certificate, and a letter from Julian.[35] The end of *The Monastery* seems to point in this direction. Mary

---

[34] *The Abbot*, Border, 625.
[35] See R. A. Houston, *Scottish Literacy and the Scottish Identity: Illiteracy and Society in Scotland and Northern England, 1600–1800* (Cambridge: Cambridge University Press, 1985), 239–40, for the ways in which written transactions concerning marriage and paternity can be used to the advantage of the literate.

Avenel, as Murray points out, becomes particularly interesting as a marriage partner when she regains her property after the death of Julian. Perhaps like the authority of the Author of Waverley, the glamour of birth turns on economics after all.

Such possibilities remain, but the earlier volume is less certain, refusing to pinpoint the exact location of authority. Even in its marked anti-Catholicism, *The Monastery* does not offer an complete polarization of written word into natural and contingent authority. Or, more precisely, the novel's anti-Catholicism forces the assertion of a better natural authority than the simple idea of grammar as glamour. Yet even so, *The Monastery* manages to evade a final decision on the matter. The novel is after all about a text which is both the magical Black Book and the Protestant Bible. As Black Book it really is magic; the novel does not offer a simple dismissal of glamour in favour of an awareness of political and contingent power. Despite the apparent ignorance and gullibility of the illiterate characters, their point of view is upheld. In charge of the natural magic of the Black Book is the conspicuously illiterate White Lady—part nature spirit, part equivocal guardian of the Avenel family fortunes—who ensures that the book is magically transported back if any of the monks attempt to seize it. An early attempt is made by the Sacristan, Father Philip, which duly ends in disaster for him. After unceremoniously depositing Father Philip in the Tweed, the White Lady gleefully proclaims the magical authority of the book itself over its enemies: 'Landed—landed! the black book hath won' (p. 61).

Even the bifurcation of the book into Black Book and Bible is not straightforward as this Bible is both a natural sign and an interpretable one.[36] When Mary undergoes her conversion to Protestantism merely reading the Bible causes her spontaneously to confirm 'Surely this is the word of God' (p. 423), yet it is not exactly 'the word of God' she is reading, but a version which has

---

[36] For an important discussion of natural signs and their exegesis in relation to Calvinist thinking in Scotland, see Susan Manning, *The Puritan-Provincial Vision: Scottish and American Literature in the Nineteenth Century* (Cambridge: Cambridge University Press, 1990), esp. 12–15. For Calvinism in relation to the problematics of Scotland's national identity see Caroline McCracken-Flesher, 'Thinking Nationally/ Writing Colonially? Scott, Stevenson, and England', *Novel*, 24 (1991), 296–318.

other texts interwoven into it. Mary's mother has prepared the volume for her by interleaving it with slips of paper which reveal 'by an appeal to, and a comparison of, various passages in holy writ, the errors and human inventions with which the Church of Rome had defaced the simple edifice of Christianity' (p. 422). The naturalness of the sign is itself dependent not only on interpretation, but on one exegesis constructed in opposition to another.

Thus, in *The Monastery*, the sources of authority are difficult to trace. Not surprisingly, Halbert's acquisition of it is fraught with anxiety as he is caught between ideas about essential and contingent power. If the low-born Halbert is to be a self-made man he must cross over from belief in the absolute magic of the book to the provisional literacy of social status. But, like the self-made lads of parts of the nineteenth century, he is encouraged to see literacy as an inherently good thing. Glamour, the essential power of the written text, is held to be intrinsic and so cannot be questioned. Halbert's own inability to progress beyond this point hampers his aspirations. Perhaps like the novel itself, he does not quite shake off the two extremes of natural magic and the status of blood in favour of a democratic and Enlightened third option.

Halbert, reluctant to learn to read, tries to evade the problem by redrawing the conditions for union with Mary Avenel (literate because of her 'rank and expectations') and seeking the magical power of the White Lady:

'It is the season and the hour,' said Halbert to himself; 'and now I—I might soon become wiser than Edward with all his pains! Mary should see whether he alone is fit to be consulted, and to sit by her side, and hang over her as she reads, and point out every word and every letter. And she loves me better than him—I am sure she does—for she comes of noble blood, and scorns sloth and cowardice.' (p. 138)

Halbert here separates out literacy and social status. Mary's privileged reading is to be incidental to that 'noble blood' which alone will guarantee her suitability as a lover for Halbert. But he continues to use the concept of literacy as a touchstone for an absolute authority whose uses cannot be questioned. Having rejected his schooltexts, Halbert goes off in search of 'a better book' (p. 136), the English Bible which he knows to be in the possession of the White Lady. Descending into a subterranean cavern with her, he undergoes a ritual test during which he has to seize the book from a magical fire. After this episode, Halbert is mysteriously elevated in the eyes of the other characters who notice that he 'bore himself with a manner which appertained to higher rank' (p. 183). Social advantage seems to be conferred by something even more intrinsic than an accident of birth—the magic of essences.[37] Literacy is deemed a state of power that has nothing to do with the processes of reading but which is nevertheless seen as a condition of literacy. Halbert's subterranean activities parody the status of reading in Scotland's evaluation of education.

The novel's unsettled exploration of literacy and power does not end here, but continually offers alternative ways of establishing authority until none can seem unique. The White Lady, herself illiterate, is a spokesperson for the social advantages of literacy, and gives Halbert a lecture on how his failure to become literate is tantamount to scorning 'the nurture of gentle blood' (p. 142). Such blood may not then be in nature if it can be nurtured. Perhaps Halbert should have learned to read after all. His bypassing of learned grammar turns out to be glamour in the sense offered by Scott in a note to *The Lay of the Last Minstrel*: '*Glamour*, in the legends of Scottish superstition, means the magic power of imposing on the eyesight of the spectators, so that the appearance of an object shall be totally different from the reality'.[38] But to sustain the belief in the deceptive qualities of glamour, such superstition remains underpinned with a faith in the essential nature of things: if an object is not in reality one thing, it must be in reality something else.

Yet in the novel's sequel, which is the second part of the Benedictine's manuscript, Halbert's social elevation does not make him happy. His marriage to Mary at the start of *The Abbot* is beset with unease about the difference in their ranks

---

[37] Judith Wilt points out that in this episode Halbert progresses from regarding the Bible as 'text-talisman' to a position where he must 'read the texts of his changed character, the characters of his changed text, and their Protestant paraphrases' (*Secret Leaves: The Novels of Walter Scott* (Chicago: University of Chicago Press, 1985), 92).   [38] *PW* vi. 258.

and the legitimacy of his acquisition of the Avenel lands. His promotion to the aristocracy is uncomfortable, and it is not until the revelation that Roland Graeme is the son of Julian and Catherine, whose union is retrospectively legitimized, that the Avenel succession can rest on a sure footing. Glamour fails to work: Adam Woodcock, the Avenel falconer, comments on a gift from Roland that 'It is not fairy-money';[39] that is, it is unlikely to revert to its real essential nature (often, in the case of money given by the fairies, dead leaves).[40] The money on which social authority rests cannot revert to any prior existence, being endlessly transferable into whatever it can buy. *The Monastery* plays with this possibility without ever quite confirming it: that the authority of the written word is arbitrary, just as the Author of Waverley's legitimizing of the novel might be a socially determined force having little to do with the intentions of the author of *Waverley*.

[39] *The Abbot*, Border, 615.
[40] For Scott's account of the insubstantiality of fairy gifts, see his 'Letters on Demonology and Witchcraft', *MPW* xxix. 21–2.

3

'Living, and Life-like': Storytelling in The Three Perils of Man

FOR a self-taught writer, very little of James Hogg's literary career seems to have been under his own control. Whereas Scott, a partner in his own printing house, was able economically to control the activities of 'The Author of Waverley' at least until the crash of 1826, 'The Ettrick Shepherd' and his fortunes were much more at the mercy of the Edinburgh literati and their influence on the reading public. To some extent, Hogg participated himself in the decentring of his own name by offering it to other writers, most famously in his letter to Lockhart after Scott's death, proposing that Lockhart write Scott's *Life* under his name. Yet more commonly the identity of the Ettrick Shepherd was constructed by the literary culture of Edinburgh.[1] Hogg's life, as figured in the commentaries of his acquaintances, is bound up in the construction of orality in the period. As both a pastoral and an actual shepherd he seemed to embody both the idealized orality of the Romantic poet and the taint of a class more commonly associated with illiteracy. Lockhart's brief sketch of Hogg's character in the *Life of Scott* holds the two in tension: 'Under the garb, aspect, and bearing, of a rude peasant—and rude enough he was in most of these things, even after no inconsiderable experience of society—Scott found a brother poet, a true son of nature and genius, hardly conscious of his powers.'[2] Lockhart gives us the construction of a poet whose genius precedes the act of writing, much as Wordsworth

---

[1] For a comprehensive account of the construction of 'The Ettrick Shepherd' by Hogg and others, see Silvia Mergenthal, *James Hogg: Selbstbilt und Bild: Zur Rezeption des 'Ettrick Shepherd'* (Frankfurt am Main: Peter Lang, 1990). For Hogg's poetic and journalistic personae see also Peter T. Murphy, *Poetry as an Occupation and an Art in Britain, 1760–1830* (Cambridge: Cambridge University Press, 1993).   [2] *Life*, i. 329.

had claimed for the generation of 'Tintern Abbey',[3] and in fact Hogg was seen as a kind of Scottish Wordsworth, as in Wilson's summation of his genius: 'And living for years in the solitude, he unconsciously formed friendships with the springs—the brooks—the caves—the hills . . . His mind, therefore, is stored with images of nature dear to him for the recollections which they bring—for the restoration of his earlier life.'[4]

More frequently, however, the reader of the *Life of Scott* is invited to peruse the 'most legible marks of a recent sheep-smearing' as Hogg embarrasses himself yet again in Scott's household by reclining on Charlotte Scott's sofa in imitation of 'the lady of the house'.[5] Hogg was in the world of the Edinburgh literati but not of it; the odour of sheep pursued him, and not only in Lockhart's gleeful tallying of his social blunders. In the first of the *Noctes Ambrosianae*, before he makes an appearance in person, Hogg is introduced by the Editor, Christopher North (Wilson's persona), first as the author of *The Three Perils of Man*, and then, immediately afterwards, as someone 'to be seen, about five in the morning, selling sheep in the Grassmarket'.[6] Like the 'recondite' printed ballads which infiltrated Constable's bookshop, Hogg, similarly touched by the unreconstructed oral, is an alien in the early nineteenth-century literary world, pointedly left out of Christopher North's list of the really important poets of the age.

Thus the paradox of orality made Hogg's position precarious. On the one hand, there is the 'natural genius' of the Ettrick Shepherd, on the other, the 'boozing buffoon' in literary circles. If Hogg was to succeed as a literary figure, it might seem important for him to establish a clear demarcation between the purity of orality and the corruption of illiteracy. But Hogg's tactics were rather different; instead of abstracting an

---

[3] Current research is indicating that not all Hogg's texts were so spontaneous, as will be made apparent by the forthcoming Edinburgh Edition of Hogg's work.

[4] [John Wilson], 'Burns and the Ettrick Shepherd', *BM* 4 (1818–19), 521–9 (p. 527). [5] *Life*, i. 408.

[6] *The Tavern Sages: Selections from the 'Noctes Ambrosianae'*, ed. J. H. Alexander (Aberdeen: Association for Scottish Literary Studies, 1992), 12–13. This conversation originally appeared in *Blackwood's* in March 1822. See also J. H. Alexander, 'Hogg in the *Noctes Ambrosianae*', *Studies in Hogg and his World*, 4 (1993), 37–47.

immaculate orality from the assumed social depravity of the oral world, he sought to subvert the distinction altogether. Hogg's characteristic play with the way primitive people are supposed to use language and stories and a conversely 'sophisticated' attitude to them is well illustrated by the short story 'The Unearthly Witness'.

'The Unearthly Witness' is the story of William Tibbers, who, after a dispute with the local laird, is believed murdered; a body is found dressed in Tibbers's clothes but otherwise unrecognizable. The laird's heir engages with Tibbers's daughters in a lawsuit, turning on a missing duplicate of a legal document, over the family property. Tibbers's 'ghost' then appears to persuade an attorney in the case, Johnie Gaskirk, to 'remember' the existence of this disposition, which he had conveniently forgotten. When Gaskirk recounts this visitation to the court, Tibbers is officially summonsed and what is believed to be his grotesquely decomposing ghost duly appears, to the consternation of all present who flee the courtroom, causing deaths and injuries in the panic.

The story explores some of the questions about language and power raised in *The Monastery*'s inquiry into literacy as it challenges the easy identification of the oral with nature. The narrator of the story, whom Hogg identifies in a note as the Reverend Walker, is an Episcopalian minister with some of the same prejudices as the editor of *Confessions of a Justified Sinner*. Walker groups the participants of the story into two sides: the 'country gentlemen' and 'the common people'. The latter group is convinced of the supernatural reality of the ghost's return, but Walker himself remains undecided; he is unconvinced that Tibbers is really dead, feeling that there is no 'decisive proof', and having little faith in the evidence of 'simple and credulous natives'.[7] The whole issue turns on another case of grammar and glamour or rather, this time, summonsing and summoning: does Tibbers appear because he is legally summonsed, or does the summons read out in court act as a magical summoning of the dead? The question is really a linguistic one, hovering between a conventional use of speech

[7] *Stories*, 142. All stories by Hogg referred to in this chapter are in this edition and further references appear in the text.

acts, apparently the province of the educated, and a belief in magic language, associated with 'the common people'.

At first there seems to be quite a difference between these two views of language. A legal summons is a classic speech act as defined by J. L. Austin in that it is dependent on a conventional context for its operation.[8] When the summons is pronounced, the legal position of the person summonsed is thereby altered; he or she must attend the court or be held in contempt. For the speech act to work, certain social conventions have to be in place; in this case the summons has to be uttered by a speaker socially empowered to do so, and in the appropriate place. However, once the empowering circumstances are exhausted the speech act ceases to be, to use Austin's term, felicitous; dead people, for example, are not usually subject to being summonsed. Magic language, such as the summoning of the dead, comes with no such qualifications; it will work whatever the circumstances as it is so intimately bound up with its object that there appears to be no difference between them. In this sense, magic language is not a system of signs but a rite.

Sometimes, however, it is not easy to determine the difference between the status of a speech act and that of magic language. This situation is neatly illustrated by an interesting debate between two speech act theorists over the question of whether or not the utterance of magic language can itself be called a speech act, centring on the case of supernatural declarations. John Searle claims that God's utterance 'Let there be light' is a declaration and therefore a speech act.[9] Sandy Petrey, on the other hand, argues that divine utterances cannot be speech acts as they are wholly independent of the social circumstances which produce 'the reality-transforming utterances institutions make possible'.[10] The theoretical situation is further complicated by Derrida's challenging of the very grounds of speech act theory, as he argues that speech act theory ignores the always arbitrary nature of signs. Classic speech acts like 'I now

---

[8] J. L. Austin, *How to Do Things with Words* (Oxford: Clarendon Press, 1962).

[9] John Searle, *Expression and Meaning: Studies in the Theory of Speech Acts* (Cambridge: Cambridge University Press, 1979), 18.

[10] Sandy Petrey, *Speech Acts and Literary Theory* (New York and London: Routledge, 1990), 64.

pronounce you man and wife' can, according to speech act theory, mean only one thing, leading Derrida to detect in them 'the self-presence of a total context, the transparency of intentions, the presence of meaning for the absolute singular oneness of a speech act'.[11] Walker admits that he reproduces in his account an 'indistinct recollection' (p. 143) of the words of the summons, but if an utterance is to work as a classic speech act the words must be 'correct', just as it is the power of words themselves that is effective in magic language.

Similarly, in the case of 'The Unearthly Witness', we are not offered a free choice between speech acts and magic language; Hogg typically denies the reader the possibility of arbitrating between dualities. Both a summons and a summoning are manifestations of power, one the power of the law and the other of magic, or nature, but which power is effective here? Does Tibbers appear because he is summonsed, or because he is summoned? Are things brought into existence through the conventional and societal functions of language, or because words are magically connected to things in nature, so that merely to utter a word is to call its referent into being? Hogg's enlightened readers might dismiss the latter, yet before the reader can decide that he or she is not subject to superstitious beliefs, Hogg has removed the option of faith in the power of speech acts by pointing out that they are no more, or no less, authoritative than magic language. Before his spectacular appearance in court, the ghost of Tibbers pressurizes Gaskirk to swear to the existence of the missing document, asserting: 'your three oaths will prove its existence' (p. 142). The belief in the power of conventional utterances to bring things into existence turns out to be no more, or less, real than the superstition of 'the common people'.

If social speech acts are really not so different from magic language, then 'The Unearthly Witness' can be seen to whittle away the distinction between 'natural' and 'artificial' language, which, in the Scottish Enlightenment, was a social as well as a linguistic judgement. Thomas Reid had argued for a historical view of language in which artificial signs must be preceded by

---

[11] Jacques Derrida, 'Signature Event Context', in *Margins of Philosophy*, trans. Alan Bass (Brighton: Harvester Press, 1982), 325.

natural ones: 'if mankind had not a natural language, they could never have invented an artificial one by their reason and ingenuity.' Natural language is produced by primitive people or 'savages': 'The elements of this natural language of mankind, or the signs that are naturally expressive of our thoughts, may, I think, be reduced to these three kinds; modulations of the voice, gestures, and features. By means of these, two savages who have no common artificial language, can converse together . . .'[12]

Like the Ettrick Shepherd himself, the user of natural language is caught up in the paradox of orality. Natural signs are the purest of all expressions, being 'naturally expressive of our thoughts', and Reid regrets their loss, but they are also the province of savages, who have to wait for the development of artificial language to make full use of their 'reason and ingenuity'. But if the opposition between natural and artificial signs is deconstructed, as it is in 'The Unearthly Witness', then savage and civilized peoples, or peasants and literati, are not so easily distinguished. But this is not to say that Hogg entirely abandons the concept of magic language in favour of the multiple puns and sliding signifiers of *Confessions of a Justified Sinner*. Continually challenging the assumptions of his readers, he will not quite allow the matter to rest on whatever the reader may chose to believe. The story 'The Barber of Duncow', tantalizingly subtitled 'A Real Ghost Story', makes further play with the literary status of speech acts and/or magic language. Like 'The Unearthly Witness', this story, told by Raighel Gordon to her family on a winter's night, concerns the appearance of the ghost of a murdered person but this time the possibility of summoning up the spirit is extended to the reader. Raighel warns that 'when any body hears [the story], an disna believe it, the murdered woman is sure to come in' (p. 169). The summoning of the ghost here depends not on superstitious belief but on rational disbelief as we are invited to imagine ghosts walking into the houses of the Metropolis.[13] The story ends with its fictional audience glancing nervously towards the door as Raighel repeats that the ghost will reappear

---

[12] Thomas Reid, *An Inquiry into the Human Mind on the Principles of Common Sense* (Edinburgh: A. Kincaid and J. Bell, 1764), 103, 105.

[13] The story was first published in the London-based *Fraser's Magazine*.

'if the tale be accurately tould' (p. 179) yet not believed. Ironically, the more sophisticated the use of language—and the 'hearing acts' in 'The Barber of Duncow' form a hall of mirrors of complexity—the less sure the reader becomes that magic language is a primitive superstition. This effect is achieved through Hogg's challenging of the inefficacy of fictional speech acts. Austin claims that speech acts spoken, for example, on stage, are merely imitative of the real variety and thus can never be felicitous. Hogg's answer to this is to unnerve the position of the reader who might take such a view; it is precisely the situation in which the fiction places the reader that causes the grounds for his or her disbelief to falter.

The relationship between language, magic, and reading is the basis for one of Hogg's more extended analyses of storytelling, *The Three Perils of Man*, published in 1822. This novel defeats any attempt at categorization; its plot alone is composed of so many strands and individual stories that it is not easy to give a coherent account of it.[14] Outwardly a historical novel (although Hogg pays little regard to recorded historical events or their generally accepted dates),[15] *Perils of Man* tells the story (or rather stories) of a Border conflict in which the Scots and the English vie for possession of Roxburgh Castle. The opening and closing sections of the narrative are concerned with the successes and failures, in love and war, of the chief parties concerned. The principal combatants here are the Earl of Douglas (who wins) and Lord Musgrave (who kills himself). The men's activities are interspersed with those of their lovers, Margaret Stuart and Jane Howard, who spend portions of the novel disguised as boys.

The greater part of the narrative, however, follows the adventures of socially less elevated characters. In order to determine on which side his loyalties should lie, Sir Ringan Redhough, a Border baron, sends a disparate group of his

---

[14] Douglas Mack gives an account of Hogg's intention to split the work into 'seven distinct tales' in 'James Hogg's Second Thoughts on *The Three Perils of Man*', *Studies in Scottish Literature*, 21 (1986), 167–75.

[15] Anachronisms in the novel are detailed by Douglas Gifford in his edition (*PM* 466–9), and addressed in John MacQueen, *The Rise of the Historical Novel* (Edinburgh: Scottish Academic Press, 1989), 218–20.

followers to visit the warlock Michael Scott, a relative of his, in order to ask him to foretell the outcome of the siege of Roxburgh Castle which will allow Sir Ringan to align himself with the winning side. The warlock turns out to be somewhat less than accommodating, but eventually supplies the required prophecy out of his magic book. The many, varied, and extremely odd adventures of Sir Ringan's embassy, led by Charlie Scott of Yardbire, in Michael Scott's castle of Aikwood form the middle part of the story which returns at the end of the novel to Roxburgh, now in the possession of Douglas and the Scots. Here some of the surviving characters marry each other and we witness the spectacular end of the warlock.

Despite, or more probably because of, the novel's seemingly chaotic structure and multiple narrative strands, *The Three Perils of Man* is a compendium of ideas about language and storytelling. These explorations into the nature of narrative are described and practised by a wide range of characters within the novel, and by the novel's principal narrator. Hogg, however, is never an author to divulge a unified theory which his readers might apply to his works, and the novel does not reveal an overarching principle of narrative beneath which other views of storytelling can range in any hierarchical order. Rather, *The Three Perils of Man* embraces diversity; it offers a range of ideas about language and storytelling; its characters argue about what is, or is not, worth the name of a story and throughout the narrator maintains an amused, equivocal presence.

The novel's structure seems to invite an opposition between the world of courtly sophistication and the primitive world of magic and storytelling. Yet, as in *Confessions of a Justified Sinner*, binary oppositions in this novel, though very frequent, turn out to be highly deceptive, typically abandoning the reader after he or she has been drawn into a pattern of dualities. Hogg attacks the cultural division into primitive and sophisticated, of which he was himself a victim, by setting up such bifurcations, only to reveal how untenable they are. The keystone of construction of orality in the early nineteenth century is the identification of the oral with nature and, not surprisingly, *The Three Perils of Man* has a great deal to say about the natural.

When the warlock, Michael Scott, asks his demonic pages, Prig, Prim, and Pricker, 'What is the most hateful thing in nature?',[16] he is asking a more precise question than simply 'What is the most hateful thing?' Michael inhabits a world in which things may have identities which remain prescribed and fixed in nature, a world consisting of the four basic elements which are presided over by 'potent elemental spirits that rule and controul the earth, the air, the fire, and the waters' (p. 177). Michael is subscribing to a conception of the cosmos in which all of nature is infused with magical properties. The practice of 'natural magic' therefore does not impose upon the natural world, but harnesses the energies already within it; in a world imbued with magical properties, power can be achieved through an understanding of 'natural' processes. Charlie Scott, for example, makes use of this in Aikwood when he is in grave danger of being slaughtered by the imps Prig, Prim, and Pricker, remembering 'that, by certain laws of nature, and the use of holy rites, wicked spirits were restrained' (p. 164).

The novel offers what at first looks a paradigm for the opposition of the essentially natural to the non-natural. During the residence of Charlie's band at Aikwood, Michael Scott is much troubled by the friar, a member of the embassy, who, not surprisingly, takes exception to Michael's occult practices. Their antagonism points up a contrast between a belief in an objectively present universe of fixed identities, and an acknowledgement that the world is subject to human perception. The friar is able to produce effects that do not directly reflect things that exist in nature, using magnification and light effects to create spectacular 'phantasmagoria' (p. 179) and he manages, by similar means, to create the 'optical delusion' (p. 183) that the Cope-Law mountain has been divided by him into three. His effect is based not only on the properties of the refraction of light, but also on the fact that nobody thinks it necessary to inspect the mountain itself. His trick succeeds because the spectators believe it to have succeeded; the 'natural' status of the mountain (whether or not it is 'really' split) is not at issue here.

So impressed is Michael with the friar's apparent magic that he dispatches Prim, Prig, and Pricker, with spades and shovels, to achieve the same result with Eildon Hill. Yet despite their

---

[16] *PM* 291. Further references appear in the text.

magical powers, the pages have a difficult task as they are obliged to deal with the natural properties of a mountain, which are to be large and solid. The pages are forced really to split Eildon Hill, whereas the friar gets away with a trick of perspective. Michael Scott's magic deals in the natural properties of things, their identities 'in nature', but the friar's methods exploit how things can appear to the susceptible human eye. What matters in the friar's arrangement of things is the way they are transmitted—there is no need to enquire into any underlying reality as everyone is perfectly satisfied with the optical effect.

This is just one example of what at first looks like a division common in Romantic thinking about the primitive: an older world of natural magic constructed against a new one of culture, a magic of essences as opposed to one of appearances, pre-social nature contrasted with a newer and more sophisticated literary and social culture. Such a pattern recurs in the disguises and transformations which proliferate in the novel. In the courtly world, characters prefer disguise to transformation. Some of these disguises are not penetrated by the reader: in the Roxburgh Castle strand, the reader learns of the executions of Richard, the younger brother of Lord Thomas Musgrave, who has been captured by Douglas, and of a person whom we believe to be Margaret Stuart disguised as a page. We are later informed that the man executed was not Richard (Douglas having been reluctant to part with his bargaining power over Thomas Musgrave) and that the dead 'page' was in fact a tailor's apprentice whom Margaret had dressed in her own boy's disguise. Although everything turns out well for the principal characters, their unfortunate substitutes are not rescued by the emergence of their 'true' identities. Unlike Gibbie Jordan (who, amazingly, manages to survive being eaten several times), the supposed page and Richard Musgrave's substitute are actually put to death in a world in which how things appear determines their identities.

Magical though they may be, however, the supernatural transformations in this part of the story are rather less effective than the simple disguises adopted, either willingly or by force, by various of the characters. The friar quickly recognizes his friends in the bulls that are delivered to him, the devil-as-dog gives himself away, and the retainers sent to meet Charlie's embassy keep their 'ratten faces', betraying their rodent origins. Disguise, on the other hand, works in a different way to transformation and is much harder to see through. In order to get into Roxburgh Castle, Sir Ringan's men, who have acquired some skins in a skirmish with English traders, disguise themselves among a herd of cattle which Musgrave's starving troops let into the besieged castle.

Some people in the novel seem to have essential natures which survive the process of transformation of which there are many, from animals into humans, and, more frequently, from humans into animals. Gourlay and Gibbie Jordan are both turned into a sequence of different beasts, Charlie's entire party is turned into bulls, the Devil sometimes appears as a dog. The magical changes wrought upon material objects do not effect their nature: the food and drink which Charlie and his associates are served in Michael Scott's castle does not satisfy their hunger, however much they consume, and indeed this meal turns out not to be the wine and sirloin of beef which it appears as. When blessed by the friar, the food is revealed as 'a small insignificant thing resembling the joint of a frog's leg, or that of a rat; and perhaps two or three drops of gravy' (p. 172). The magical transformations alter shapes, but not the essential characteristics of things in nature. Characters too seem to have essential natures which are unaffected by the metamorphoses to which they are subjected. The transformation into bulls barely works at all as the friar immediately recognizes his erstwhile companions, but when Charlie's party disguise themselves as bulls it is a triumphant success for the Scots.

Again, the novel seems to be proposing an opposition between nature and social assumptions. The magic world deals in the essential nature of things which are constant and are subject to material presence. The social world is one of representation: the way this world is read is the way it is. Yet the opposition is not sustained, transformation and disguise come together in the incidents first, of Michael Scott's turning Charlie and friends into bulls, and secondly, in the adoption of the bull disguise to get into Roxburgh Castle. This time, it is not so easy to identify what is 'in nature'. When Michael effects the transformation of the men into cattle he remarks, 'I have now given you your own proper shapes, and showed you in frames suited to your natures' (p. 344). This has led a number of commentators to assume an allegorical basis for the novel. David Groves argues that both the transformation and the bull disguise point to a necessary recognition of man's physical nature, suggesting that the disguise episode offers an explanation of the earlier transformation:

The act of dressing in ox hides is the turning-point in the romance, the action that leads from despair to triumph and harmony: allegorically, it implies that mankind may reascend to its rightful place in an improved world only after fully accepting its universal, common bond in the physical or animal side of its nature.[17]

The novel as a whole, however, tends to resist a straightforward allegorical explanation. Allegory itself points to stable and essential qualities that exist in nature and with which the allegorical symbols can be fully identified, a state of affairs which is never the full story of *The Three Perils of Man*. Contrary to Michael's claims, the narrator suggests that it is after Charlie and friends have changed back to their human shapes that they correspond to nature: they will then be able to 'regain their natural shapes' (p. 347). To confuse the opposition further, the bull disguise is the only one to be penetrated by an observer, a little boy whose warnings about 'how yon great black stott stood straight up on his hind legs' (p. 387) are fatally ignored by the English camp. The astute reader, however, might not ignore this incident, which subtly undermines the disguise/transformation opposition which the novel had seemed at such pains to draw up.

The material changes in the novel act as linguistic metaphors, bringing us back to the problem of the speech act and its difference, if any, from magic language, and *The Three Perils of Man* explicitly addresses the question by providing examples of each. The novel seems to contrast two worlds—one of courtly

---

[17] David Groves, *James Hogg: The Growth of a Writer* (Edinburgh: Scottish Academic Press, 1988), 103. Douglas Gifford also detects allegory at work in the novel and identifies 'Charlie as Honesty and Strength, the Friar as Faith, Gibby as Clown and Weakness ... and Tam as Greed and Fleshly Lust' (*James Hogg* (Edinburgh: Ramsay Head Press, 1976), 110). For this approach, see also W. G. Shepherd, 'Fat Flesh: The Poetic Theme of *The Three Perils of Man*', *Studies in Hogg and his World*, 3 (1992), 1–9.

behaviour and the other of the magical adventures of characters further down the social order. These two worlds are characterized by, among other things, different usages of language. The first is determined by social convention: the long and bloody siege of Roxburgh Castle originates in a vow taken by the king of Scotland that he will give his daughter's hand in marriage to any lord or knight who can take Roxburgh from the English before the end of the Christmas holidays. The vow is a popular example of the classic speech act—a promise which creates a future obligation for the speaker. Furthermore, the specific obligation involved in this vow constitutes the transference of power and status to the successful knight in the form of marriage to the king's daughter. In order to be able to award this status the speaker, clearly, has to be the king, and in making the speech act King Robert draws attention to the social institution that legitimizes it, vowing 'By this sceptre in my right hand' (p. 3). At the end of the novel we are returned to the world of socially determined speech acts where a number of the characters are married by being 'pronounced husband and wife' (p. 444) by the friar. This is a world, then, where language is used to create or reinforce social institutions, and such language, in turn, gives shape to the world which employs it.

In between leaving and returning to the court, however, we encounter another use of performative language. Magic language has the power to transform reality in a physical rather than a conventional way; it is effective not because of the power conferred upon it by institutions, but by an internally generated force. Like 'The Unearthly Witness', *Perils of Man* contains a summons which is successful through magical rather than social means. Gourlay, Michael Scott's monstrous but long-suffering seneschal, is commanded by his master to provide a retinue to meet Charlie's embassy. Gourlay complains that there is 'no mortal thing in the castle, but the old witch, and perhaps two or three hundred rats' which are unlikely to accomplish the task. Michael Scott, however, has other ideas: ' "Take that then," said the Master, "and put it above the lock-hole of the door; it shall serve you as a summons, and Prig, Prim, and Pricker shall marshal your array." With that he gave him a small piece of parchment written in red characters' (p. 149).

The narrator observes that 'The charm was effective' as the

castle's rats are instantly transformed into a column of men, grammar acts as glamour again (and, in this case, spelling as spelling). This kind of magic language foregrounds the special properties of writing which, in *The Three Perils of Man*, often take the form of an extreme kind of performative language. In such magic language words become objects which can forgo referential significance. Many of the characters in *Perils of Man* evince respect for the magical powers of writing. One of Michael Scott's principal sources of power is his Black Book, the written words of which will apparently have dire consequences for the wrong reader. Michael warns:

Before I open this awful book, it is meet that every one of you be blindfolded. I ask this for your own sakes. If any one of you were to look but on one character of this book, his brain would be seared to a cinder, his eyes would fly out of their sockets, and perhaps his whole frame might be changed into something unspeakable and monstrous.

(p. 335)

Writing here has a force that has little or nothing to do with its referential function: merely to look at one letter of the book will be catastrophic. This use of language echoes the idea of the identity of things in nature: Charlie Scott associates the laws of nature with the power inherent in language in his attempts to escape death at the hands of Prig, Prim, and Pricker: ' "But what law of nature, or what holy word or sign," thought he, "can restrain the arm of a wicked man?" ' (p. 164), immediately discovering the answer to be a prayer which apparently summons the friar to his assistance. In contrast to the socially activated speech act, the power of magic writing is inherent in the writing itself; it is not contingent on social institutions or any other external circumstances. The words which marry Charlie and Jane Howard are dependent on their being spoken by the friar. The magic book, however, has a physical power which is independent of Michael's 'status' as a warlock; the summons will presumably transform the rats into men irrespective of whoever places it above the lock-hole of the door. Magic language works because it is in its nature to do so; speech acts will only be felicitous if the circumstances are right (just as the friar's trick is only successful because his illusion is accepted). Magic language, like natural magic, is subject to laws of its own, but speech acts are dependent on external factors and social consensus.

Not surprisingly, however, Hogg refuses to sustain these separate language worlds. Like *The Monastery*, this novel features a Bible and a Black Book. Unlike in Scott's novel, these are two different volumes, yet the difference is deceptive. Like *The Monastery*'s Alice of Avenel, the friar is in possession of a translation of the Bible from Latin into English, a dangerous object in the fourteenth century. Tam Craik, a member of Charlie's party, informs us that the friar has been persecuted for his translating activities, although he still carries with him 'some auld-fashioned beuk . . . that he has pored on a' his days, an' translatit out o' other tongues, till he was nearly hanged for it' (p. 122). Tam Craik believes that the friar's book of the gospels has the same capabilities as Michael Scott's book of magic, which can make people's eyes fly out of their sockets by being looked at. Tam Craik tells the assembled company that the friar's book has mysterious powers: mere possession of this 'book o' black art' has so far magically preserved the friar from hanging, decapitation, drowning, and burning (p. 132). And in some respects this Bible does resemble Michael Scott's magic book as their owners share a belief in the essential power of words. Unlike his persecutors, the friar is of the opinion that translation has no effect on the content of the text. He believes that the individual words of a translation can express the primary Word of God, and, as suggested by the argument between Searle and Petrey, the Word of God blurs any easy distinction between speech acts and magic language. Any individual utterance, even if translated into another language, can be said to express this primary Word. The essential meaning remains constant because, while it can be expressed by them, it is not dependent on specific human utterances (just as Michael's spells will have power whoever pronounces them), giving the power they represent an independent existence: 'The mountains may depart, and the seas may pass away, the stars, and the heavens in which they shine, may be removed, but the words of that book shall remain for ever and ever!' (p. 131).

The independent deep structure of the friar's language is bound up in the novel's inquiry into storytelling and the narratological distinction between story and discourse in turn becomes a way for Hogg to interrogate assumptions about the uses of orality. Hogg challenges Scott's view of stories as stable narrative structures which can be corrupted by faulty transmission, according tellers no rights to their own stories which, Scott believes, pre-exist any individual telling. For many ballad-collectors, antiquarians, and folklorists coming after Scott, the typographic grouping of plot-structures, or 'tale-types', has been central to their methodology. However, another line of approach is also possible. Scott's distrust of ballad transmission serves greatly to devalue the idea of stories as performances, as performance is a concept in which story and discourse are not easily separable. In his essay on storytelling, Walter Benjamin makes the point that the moment of storytelling is not only a transmission of experience but also the generation of it: 'The storyteller takes what he tells from experience—his own or that reported by others. And he in turn makes it the experience of those who are listening to his tale.'[18] In Benjamin's opinion, stories are the stuff of people's lives; they do not enclose or describe experience, they *are* that experience. 'Real tales', argues Benjamin, offer 'counsel', but such counsel does not constitute an extractable or portable moral: 'counsel is less an answer to a question than a proposal concerning the continuation of a story which is just unfolding. To seek this counsel one would first have to be able to tell the story.'[19] Anything that the story might be about is woven into the fabric of the telling.

Benjamin's essay can seem unrealistically nostalgic for a pre-modern oral past that may never have existed in the first place, but in fact recent anthropological studies of storytelling have confirmed his view that stories function in communities as performances. Richard Bauman's study of Texan dog-trading stories argues against the narratological division into concepts of story and discourse which are seen as being organized on entirely different principles. According to this commonly held view, Bauman writes, 'Events are action structures, organized by relationships of causality, temporality, and other such linkages; narratives are verbal structures, organized by rules of discourse.'[20] Bauman, on the contrary, argues for a concept

---

[18] S 87. [19] Ibid. 86.
[20] Richard Bauman, *Story, Performance, and Event: Contextual Studies of Oral Narrative* (Cambridge: Cambridge University Press, 1986), 5. An analysis of

of performance in which 'we can comprehend narrated event as well as narrative event within our overall concern with the interplay between the given available resources and patterns of narrative performance and the emergent functions and outcomes of that performance.'[21] In order, then, to see how the distinction between events and their narration becomes blurred in performance, performances must be sited as functions of a storytelling community, such as that in *The Three Perils of Man*. Amy Shuman's work observing storytelling among American high-school students leads to her making a comment which could be describing the way stories work in *Perils of Man*: 'personal narratives in which the world of the storytelling situation and the world in which the story takes place are so close together that one can forget that they are different worlds in which knowledge is differently distributed.'[22] Shuman's work is based on the premiss that the status of stories has to be negotiated, particularly the question of who is in a position to tell what about whom, and Richard Bauman similarly argues that 'considerations of truth and belief will vary and be subject to negotiation within communities and story-telling situations'.[23]

Perils of Man offers us just such a process of negotiation in the storytelling contest, the loser of which is to become the first meal for the others imprisoned without food in Michael Scott's castle (the friar having inadvertently blown up the exit with gunpowder). This contest provides one definition of a story as a kind of speech act: a narrative with a chiefly performative function, serving a particular purpose. To look at a story in this

storytelling along the axes of 'event structure' and 'discourse structure' can be found in William F. Brewer, 'The Story Schema: Universal and Culture-Specific Properties', in *Literacy, Language and Learning: The Nature and Consequences of Reading and Writing*, ed. David R. Olson, Nancy Torrance, and Angela Hildyard (Cambridge: Cambridge University Press, 1985), 167–94.

[21] Bauman, *Story, Performance, and Event*, 6.
[22] Amy Shuman, *Storytelling Rights: The Uses of Oral and Written Texts by Urban Adolescents* (Cambridge: Cambridge University Press, 1986), 25–6.
[23] Bauman, *Story, Performance, and Event*, 11. Similar conclusions to those arising from Bauman's empirical work are also finding favour in narrative theory. See, for example, Marie Maclean, *Narrative as Performance: The Baudelairean Experiment* (London and New York: Routledge, 1988).

way is to throw all the emphasis on to the act of its narration and its accompanying circumstances; what matters is not what the story is about, the events it seems to describe, but how and by whom it is narrated and heard. This is a view of narrative at the opposite extreme from Scott's theory in relation to ballads. Here the stories are epitomized as performatives (as distinct from performances) which form the human interaction of the characters. The audience of these particular stories, however, is not content with such a concept alone. Gibbie Jordan is of the opinion that if a story is reduced to a purely performative function, it is no longer entitled to the status of a story. Gibbie complains of Tam Craik's contribution: 'It is turning out no tale at all, but merely an offputting of time, till we shall all perish of hunger' (p. 274). A story which is pure form is not satisfactory to this audience and later Gibbie objects to the poet's tale because it does not seem to be about anything, its narration describes nothing: 'It brings me amind o' our host's dinner, that was a' show but nae substance' (p. 316).

In the discussion following Tam Craik's story, the friar, while admitting that Tam's tale is rather lengthy, offers a view of storytelling which legitimizes that length. The friar argues that a story cannot be identified by the way in which it is told, but by its events. In his view, Tam Craik is entitled to continue as long as he has events to narrate. The events are therefore primary and will determine the story: ' "Lo, the tale is good," said the friar; "but it goeth here and there, without bound or limit; and wherefore should not a man relate all that befalleth unto him" ' (p. 274). According to this view, stories themselves might be said to be 'in nature', being identified with a sequence of events.

These two extremes—the story primarily as its narrated surface and as its events—meet, and become blurred, in Gibbie Jordan's own entry into the storytelling contest, which in turn instigates an animated discussion among its hearers, both as to what kind of story it is, and as to what its meaning might be. This is the story of Marion's Jock, which ends with Jock going on the run, and Gibbie, the narrator, wondering what has become of him since then. When Gibbie has finished his narration, the others discuss it. The first to express an opinion, albeit covertly, is Tam Craik who is, as we later discover, Jock himself. He offers the opinion that a story is the account of real people who enact real events. Stories are thus not bounded by their narration, but continue with the life of their characters.

Perils of Man takes place in a world which is made up of stories and which is continually generating them. Because most of the stories concern the experiences of the people who are listening to them, the transition between telling and acting is a smooth one. When the storytellers have finished their narration, the story passes back into the experience of the characters. No one objects to the way their past has been narrated. Indeed, Tam Craik identifies himself in terms of the events of the story about him just told by Gibbie Jordan: 'I am neither less nor mair a man than just Marion's Jock o' the Dod-Shiel, that sliced the fat bacon, ate the pet lamb, and killed the auld miser' (p. 252). His sense of himself, that is, is mediated through the narrated structure of a story. Tam goes on himself to give an extensive account of his subsequent experiences. In his own opinion, he remains a constant in his transition in and out of stories, being unchanged by the individual tellings. Charlie, also believing stories to be naturally shaped by the lives of their characters, asks for the end of Jock's story but does not get to hear it: ' "But what an it shouldna be endit yet, Yardbire," said Tam: "Marion's Jock is perhaps living, and life-like, to tell his ain tale" ' (p. 230). Tam's choice of words is interesting here: the phrase 'living, and life-like' conflates the terms of literature ('life-like') with those of life ('living'). It is impossible to tell where the events end and the narration begins as the two merge seamlessly and are interdependent; the story will not end as long as Tam is alive, and while he is alive he will 'tell his ain tale', as he in fact does a little later on.

Stories in *Perils of Man* function in their community of tellers (which Benjamin believed to be the only site for the communication of experience in 'real tales') because of their ability to perform people's lives and be performed by them. Stories do seem to have a life 'in nature', and an autonomy irrespective of individual tellings, but such a natural pattern can, paradoxically, only emerge in the act of storytelling. The seemingly random stories prove to be linked in ways unexpected at the time of telling as characters who appear in these stories turn out to be members of the audience. Tam Craik is not alone in being both a character in a story and a member of the audience. Tam observes, 'we seem to ken mair about ane anither than ony ane o' us kens about ourselves' (p. 252). The storytelling competition works by drawing on pre-existent stories which the various tellers tap into, but the very existence of those stories is dependent on the storytelling situation.

The storytelling contest is eventually abandoned and the participants decide to draw lots instead. With no winner emerging, no criteria are ever finalized which might make a judgement possible. *The Three Perils of Man* is itself like the contest, throwing up ideas in an active process of exploration. It is impossible to draw a clear division between stories which are 'in nature' and stories which are the product of narrators. The novel appears to set up such oppositions and then blurs the distinction between them. Any attempt to apportion 'natural' stories into the realm of orality and self-conscious narratives into a literary and novelistic tradition is thwarted by the fact that both the internal oral storytellers and the narrator subscribe to both theories at various points.

When discussing the nature of the stories they have heard, the characters exchange a wide range of opinions but seem uninterested in fighting them out between each other. Furthermore, none of the individual storytellers feels obliged to subscribe to any consistent theory about narrative. Like the characters' discussions, the novel itself is less a contest between competing ideas than a multiplicity of possibilities. In fact, the narrator's exact status as regards the story is highly problematic. He refers to himself as an 'Editor' who is conveying the story of an old curate named Isaac. However, the specific wording of the narrator's description of the transmission of the text raises a further problem. This 'Editor' covertly absolves himself from the word-for-word reproduction of Isaac's narrative, claiming that the tale 'was taken down from the manuscript of an old Curate, who had spent the latter part of his life in the village of Mireton, and was given to the present Editor by one of those tenants who now till the valley where stood the richest city of this realm' (p. 2).

The reader is liable to miss the participation in the transmission of the story of the intermediary tenant, or whoever 'took down' the tale from the manuscript, as the Editor subsequently mentions only Isaac. Nevertheless, it is the story taken down *from* the manuscript and not the document itself which is here said to be passed on to the Editor. Thus, with one hand Hogg sets up a quasi-factual state of affairs while with the other he awards himself the freedom to make the whole thing up as the documentary evidence appears to be no longer available. The narrator may not be the editor of Isaac's story but its author. This 'Editor' is thereafter able to manipulate the circumstantial evidence as it suits him. At the start of the book, he hints that Isaac is a storyteller rather than a documentary historian: 'There were once a noble king and queen of Scotland, as many in that land have been.—In this notable tell-tale manner, does old Isaac, the curate, begin his narrative' (p. 2). Later on he refers confidently to the time 'when Isaac the curate wrote this history' (p. 327). Story and history are so far merged that it is impossible for the reader to disentangle them.

Unsurprisingly, the narrative stance adopted by this ambiguous figure further complicates the novel's already multiple exploration of storytelling. Like the characters, the narrator resists any one narrative theory which might be said to underpin his story. One of the guises adopted by the editor/ narrator sounds like an eighteenth-century novelist teasing the reader with concepts of verisimilitude. Like Fielding, he is fond of textual metaphors drawn from transportation. In *Tom Jones*, Fielding compares his 'history' to a stage-coach which 'performs constantly the same Course, empty as well as full'.[24] The writer is obliged to record faithfully what happens even though this may involve the documentation of long periods of dullness in which not much is going on. The narrator of *Perils of Man*, also describing his work as a history, similarly complains of the obligation to be faithful to the events and the uncompromising nature of time:

A story is like a waggoner and his horses travelling out the king's highway, his machine loaden with various bales of rich merchandise. He goes smoothly and regularly on, till he comes to the bottom of a steep ascent, where he is obliged to leave a great proportion of his loading, and first carry one part of it to the top of the hill, then another, and then another, which retards him grievously on his way. So it is

[24] Henry Fielding, *The History of Tom Jones, A Foundling*, ed. Fredson Bowers (2 vols., Oxford: Clarendon Press, 1974), i. 76.

with the writer of a true history such as this; and the separation of parties is as a hill on his onward path. (pp. 157–8)

In the very act of seeming to epitomize a story as a sequence of events which narration must follow in a secondary capacity, Fielding and Hogg ironically undermine the whole concept. The more they protest the 'truth' of their history and the primacy of its events, the more they expose to the reader how such supposed events are abstractions which the reader makes from the narration. The more Hogg's narrator complains of the difficulty of having to organize all the strands of his story, and all the individual tales contained within it, into their 'proper places', the more we realize that such strands have no inherently or naturally appropriate places. In one sense this is a Shandean tactic designed to reveal the futility of imposing an artificial narrative order on to the unformed, multifarious experience of life: 'there were so many truths, that any body may see it was scarcely possible to get them all narrated in their proper places' (p. 190).[25] Such novelistic games seem very far removed from the concept of the real-life story. Whereas Charlie and Tam happily (though not necessarily consistently) accept the essential and determining power of events, the narrator's bantering with the reader reveals his own control of them. However, there are other things in *The Three Perils of Man* which move the narration away from these sophisticated literary jokes which reveal stories as constructions. Hogg will not allow an opposition to stabilize itself between oral stories which are 'in nature' and written ones which are literary constructs.

When Tristram Shandy, unwilling spokesman for the ever-unbridgeable gap between events and their narration, writes about chapters he exposes their artificiality, arguing that the allocation of a narrative division to a unit of action is a contrivance designed solely for the assistance of the reader: 'chapters relieve the mind'.[26] But when the narrator of *Perils of*

[25] For Hogg's affinities with Sterne, see also H. B. de Groot, 'The Imperilled Reader in *The Three Perils of Man*', *Studies in Hogg and his World*, 1 (1990), 114–25.

[26] Laurence Sterne, *The Life and Opinions of Tristram Shandy, Gentleman*, ed. Ian Campbell Ross (Oxford: Oxford University Press, 1983), 225.

Man observes that his chapter cannot proceed 'as an extra-ordinary incident befel, which naturally brings it to an end' (p. 280), we cannot be so confident about any ironic intent. Taken in the context of the book as a whole, the narrator's apparent exposure of the shortcomings of fictionality is not as it seems. In the 'living and life-like' theory of storytelling, narratives *can* be brought naturally to an end by means of the death of their protagonist. In this sense, stories are given their narrative shape by the events they contain and not by authorial manipulation. If events can naturally end stories, why not chapters also? But this question is unanswerable—like Tam Craik, the novel is itself 'living and life-like', as Hogg refuses to make an absolute distinction between the tropes of oral storytelling and those of literary narratives.

Like Tam's life/story, the novel itself is never quite 'endit', a state of affairs which directly addresses itself to the reader. Just as, in Benjamin's formulation, a story is dependent on the context of its reception, so *Perils of Man* draws the reader into its narratological debates. Again, we are offered a model which seems at first to contain the oral in a world of nature, offering the comforting prospect of closure: the status of prophecy within the novel. The issue of prophecy is closely related to the nature of story in *Perils of Man*. The main prophecy in the novel, Michael Scott's forecast of the outcome of the siege, works as a metaphor for the shifting relationship between events and narration. A belief in prophecy, the idea that 'a particular event will happen' rather than that 'anything might happen', reinforces confidence in a world of fixed identities. Future events are accorded an existence which cannot be altered; one of Sir Ringan's followers remarks of Michael's skills that there is 'no event so closely sealed up in futurity, but that he can calculate with a great deal of certainty on the issue' (p. 95). The event may be sealed up in the future but it is also conceived of as *already* existing. Prophecies posit a view of the world in which events may be made known through language but are not dependent on it—a fixed future will arrive whether prophesied or not.

So far this seems in accordance with the idea of stories that take place 'in nature' and which are lived independently of their narration. But, of course, *The Three Perils of Man*, being itself a construction of language, can offer no enacted examples of such stories. In Tam Craik's phrase, the living are constantly becoming lifelike, while the lifelike are offered as enactments of their living selves. The movement of experienced events into stories and abstracted events out of stories is a continuous one, never coming to a rest where it might stabilize into a theory of storytelling. The prophecy in the novel enacts this movement.

Michael Scott's prophecy contains the crucial lines, 'He that drives shall feel the gin, | But he that's driven shall get in' (p. 336). In the retrospective position of having read the novel, we might assume that these lines refer to the successful penetration of Roxburgh Castle by Sir Ringan's troops disguised as beasts, the idea which occurred to Charlie as a good plan of action. However, the whole prophecy causes some considerable confusion to those who hear it and much time is spent puzzling over it when it is reported back to Sir Ringan. The narrator is initially rather cryptic about what happens next:

But the precise meaning of the destiny, read for him out of the book of fate, puzzled and interested him most of all. It was dark and full of intricacies; and it was not till after long consultation with wise men, as well as women, that any thing like a guess could be formed of its tendency. By making words and actions to coalesce, a mode of procedure was at the last pitched on as the only one reconcileable with the predictions. (pp. 348–9)

The exact relationship of 'words and actions' is ambiguous here, although, importantly, it is open to 'consultation' or negotiation. It does not look as if the language of the prophecy refers very clearly to any pre-existent events which might be sealed up in futurity. On the contrary, the prophecy's 'meaning' is something which has to be constructed by a process of guesswork and reconciliation, a process, in fact, very like the act of reading stories, in which the reader creates, from the narration, a version of the events which that narration purports to be describing. The narrator drops a sizeable hint that events are abstracted from narratives by readers, who are here invited to decide whether they think Charlie's scheme accords with the actions they themselves construct out of Michael's prophecy. When the subsequent events are unfolded, readers will be able 'to judge whether or not the Redhough and his sages understood the Master's signs and injunctions properly' (p. 349). When he asks the reader to guess the meaning of the prophecy the narrator focuses on the reading process itself. In concealing the identities of disguised persons from the reader, Hogg draws attention to parallels between our experience of reading *The Three Perils of Man*, and the characters' attempts to make sense of what happens to them within the novel. As readers, we are not always the privileged recipients of additional information from the narrator, particularly as this narrator cannot be said to be very reliable. Readers may have a sense that narratives describe anterior events, but because these events are not identical with happenings that actually occurred, a compromise has to be reached so that the reader may proceed with the plot. Like Sir Ringan Redhough, the reader is obliged to *make* words and actions coalesce in a situation where they may not naturally do so.

Sir Ringan himself, when trying to make up his mind about the prophecy, evinces an interesting view of 'facts' which are to him not things which exist 'in nature' but things which are constructed out of a consensus of societal views. He is rather like one of Jonathan Culler's hypothetical readers for whom 'meanings' are whatever 'they are willing to accept as both plausible and justifiable when they are explained'.[27] Sir Ringan, according to the narrator, has a philosophy which 'taught him to estimate facts and knowledge as he found them developed among mankind, without enquiring too nicely into the spirit of their origin' (p. 395). In the world of *Perils of Man*, however, narratology is never an easy matter. The relationship between Michael Scott's prophecy and Charlie Scott's trick is never precisely established. It is impossible to say whether the prophecy describes the penetration of Roxburgh Castle, or whether Charlie constructs his plan out of it. As a metaphor for the ontological status of stories, the prophecy refuses to be pinned down. In *The Three Perils of Man* we can never say absolutely what stories are, but only that they are open to negotiation by a community of interested parties of which the reader is one.

[27] Jonathan Culler, *Structuralist Poetics: Structuralism, Linguistics and the Study of Literature* (London: Routledge, 1975), 124.

4

Not Proven: Scott, Hogg, and Storytelling

HOGG'S story 'Seeking the Houdy' ends with the observation that oral stories are under threat because of the demise of the social groups which had hitherto ensured their circulation:

I am exceedingly grieved at the discontinuance of midwifery, that primitive and original calling, in this primitive and original country; for never were there such merry groups in Scotland as the midwives and their kimmers in former days, and never was there such store of capital stories and gossip circulated as on these occasions. But those days are over! and alack, and wo is me! no future old shepherd shall tell another tale of

SEEKING THE HOUDY![1]

Such laments frequently accompany the discussion of traditions of oral storytelling. Although orality is often used to underwrite myths of origins, it can equally well be employed in the constructions of endings and the boundaries these represent. Throughout the nineteenth century—and into the twentieth— the death of orality is something always just about to happen. The oral is frequently on the verge of extinction yet each time manages to survive long enough to be threatened again with its imminent demise. The oral becomes identified both as a tenuous link with the past, and as a sign of a vanished order; to hear its traces is both to come into contact with that order and to witness its disappearance. The phenomenon of the precarious oral springs from two recurring and closely related assumptions about it: first, that orality is destroyed by writing, and secondly, that the oral and the written or printed are sustained by very different cultural forces, to the extent that we sometimes refer to 'the oral world' and 'print culture' as if these were two quite

[1] *Tales*, 175.

unrelated spheres. According to this view, speech is both materially and experientially different from writing: speech (as in the Rousseauist paradigm) is experience itself, writing a second-order experience which alienates the reader from the world about which he or she reads. The very act of reading is described by John Wilson ('Christopher North') as an artificial medium offering a synthetic rendition of experience which disrupts the more natural temporality of 'real life':

Reading ... supplies us artificially with a far more rapid series of impressions and causes of feeling, than any human being could ever be subjected to by his own individual experience. In real life, objects approach and depart by degrees; and suggestions follow each other at long intervals; at least, such would be the case before the invention of printing, and among men who had few books. But reading now subjects the mind, at once, to the action of a crowd of thoughts, which of old could only have been gathered slowly, and separately, during the course of a whole existence.[2]

The oral here seems under assault by the increased speed of modern communications—a familiar anxiety. In the story 'My Aunt Margaret's Mirror' Scott observes: 'In all our modern improvements, there are none, perhaps, greater than in the accuracy and speed with which intelligence is transmitted from any scene of action to those in this country whom it may concern'.[3] The supernatural element of story, ostensibly set before the days of accurate communication, depends upon the *slowness* of the transmission of news. Lady Forrester is shown by a clairvoyant the image of her husband bigamously wedding another woman. The narrator, interrogated by Scott, admits that the wedding had actually taken place 'some days sooner than the apparition was exhibited' and concedes that it was possible 'that by some secret and speedy communication the artist might have received early intelligence of that incident'

    [2] [John Wilson], 'On the Effects of Knowledge upon Society', *BM* 4 (1818–19), 80–4 (p. 83).
    [3] Walter Scott, *'The Two Drovers' and Other Stories*, ed. Graham Tulloch (Oxford: Oxford University Press, 1987), 284. All the Scott stories in this chapter except 'Wandering Willie's Tale' are quoted from this edition and further references appear in the text.

(p. 304). Yet if this is the case, the story as it is told will be less satisfactory: to admit to technological advances is 'to be obliged to maim one's story' (p. 303).

This chapter is about Hogg's and Scott's different attempts to represent oral storytelling in print. The sense of alienation expressed by Wilson and Scott raises problems for authors who perceived themselves to be writing at a point of transition between oral and written narratives. Indeed, Walter Ong sees an anxiety about the alienating effects of writing as particularly intense for nineteenth-century novelists who 'self-consciously intone, "dear reader", over and over again to remind themselves that they are not telling a story but writing one in which both author and reader are having difficulty situating themselves.'[4] In his 1831 introduction to the story 'The Tapestried Chamber', Scott seems prey to just such an anxiety as he worries that oral storytelling is context-dependent and cannot fully survive the transition to print:

> it must be admitted that the particular class of stories which turns on the marvellous, possesses a stronger influence when told than when committed to print. The volume taken up at noonday, though rehearsing the same incidents, conveys a much more feeble impression than is achieved by the voice of the speaker on a circle of fireside auditors, who hang upon the narrative as the narrator details the minute incidents which serve to give it authenticity, and lowers his voice with an affectation of mystery while he approaches the fearful and wonderful part. (pp. 310–11)

This sounds very like Rousseau's dismissal of writing as a feeble imitation of the bodily authenticity of speech. However, before dismissing such attitudes as another example of the irresistible attraction between the oral and logocentrism, we might consider that the 'real life experience' of which speech is supposed to be a part need not be sought in authentic, primary utterances whose self-present meaning can only be weakly represented in writing. Oral storytelling can be characterized in two ways which move it very far from the metaphysics of presence. First, oral storytelling is associated with repetition and

---

[4] Walter J. Ong, *Orality and Literacy: The Technologizing of the Word* (London and New York: Methuen, 1982), 31.

alterity, a process of gradual deposits and erosion that dislocates the story from any single originating voice or intention. Oral stories have no fixed form but circulate in a variety of versions and retellings. Instead of authorship and meaning there is only the constantly renewed act of storytelling. Thus, in Walter Benjamin's words, a story 'does not aim to convey the pure essence of the thing, like information or a report'.[5] Orality thus comes to represent not a direct access to an imagined source, but its opposite: spoken words' continual erasure of their origins: 'They have no focus and no trace (a visual metaphor, showing dependency on writing), not even a trajectory. They are occurrences, events.'[6]

If stories are events they lose their referential power, and thus, partly as a result of the untraceable origins of oral narration, the story takes on a second characteristic: it blurs the distinction between truth and fiction. It is the social superiority and apparent permanence of writing which offer to determine between what is real and what is not: the talismanic truth-status of the book which I discussed in earlier chapters introduces the idea of a unalterable authority which can be appealed to in any given instance. Such a destabilizing of the grounds for proof afforded nineteenth-century authors a way of drawing on a seemingly precarious oral tradition. Paradoxically, it is the very impermanence and provisionality of the oral—those qualities which seem to make it least graspable by writers—which most inform the work of Hogg and Scott. In their writing, stories question the claims of history and science to provide true narratives that will explain a prior state of affairs. In all the stories discussed in this chapter, the aspiration to resolve matters into the either/or polarity of proof is seen to be not absolute but culturally determined. Proof is something that results either from the imposition of rules from outside a community, or from the breakdown of shared social assumptions within the community. By looking closely at some stories by Scott and Hogg, we can see what happens when the negotiations of storytelling encounter the demand for true narratives.

[5] S 91.   [6] Ong, *Orality and Literacy*, 31.

The Proof of the Story: 'Wandering Willie's Tale'

Scott's relationship with oral history is a complex one. In his editorial work on the *Minstrelsy of the Scottish Border*, Scott complains about the limitations of oral memory when it is required to constitute history. If ballads are to be a documentary representation of the past, then oral recollections with their fluctuating texts are bound to be found inaccurate. In his non-fictional writing, however, Scott tentatively explores the possibility that oral memory may not be a weaker version of written history, but an alternative to it.[7] In *Guy Mannering*, the oral surfaces as an act of memory which almost succeeds in taking precedence over the social superiority of the written account. Harry Bertram, on his return to the old castle of Ellangowan, is on the verge of remembering his former life, prompted first by the memory of the locality itself and then by oral memory as he remembers 'the remnants of an old prophecy, or song'. He cannot make much sense of it but the reader knows that it signals the restoration of the Bertram property rights. Other songs from his past begin to return to him and as Bertram plays through the tune of one, it is taken up by a passing woman who sings the continuation of the ballad. On this occasion oral memory is interrupted by Gilbert Glossin who expresses the usual evaluation of the social status of ballad-singers: 'the devil take all ballads, and ballad-makers, and ballad-singers! and that d—d jade too'.[8] Censoring the oral, Glossin steers Bertram away from the prophecy which remains 'a strange jingle of sounds' until it re-emerges, completed, in Meg Merrilies's written epistle.[9] Though socially marginalized, orality is seen here to have strange powers of recalling—or re-creating—past experiences not by offering an accurate *report* of the past but by the *process* of recollection: Harry Bertam is much more conscious of the act of remembering than he is of any particular thing remembered.

---

[7] On history and memory in Scott, see Jina Politi, 'Narrative and Historical Transformations in *The Bride of Lammermoor*', *Scottish Literary Journal*, 15/1 (1988), 70–81.   [8] *Guy Mannering*, Border, 413.

[9] Ibid. 412, 411.

Scott returns to the subject of oral memory in the later novel *Redgauntlet* whose hero, Darsie Latimer, is, like Harry Bertram, ignorant of his family and his inheritance for much of the novel. *Redgauntlet* is made up of many different textual media: letters, a personal journal, third-person narrative, oral inset tales; none of these takes narrative precedence but together they explore the conditional nature of historical recollection. Among them is 'Wandering Willie's Tale', Scott's most famous representation of oral storytelling and a text which investigates the possibilities offered by oral re-creation—as opposed to written reproduction—in the construction of history.[10] Wandering Willie is an experienced and accomplished oral storyteller who narrates the following tale to Darsie: Steenie Steenson, a piper, owes money to his landlord, Sir Robert Redgauntlet, and borrows the sum from a neighbour. Steenie arrives at Redgauntlet Castle to pay the rent, but before Sir Robert can write out a receipt the laird suddenly and mysteriously dies and Steenie flees the castle. Sir Robert's heir, Sir John Redgauntlet, demands either the money or the rent from Steenie who, unable to raise any more cash, wanders dejectedly into a wood where he meets a mysterious stranger with demonic characteristics. The stranger guides Steenie back to the castle, now once again occupied by the deceased Sir Robert and some notorious characters from Scottish history. Here Steenie obtains a receipt and discovers the whereabouts of the money.

The tale is about the history of the Redgauntlets (of whom, unbeknown to him, Darsie is one) but it is also about the recovery of the past in a metahistorical sense. How can a text like the receipt 'prove' a version of the past? What is the difference between acting and narrating? These questions, which we have already seen raised in *The Three Perils of Man*, are particularly relevant to oral storytelling in which the

---

[10] For historiography in the novel as a whole, see Mary Cullinan, 'History and Language in Scott's *Redgauntlet*', *Studies in English Literature*, 18 (1978), 659–75; Margaret M. Criscuola, 'Constancy and Change: The Process of History in Scott's *Redgauntlet*', *Studies in Scottish Literature*, 10 (1985), 123–36; James Kerr, *Fiction Against History: Scott as Storyteller* (Cambridge: Cambridge University Press, 1989); and H. B. de Groot, 'History and Fiction: The Case of *Redgauntlet*' in *Scott in Carnival*, ed. J. H. Alexander and David Hewitt (Aberdeen: Association for Scottish Literary Studies, 1993), 358–69.

narration is itself an event: a story does not prove what happened in the past but performs a version of it that is relevant at the moment of narration. Benjamin sees this quality of storytelling as its most valuable social function, which he describes as the characteristic of a 'real story':

It contains, openly or covertly, something useful. The usefulness may, in one case, consist in a moral; in another, in some practical advice; in a third, in a proverb or maxim. In every case the storyteller is a man who has counsel for his readers. But if today 'having counsel' is beginning to have an old-fashioned ring, this is because the communicability of experience is decreasing. In consequence we have no counsel either for ourselves or for others. After all, counsel is less an answer to a question than a proposal concerning the continuation of a story which is just unfolding. To seek this counsel one would first have to be able to tell the story. . . . Counsel woven into the fabric of real life is wisdom.[11]

For 'counsel' to be effective, it must be 'less an answer to a question than a proposal concerning the continuation of a story which is just unfolding', and this is how 'Wandering Willie's Tale' operates. Benjamin's 'real story' is one which, rather than addressing a predetermined question, will deliver its possible meanings as and when they are formulated by readers. A story 'does not expend itself. It preserves and concentrates its strength and is capable of releasing it even after a long time.'[12] But whatever is thereby released exists as it is assimilated into the experience of its receptors. Like Wilson's idea of preliterate experience which is 'gathered slowly, and separately, during the course of a whole existence', 'Wandering Willie's Tale' uses a sense both of cumulative narration and of a gradual release of its meanings in its telling.

The story makes itself freely available to any subsequent hearer or narrator. Wandering Willie, Steenie's grandson, inherits the tale from his family and passes it on to Darsie, the 'final' narrator, who retells the story in a letter to his best friend, Alan Fairford. The two narrators, Willie and Darsie, allow its passage from oral narration to written text by entering into the act of narration without laying claim to any unique authorship. When the tale is over, Willie and Darsie mull over possible

---

[11] S 86–7.   [12] Ibid. 90.

meanings which are not mutually exclusive. The inexperienced Darsie offers a moral interpretation; Wandering Willie, who knows what happened next, has a more superstitious explanation, but he expresses it as an alternative, rather than an opposed meaning to that of Darsie: 'Ay, but they had baith to sup the sauce o't sooner or later'.[13] Steenie himself, Willie says, may have had a more practical purpose for telling the tale, being 'obliged to tell the real narrative to his friends, for the credit of his good name. He might else have been charged for a warlock' (p. 116). Another possibility remains: James Kerr points out, in a telling phrase, that 'The "real narrative" is "Wandering Willie's Tale" itself, a fact which would seem to do the teller "credit" only by enhancing his reputation as a taleteller'[14] and Richard Bauman, in a modern ethnological study, sees this as characteristic of oral storytelling: 'whatever its referential and rhetorical functions, it constitutes a form of verbal art. That is, it is characteristically *performed*, subject to evaluation, both as truth and as art for the skill and effectiveness with which it is told.'[15] Like the storytelling contest in *The Three Perils of Man*, 'Wandering Willie's Tale' is at the same time a performative act and a story with real relevance for the lives of its actants and its hearers.

The tale itself contains a warning about the results of trying to turn a tale into an answer to a question. A very different version of storytelling is offered to Steenie by the new laird, Sir John Redgauntlet, an Edinburgh lawyer who comes from outside the immediate circumstances of the tale to insist on the importance of verifiable fact. He attempts to impose upon Steenie a concept of storytelling which is alien to the progression of the tale. That is, Sir John expects Steenie to produce a version of past events (the disappearance of the money) which can objectively describe and account for them. In his interview with Steenie he insists upon this again and again: 'Where do you suppose this money to be?—I insist upon knowing'; 'Somewhere the money must be,

[13] Walter Scott, *Redgauntlet*, ed. Kathryn Sutherland (Oxford: Oxford University Press, 1985), 177. Further references appear in the text.

[14] Kerr, *Fiction Against History*, 117.

[15] Richard Bauman, *Story, Performance, and Event: Contextual Studies of Oral Narrative* (Cambridge, Cambridge University Press, 1986), 21.

if there is a word of truth in your story . . . I ask you where you think it is—and demand a correct answer'; and, most significantly, 'if there be a knave amongst us, it must be he that tells the story he cannot prove' (p. 109). Sir John supposes that a story can only be called 'true' if it is a direct reflection of observable phenomena, and that it can be 'proved' by reference to factual evidence.

Steenie is, however, another kind of storyteller and resists the imposition of Sir John's theory of narrative for as long as possible. He becomes disoriented, desperate, and 'driven almost to his wit's end' as he finds himself unable to answer Sir John on the laird's own terms and refuses to be drawn into his mode of storytelling. Sir John tries to enforce an argument based on an absolute distinction between truth and fiction, while Steenie tries to resist one:

'Speak out, sir! I *will* know your thoughts;—do you suppose that I have this money?'
'Far be it frae me to say so,' said Stephen.
'Do you charge any of my people with having taken it?'
'I wad be laith to charge them that may be innocent,' said my gudesire; 'and if there be any one that is guilty, I have nae proof.'
(p. 109)

Sir John demands an exactness and a precision in the relationship between events and their narration. He assumes that a story can answer a specific question (here the where-abouts of the money) and can therefore be interpreted in only one way. But in view of the strength of other modes of storytelling in the tale, Sir John's demands seem anomalous and redundant. 'Wandering Willie's Tale' is not so much a story that can be proved, as a story which is itself its own proof. After his argument with Sir John, Steenie becomes taken over by the tale in an extrarational way that is not easily interpretable. The tale offers itself up for interpretation but it also exists without the need for any explanation at all. Like Hogg, Scott explores the borders between the living and the lifelike; 'Wandering Willie's Tale' is on the one hand a narrative which takes place in its telling and re-telling, but on the other it is Steenie's tale and the story is whatever he does.

As the story moves towards the supernatural world, it seems

that the 'proof' of the story lies not in the recounting of it but in its action. Wandering Willie relaxes even his narrative responsibility. As Steenie rides home through the suggestively named wood of Pitmurkie, Willie remarks: 'I ken the wood, but the firs may be black or white for what I can tell' (p. 110). The word 'tell' is apt in its double meaning: Wandering Willie cares neither to distinguish nor to report the nature of this wood. He does not relinquish his cordial relationship with the reader, but he or she is invited to attend less to Wandering Willie and more to Steenie's activities. As Steenie rides through the wood letting his horse 'take its ain road' (p. 110) a figure suddenly appears who bears a striking resemblance to the devil. The demonic stranger offers Steenie a very different concept of proof from that of Sir John Redgauntlet—one based not on *telling* a story but on *acting* it. Mysteriously, he seems to cause Steenie's worn-out horse first to 'spring, and flee' and then to return to 'its auld heigh-ho of a stumbling trot' and remarks, 'and that is like mony a man's courage, that thinks he wad do great things till he come to the proof' (p. 110). In entering the dangerous, supernatural inner world of Redgauntlet Castle and confronting what he finds there, Steenie also enters into the story in a very physical way: he 'proves' a tale about him by means of his own action in it.

History is itself something to be enacted in this story. It is closely allied to memory, and both personal and collective memories work together in their uses of the past. Wandering Willie opens his narration with: 'Ye maun have heard of Sir Robert Redgauntlet of that Ilk, who lived in these parts before the dear years. The country will lang mind him; and our fathers used to draw breath thick if ever they heard him named' (p. 102). This opening contains an assumption of shared knowledge: Wandering Willie is including Darsie (and the reader) in a localized community of listeners who are familiar with the circumstances of the tale. Yet there is nothing exclusive about such an assumption: Wandering Willie will tell the tale even if we have not heard of Sir Robert Redgauntlet, and it will be equally accessible. In 'Wandering Willie's Tale' the continuity of history is available to the storyteller; in spite of the intervention of a period of want ('the dear years'), the tales of the past survive to be given, by the storyteller, the sense of living in the present. Wandering Willie can dramatize or revive individual moments from the past: 'our fathers used to draw breath thick if ever they heard him named'.

Steenie's trip to hell is another crossing of history and memory, enacting, like the story itself, ways in which the living can enter the past. Memory becomes not a means to an end as Sir John would have it, but an activity, and the tale moves closer to Tam Craik's reclamation of his own story in *The Three Perils of Man*. Serving as the site of memory for both Wandering Willie and Darsie, the tale is also an account of how Steenie deals with his personal past and with a larger historical one. Steenie has to return to the castle, not knowing what he will find there, in the attempt to probe the past and there to acquire the receipt owed to him, but the act of finding is as important as the receipt itself. While in the tale's inner world, Steenie enacts the 'proof' of the story as suggested by the stranger, and his success in recovering the past by acting in it is brought about through an amalgamation of personal, collective, and historical memory. The castle's oak parlour, which now bears a striking resemblance to hell, is filled with some of the most bloody and treacherous characters from Scottish history, all feasting and revelling. Steenie nevertheless manages to negotiate a path through the castle's dangers. Like the folk-tale narrative in which human characters are tricked into remaining in fairyland, or hell, or the underworld, Steenie has to avoid a number of traps laid for him. First he is asked by Sir Robert to play a particular tune on the pipes, but remembers that it was one he had learnt from a warlock and excuses himself. The dead, both Steenie's personal acquaintances and historical characters, supplement his personal memory. Next Steenie is offered a pair of bagpipes, but after a nudge from Dougal MacCallum, the butler and Steenie's 'auld acquaintance' (p. 111), he notices that the chanter is white hot. Finally he is invited by Sir Robert to eat but the invitation is framed in 'the very words that the bloody Earl of Douglas said to keep the King's messenger in hand, while he cut the head off MacLellan of Bombie, at the Threave Castle' (p. 113) and Steenie is warned off. Political history and personal memory are as inseparable as action and narration.

In his historical reminiscences of his own childhood in Berlin, Benjamin observed: 'Language shows clearly that memory is not an instrument for exploring the past but its theatre. It is the medium of past experiences, as the ground is the medium in which dead cities lie interred. He who seeks to approach his own buried past must conduct himself like a man digging.'[16] In the same way, language in 'Wandering Willie's Tale' shows us how oral memory can act as the theatre of history which Steenie can enter to excavate the past by reliving it. Benjamin further insists that 'remembrance must not proceed in the manner of a narrative or less still a report'; Steenie's remembrance is as little like a report as any narrative can be.

The Anxiety of History: 'The Highland Widow'

'Wandering Willie's Tale' uses the oral to multiply, and thus to confuse, the origins of history. The plurality of the tale's narration, its disruption of temporality, and its relaxing of the demands of historical realism all decentre history, making it conditional upon the dynamics of the storytelling situation. Scott was not always so optimistic about the successful challenge of the oral to an official history associated with writing, and orality remained vulnerable to fears of a modernity which cuts off the possibility of negotiated exchange and shared narration. The late story 'The Highland Widow' enacts an opposite process to Wandering Willie's dispersal of history as either the teleological explanation of a perceived state of affairs, or an ideological structuring of events to answer a particular question, or both. In 'The Highland Widow' Scott rejects an absolute distinction between the storytelling techniques of an oral world and a literate readership, but the demands of a more absolute realism seem to have infiltrated both worlds. 'The Highland Widow' is a bleak vision of circumstances in which storytelling is no longer possible.

Whereas 'Wandering Willie's Tale' accommodates many different interpretations of the history with which it has to do, 'The Highland Widow' works to prevent the possibility of interpretation altogether. Between them, Steenie and Wandering

---

[16] Walter Benjamin, 'A Berlin Chronicle', in One-Way Street and Other Writings, trans. Edmund Jephcott and Kingsley Shorter (London: Verso, 1985), 314.

Willie manage to accommodate large historical developments into the tale with considerable ease, but in 'The Highland Widow' history, or historical assessment, is one of the greatest frustrations for the reader. 'Wandering Willie's Tale' rewards the reader's active participation in the story, but 'The Highland Widow', even as it seems to draw the reader in to the tale, denies him or her the opportunity of responding in *any* way to the story it purports to relate. At first glance, 'The Highland Widow' seems like a similar exercise in re-creating an oral tale passed through different narrators; but where 'Wandering Willie's Tale' openly and confidently affirms its relationship with oral storytelling, 'The Highland Widow' makes ironic gestures in the direction of what Benjamin defines as a 'real tale'.

The story narrated in 'The Highland Widow' is a bleak one. Elspat MacTavish is the widow of a cateran (a marauder or freebooter with an accepted position within Highland society) and is fiercely loyal to the clan tradition. When her only child, Hamish, enlists in the British army, Elspat is appalled by this apparent betrayal of honour. After failing to persuade Hamish of her view, she drugs him so that he misses the time appointed for him to rejoin his regiment, and he thus becomes liable to be flogged as a deserter—a punishment which represents the utmost dishonour to the Highlander, and which is abhorrent both to Elspat and to Hamish. When a party of soldiers arrives for Hamish, he shoots dead their leader—a personal friend— and is duly executed.

One view of this story is that it is primarily about a clash of two historical cultures—decaying Highland feudalism and British progress. A. O. J. Cockshut, among others, has seen this historical perspective foregrounded by the tale: 'Hamish is executed and Elspat is left in a silent solitude that is both the grey aftermath of a personal tragedy and a moving emblem of the dying Highland society so vividly pictured by Dr. Johnson.'[17] But although cultural relativism certainly informs the narrative structures of 'The Highland Widow', to read the story as emblematic history presupposes concepts of historiography

---

[17] A. O. J. Cockshut, *The Achievement of Walter Scott* (London: Collins, 1969), 58. See also Seamus Cooney, 'Scott and Progress: The Tragedy of "The Highland Widow" ', *Studies in Short Fiction*, 11 (1974), 11–16.

which conflict with the narration of the tale. History in 'The Highland Widow' is at best a difficult, and at worst an impenetrable, area. If 'Wandering Willie's Tale' is about how the act of narration can constitute the transmission of experience, then 'The Highland Widow' is its opposite. Susan Manning has written of Elspat's story, 'What *can* be known of her story *is* known by others, and it is this part that we are told, but we are never allowed to mistake the recounting of the experience for the experience itself.'[18] I would further suggest that even the recounting of the experience is highly problematic.

The transmission of the story of Hamish and Elspat is both complex and uncertain. After the events have taken place, some unidentified local people communicate them, at a time and in a manner unspecified by the text, to Donald MacLeish, who acts as a guide to tourists wishing to see the Highlands. The tale is next told by Donald, in 'a few hurried words', to Mrs Bethune Baliol, a middle-class Edinburgh woman whom he is conducting through the area in which the events took place. Mrs Baliol is later asked for the tale by a friend, Chrystal Croftangry, but she elects not to tell it to him. Instead, she writes it down, again at an unspecified time, and leaves it to Croftangry after her death. Croftangry then becomes the 'final' narrator of the tale and 'publishes' it in the series of stories entitled *Chronicles of the Canongate*. To complicate the matter further, Croftangry, in his concern for the decline of the Highlands and the telling of stories about them, is disconcertingly similar to Scott himself.[19] The transmission of the tale from Hamish and Elspat to Croftangry's 'gentle reader' is thus a series of blanks and interruptions, the most obvious of which are the brevity of Donald's narration in 'a few hurried words' and the consignment of the tale to a legacy in which the story is transmitted after a narrator's death.[20]

---

[18] Susan Manning, 'Scott and Hawthorn: The Making of A National Literary Tradition', in *Scott and his Influence*, ed. J. H. Alexander and David Hewitt (Aberdeen: Association for Scottish Literary Studies, 1983), 421–31 (p. 427).

[19] The relationship between Scott and Croftangry is discussed by Judith Wilt in *Secret Leaves: The Novels of Walter Scott* (Chicago: University of Chicago Press, 1985), 201–2. See also Frank Jordan, 'Chrystal Croftangry: Scott's Last and Best Mask', *Scottish Literary Journal*, 7/1 (1980), 185–92.

[20] For the transmission of stories in the Waverley Novels, see Joseph Kestner, 'Linguistic Transmission in Scott: *Waverley*, *Old Mortality*, *Rob Roy*, and *Redgauntlet*', *Wordsworth Circle*, 8 (1977), 333–48.

'The Highland Widow' refuses its readers any point of access. Given its origins in the still largely preliterate Highlands, the tale reads almost like a parody of the traditional story which is handed down orally. The points of transition between the tale's narrators, which might elsewhere suggest acts of communication, are here frustrated. The story does not flow easily from one narrator to another and the reader is soon alerted to the tale's narrative blocks when Mrs Baliol, for no apparent reason, elects not to communicate the story orally in spite of Croftangry's requests that she should do so. Benjamin's description of the storyteller as 'a man who has counsel for his readers' embraces many of the problems of 'The Highland Widow' and the impossibility of 'counsel' is felt in every aspect of the tale. No practical advice or moral can be detected in the events themselves; the story can serve neither as an example nor as a warning, since the tragic situation is both futile and unavoidable. The absence of 'usefulness' in the events of the tale is compounded by the narrators, who render the experience of Hamish and Elspat incomprehensible. The breakdown in communication is a complex matter, as 'The Highland Widow' continually makes gestures in the direction of Benjamin's concept of storytelling, but these are immediately revealed to be further *impediments* to the easy transmission of the story. The tale is laced with an irony that closes down points of access into the story just as they appear to open up. The problem is not that the narrators communicate nothing, but rather that their knowledge of the story, and what they extract from it, are either tied up in their own preoccupations, or frustratingly ambiguous. This latter quality reflects the tale's persistent pattern of almost simultaneously opening up and closing down to the reader. In a 'real story', in Benjamin's sense, the narrator is at ease with the material, or with the conception of the events he or she is narrating; he or she makes no attempt to communicate the events exactly, but allows his or her own telling or retelling to reshape them. Certainly, the narrators of 'The Highland Widow' add to the story—the tale that is communicated to Mrs Baliol in 'a few hurried words' ends up in five chapters—but the impulses behind these narrative additions involve a variety of personal motives which run counter to Benjamin's observation that 'counsel is less an answer to a question than a proposal

concerning the continuation of a story which is just unfolding'.

Both Mrs Baliol and Chrystal Croftangry use the tale to
supply exemplars for their own ideas, creating distortion and
misappropriation. Or rather, the tale manœuvres us into a
position of *assuming* that there is a gulf between the characters'
experience and the narrators' responses, as we are never given
direct access to Hamish and Elspat. Mrs Baliol, the educated
Edinburgh woman, wants the tale to be a literary tragedy. Upon
meeting Elspat, and after she has heard the story from Donald,
she relates:

I shall never forget the look which she cast up to Heaven, nor the tone
in which she exclaimed, in the very words of my old friend, John
Home—
'My beautiful—my brave!'
It was the language of nature, and arose from the heart of the deprived
mother, as it did from that gifted imaginative poet while furnishing
with appropriate expressions the ideal grief of Lady Randolph. (p. 138)

Mrs Baliol is here imposing on to the story her interpretation
of the Romantic concept of 'the language of nature'. But, in
contradiction of Mrs Baliol's impositions, the evidence of the
tale suggests that Elspat's language, as represented throughout
the text, is far from natural, or comprehensible on the instinctive
level that Mrs Baliol implies. It is, in fact, a *literary* 'translation'
of Elspat's native language, which is Gaelic. What Elspat might
actually have said at this point, and, consequently, her real
feelings, are not ascertainable as the tale gives no clue as no
process of translation is referred to. Mrs Baliol is here allying
herself with a literary readership removed from Elspat's
experience and is giving the tale a corresponding reading, or
significance. From Donald's 'few hurried words' and her own
brief meeting with the unforthcoming Elspat, she appropriates
the narratorship of the tale to answer the literary taste of a
society very different from Elspat's own.[21] Mrs Baliol exemplifies
the problems of articulating the story: her only way of

---

[21] Graham Tulloch suggests that despite the disparity between Elspat and the
narrative voice, the story offers a pattern of natural imagery which corresponds to
Elspat's experienc ('Imagery in "The Highland Widow"', *Studies in Scottish
Literature*, 21 (1986), 147–57.

representing Elspat's words at this point is through the unlikely coincidence that Elspat is unwittingly quoting from John Home's popular tragedy, *Douglas*. But in pointing this out, Mrs Baliol also draws attention to the fact that, unlike the grief of Lady Randolph, Elspat's feelings can find no 'appropriate expressions' in the narrative of 'The Highland Widow'.

In contrast to the treatment of history and memory in 'Wandering Willie's Tale', this story's political antagonisms invite us to read the sequence of narrations not as something shared, but as something to be fought over.[22] The text is left uneasily poised between the security of a tale and the alienating modernity of the novel. The 'real' storyteller, Benjamin argues, involves himself or herself in the story in order to develop a sense of closeness between narrator and audience; he or she recounts the circumstances of his or her knowledge of the tale in order to negotiate the terms of the contextual realism which will operate within the tale. The problem of 'The Highland Widow' is that the narrators lay claim to a realism that comes from *outside* the tale in an attempt to present it as objective history. Chrystal Croftangry's bias inclines less to the literary tragedy than to the historical document. Like Mrs Baliol's reading of the story, his interpretation cannot be described as 'wrong' or morally suspect because the tale reveals no objective reading or touchstone by which the events can be interpreted. Croftangry (who seems to share some of Scott's general preoccupations) is concerned about the fate of Scotland, but as a narrator he is far from easy about the status of the tale as history. He admits that the story will serve no general historical purpose as it may be outside the comprehension of anyone but his Highland house-keeper: 'It is, however, but a very simple tale, and may have no interest for persons beyond Janet's rank of life or understanding' (p. 123). Janet's position in relation to the tale acts as an odd deflection of its transmission. Gaelic speaking and Catholic, she is illiterate, outside the realm of Scottish education, yet, as the implied audience for this highly literary artefact, she is employed

---

[22] Though published under the name of 'The Author of Waverley', the introduction to the *Chronicles of the Canongate* was signed by Scott, marking his first textual acknowledgement of his authorship of the Waverley Novels. Thus even Scott enters into the narrative contest for authorship.

to keep the story's readers at a distance. Far from negotiating positions between teller and receptor, this tale attempts to cut out the audience for whom, as a published story, it is apparently intended.

'The Highland Widow' is, of course, a far from 'simple' tale and the Baliol/Croftangry/Scott narrative voice occupies a highly ambiguous and disconcerting position in it. The narrator of a 'real story', or one in which the reader can be fully engaged, as Benjamin suggests, does not pretend to an intimate knowledge of the characters' thoughts and feelings, rather, he 'forgoes psychological shading'.[23] The narrative voice of the 'finished' version of 'The Highland Widow', however, has a habit of entering into such thoughts and feelings only to disclaim an intimate knowledge of them. The effect is a disconcerting one as the reader is encouraged simultaneously to trust and to doubt the tale's veracity. An example of this occurs after the climactic argument between Elspat and Hamish over his having joined the British army. The narrator relates how Elspat appears to be reconciled to Hamish's intentions, but comments omnisciently, 'In truth, however, nothing could be farther from her thoughts' (p. 167). Yet this narrative omniscience is a dubious commodity; no sooner has the reader been asked to volunteer his or her confidence in the narrator, than the narrator's knowledgeable presence is abruptly withdrawn as he observes, of Elspat's plan to drug Hamish, 'Whether she looked to any farther probable consequences of her unhappy scheme, cannot be known' (p. 167).

The tale as a whole is scattered with dead ends of this kind, and they are signalled in ways which intensify its unaccommodating nature. The meeting of Mrs Baliol with Elspat has a particularly disconcerting effect and Scott here plays on the reader's expectation of narrative modes. According to Richard Bauman's analysis of oral storytelling, generic expectations permit listeners to enter into the game of storytelling, either giving them a means for assessing the truth-status of stories, or allowing them to enjoy the joke of a narrator's 'establishing a set of generic expectations that the tall tale can bend exaggeratedly out of shape'.[24] But the realignments that 'The Highland

[23] S 91.   [24] Bauman, *Story, Performance, and Event*, 20.

Widow' requires of its readers serve further to prohibit their participation. We might expect our introduction to Elspat so early in the story to elicit her own narration, but Elspat does *not* tell her own tale; the only words she offers directly to Mrs Baliol are the highly ambiguous 'Daughter of the stranger, he has told you my story' (p. 138). Elspat's position in the text is frustrating: the only living 'eyewitness' to the events of the tale appears, but will not tell her own story.

Perhaps the most important of these narrative impasses is one which might serve as a metatext for the ways in which the story as a whole is told. As Mrs Baliol travels with Donald through the glen in which Hamish and Elspat formerly lived, she notices Donald's haste to leave it and demands of him the reason. If, as Benjamin writes, 'counsel is less an answer to a question than a proposal concerning the continuation of a story which is just unfolding', then Mrs Baliol poses a question and requests a story which will answer it. But, in Benjamin's analysis, 'to seek this counsel one would first have to be able to tell the story' and Donald is reluctant to embark on any storytelling—despite his alleged 'turn for legendary lore' (p. 126)—and becomes 'grave and mysterious', answering Mrs Baliol's enquiries as to whether the glen is haunted only with the telling remark, 'ye are clean aff the road'. (p. 133). Mrs Baliol attempts to reopen Donald's narrative, but to no avail: 'I was obliged to suspend my curiosity, observing that if I persisted in twisting the discourse one way while Donald was twining it another, I should make his objection, like a hempen-cord, just so much the tougher' (p. 134). If this hempen-cord, with its forebodings of execution, is a metaphor for the events of the story, then the manner in which Donald and Mrs Baliol twist and twine the discourse might suggest the action of the narrators upon the events. Any attempt to tell the story will then inevitably result in a distortion of it, and the multiple narrators, each imposing their own motives on to the tale, or posing a question of it, will be seen in conflict with one another. The hempen-cord metaphor is peculiarly chilling: although the two external narrators are twisting it in opposite directions, the effect of such an act will be for the cord to form the shape of a loop or a noose, implicating all the narrators in the story's overriding sense of death, loss, and waste.

Hamish and Elspat, as characters who interpret the events as they take place, have an internal narrative status within the story, but they each employ very different narrative modes. Elspat attempts to interpret events rigidly by admitting only her own point of view. After Hamish has left to join the British army, the first word that Elspat has of him is through a messenger who, significantly, is not immediately identified in the text. This messenger brings money to Elspat from Hamish: 'Elspat MacTavish remained gazing on the money, as if the impress of the coin could have conveyed information how it was procured' (p. 149). Already we see how Elspat's single-minded interpretation of events represents a relentless narrowing down of possible explanations to a single meaning. She extracts the meaning she desires from the evidence in her typically uncompromising manner, deciding, eventually, that 'this riddle can be read but one way' (p. 149). In treating the evidence as a riddle she arrives at the only answer possible in her mode of discourse and decides that Hamish has become a cateran like his father.

When Hamish returns from Dumbarton, Elspat notices that he is wearing the tartan, which had been proscribed after the 1745 Jacobite Rebellion but which could be worn by Highland regiments. Hamish's explanation of his dress is ambiguous: ' "Fear not for me, mother," said Hamish, in a tone designed to relieve her anxiety, and yet somewhat embarrassed; "I may wear the *breacan* at the gate of Fort Augustus, if I like it" ' (p. 156). Throughout his own account of his activities at Dumbarton, Hamish is trying to tell a story that has more than one interpretation. Here, as he tries to explain his Highland dress, he seems conscious of all that it might signify; that he has enlisted, or that, as Elspat at first believes, that he is defying British authority. In a less bleak tale, this attempt might bring a sense of freedom and openness, but here it is merely cryptic and vulnerable, and Hamish, in his embarrassment, seems aware of the futility of his narrative stance. While he attempts to liberate the 'hempen-cord' of the tale, by allowing it to be interpreted simultaneously in different ways, Elspat persists in twisting it in a single direction by assuming that Hamish wears the tartan as an act of defiance. She is effectively forcing the narrative into the twisting/twining pattern of opposing intentions, whereas Hamish's instinct is to leave it untouched. The subsequent dialogue between the two follows this fatal pattern, Hamish attempting to open out the tale, Elspat forcing it into the polarity of an argument.

When Hamish finally admits to having enlisted, his mother attempts not only to narrate the present but also to rewrite the past: ' "Enlisted!" uttered the astonished mother—"against *my* will—without *my* consent—you could not, you would not . . . Hamish, you DARED not!" ' (p. 158). Elspat's emphatic past tense can be answered only by Hamish's increasingly unsure conditional as he attempts to move her from her narrative intransigence into the position of listener: 'Would you but sit down and listen, I would convince you I have acted for the best' (p. 158). Again the tale gestures towards an impossible ideal of a storytelling in which the participants come to a negotiated understanding. But Elspat adopts a bitterly sarcastic position— one that contrasts sharply with Hamish's own ambiguity which permits a plurality of explanation: her irony serves only to emphasize her own single-mindedness by closing down all other possible interpretations. Hamish's comment that MacPhadraick 'finds his own good' (p. 160) in the army is subjected to Elspat's ruthless narrowing of the tale down to one 'true' meaning. She strikes at the centre of Hamish's narrative methods in her bitterly sarcastic reply: 'That is the truest word of the tale, were all the rest as false as hell' (p. 160). Her aim is to prevent Hamish from uttering a single word of his tale, forcing his narrative into the true/false dichotomy that 'Wandering Willie's Tale' resists. By the end of the argument, Hamish is driven into the very position of listener that he had, less brutally, attempted to persuade his mother to adopt—now he listens in passive silence as Elspat tells him Highland stories. He is accorded no more direct speech in the text until he attempts to take farewell of his mother, whereupon she tricks him into drinking the drug by which she renders him physically voiceless. Hamish is left pathetically unable to narrate anything—'I might tell my tale, but, oh, who would believe me?' (p. 182)—and his only future is the ultimate silence of death.

The anxiety of history closes down all points of transmission in 'The Highland Widow': between frame narrators, between Hamish and Elspat, and between text and reader. The course of history, even of time, is constantly disrupted or artificially preserved: Mrs Baliol creates a synthetic pastness in her narrative-as-legacy and Elspat refuses to acknowledge the passage of time altogether by both denying historical change and creating a lacuna in her son's life in which she believes time will stand still. Unlike 'Wandering Willie's Tale', in which characters happily move between a past and a present in which living is not very different from narrating, 'The Highland Widow' demonstrates the impossibility of any transaction between the past and the present. The final irony of the story is that past and present can neither coexist, nor exist independently; the bleakest aspect of the tale is its underlying denial of any life. The only survivors of this process are the cautious, wary characters like Miles MacPhadraick and Donald MacLeish who are unwilling to be drawn into the tale. They survive in history because they are not deeply involved in the experience of narration; it is Hamish and Elspat who, entering into the attempt to narrate history, are casualties of the historical process.

The reader's experience of the tale's impossible history is enacted in Hamish's shooting of Allan Breack Cameron, the sergeant in charge of the soldiers who have come from Dumbarton to arrest him. The moment at which Hamish kills Cameron is a highly complex one. Hamish awaits the arrival of the party in a limbo-like state which prevents both his narrative stance—'I might tell my tale, but . . . who would believe me'— and his influence on the action. The text supplies a peculiar insight into this latter denial of cause and effect as Hamish levels his musket at Cameron:

Instantly he rushed forward, extending his arm as if to push aside the young man's levelled fire-lock. Elspat exclaimed, 'Now, spare not your father's blood to defend your father's hearth!' Hamish fired his piece, and Cameron dropped dead. All these things happened, it might be said, in the same moment of time. (p. 195)

Clearly, from a realistic point of view, which would allow for the principle of cause and effect, Cameron can only die *after* he has been shot by Hamish, but in the context of the tale these things happen simultaneously, 'in the same moment of time', obstructing first, the normal chronological sequence of events and next, the reader's attempt to regard the action of the story as the linear progression of history. And again, the reader who attempts to interpret history as such a chronological progression extending into his or her own present, is shut out of the tale altogether.

As a result of the breakdown of cause and effect, other concepts by which the reader might make sense of the tale are denied. No accommodation is made for the sequence of guilt, blame, and retribution, a moral concept by which we might make sense of the tale. Here the pointlessness or arbitrariness of the tale is felt—the narrative itself supplies no context by which Hamish might be deemed guilty, but he is executed anyway. Scott includes the point of view of an interpreter from the 'outside' world—the anonymous general in command at Dumbarton who attempts to rewrite the events as a fable which will serve as a warning: 'here was one who had defended himself by main force, and slain in the affray the officer sent to take him into custody. A fitter subject for punishment could not have occurred' (p. 201). Yet this narrative is no more helpful than Elspat's own.

The simultaneity of Elspat's words, Hamish's action, and Cameron's death makes it impossible for the reader to establish Elspat's culpability. Significantly, the narrator remarks that her share of the blame 'was not accurately known' (p. 200). She ends the tale cursing Michael Tyrie, the bewildered clergyman who gives her the news of Hamish's execution: 'the thunder of heaven be launched against thy head and stop for ever thy cursing and accursed voice!—begone, with this malison! Elspat will never, never again bestow so many words upon living man' (p. 213). Even as Elspat renounces language, her curse on Tyrie expresses her destructive and single-minded use of it. In the impenetrable sense of history presented in 'The Highland Widow', she is unable to learn from the past. Having fatally deprived Hamish of language, she continues to silence anyone who offers an interpretation of events contrary to her own beliefs and desires. Her last alienating utterance cuts her off finally from both moral and historical scrutiny. In the end she simply disappears without trace and becomes absolutely unknowable, turning the tale's efforts to recount history into anxious and frustrated attempts at explanation.

Expressive, Ingenious, and Downright Lies: Hogg's Stories

The final transition into print of 'The Highland Widow' marks the last stage of a journey which cuts the story off from any oral source. Hogg's stories, however, return us to the incorporation of the techniques of oral storytelling in the printed text. Like 'Wandering Willie's Tale', Hogg's stories refuse to stand as proof of their subject-matter. But whereas Scott's story imitates oral storytelling without reference to its own printed status, Hogg's tales are enthusiastically aware of their own location in magazines. In fact, it is Hogg's very identification of the magazine as the site for modern storytelling that characterizes his own continuation of oral tradition. Hogg locates his stories at a transitional point, blurring the boundary between speech and writing and undermining cherished Romantic notions about nature. His strategies address questions both of the relativity of realism and of the media of circulation. The productions of 'peasant' writers, among whom Hogg was generally counted, were assumed to have to do with the idea of truth, though, divided by the social assumptions about orality, the two formulations of this relationship were diametrically opposed to each other. Hogg, caught in the centre of the paradox of orality, characteristically plays both ends against the middle.

In the idealized orality constructed for a literary readership, peasant writers were celebrated for providing access to the truth of nature. John Wilson had contributed to one of the various characterizations of Hogg by making him a representative of the truthful values of 'natural' writing. Wilson's *Blackwood's* essay on Hogg and Burns identifies in Hogg the continuation of an ancient ballad tradition and rhapsodizes effusively about the lyrics of 'peasant poets' which are 'full of tenderness and truth'.[25] Wilson's view is that Hogg's ability to reflect nature in his writing came from his physical exposure to so much of it while working as a shepherd. Hogg's reply to this treatment was his famous *Blackwood's* letter which describes the discovery of the preserved corpse of a suicide and was later incorporated into

[25] [John Wilson], 'Burns and the Ettrick Shepherd', *BM* 4 (1818–19), 521–9 (p. 521).

Confessions of a Justified Sinner. The letter satirizes Wilson's attitude to nature by offering the mummy story as a response to demands from 'Christopher North' that Hogg 'should look less at lambs and rams, and he-goats . . . and more at the grand phenomena of nature'.[26] Hogg's exposition in *Confessions* of the difficulty of saying what the phenomena of nature are, or indeed what nature itself is, has been well documented and the original *Blackwood's* letter similarly implies that what is 'natural' may not therefore be true. The mummy story leaves several questions unanswered about how the suicide could have killed himself with only a weak grass rope and who witnessed the event. Proof is sought, but the tale will not supply it.

In the case of Hogg's stories this erosion of the truth/fiction opposition is simultaneously a subversion of class demarcations. In the first appearance of the letter Hogg gleefully points up the low status of oral storytelling, calling the mummy incident a 'disgusting oral tale' and an 'ugly traditional tale' which seems to be invading the more polite space of the magazine.[27] In another story he uses a metaphor of contagion to describe the risky contact of his readers with traditional tales: 'the sophisticated gloss and polish thrown over the modern philosophic mind, may feel tainted by such antiquated breathings of superstition'.[28] Such comments are made in the face of a growing belief that 'traditional tales' were indeed ugly and their bad morals infectious. Evangelical church leaders and educationalists directed their efforts against the supposed tendency of peasants to be untruthful, a condition manifest in their superstitious beliefs and stories. In Henry Duncan's popular improving tale, *The Cottage Fireside, or The Parish Schoolmaster* of 1815, the title is suggestive: unless the cottage fireside, traditional site of superstitious immorality, is reformed by the presence of the book, it will remain (like Meg Merrilies), in opposition to the correct values of the schoolmaster, and the story subsequently confirms this. The narrator's young nephew is threatened by his mother with the bogle man and the shocked narrator comments: 'This mode of education was so contrary to all my ideas of

---

[26] James Hogg, 'A Scots Mummy', *BM* 14 (1823), 188–90 (p. 188).
[27] Ibid. 189, 190.   [28] *Stories*, 71.

propriety, that I could bear it no longer'.[29] Later on, the boy
tells lies about his schoolmaster which the narrator emphatically
ascribes to his nephew's having picked up bad habits from his
mother's handling of the bogle incident: 'I say these were
downright lies'.[30] The fireside, in Duncan's writings, is to be
purged of its tendency to foster the 'downright lies' of
superstition by the new domestic ideal of family-centred reading
around the hearth. The consumption of the kind of popular
science which the evangelical writers on education both
advocated and produced as an antidote to superstition was
designed to sustain the moral and rational working-class
thought appropriate for the transition to industrialization.

Many of Hogg's stories act in opposition to the evangelicals'
goal and his own fireside settings are an attempt to reclaim that
particular place for a storytelling neither moral, rational, nor
scientific, yet able to encompass large questions of history and
textuality. *The Brownie of Bodsbeck* opens out its broad
historical inquiry from the fireside of Walter Laidlaw and
Maron Linton. Similarly, 'The Barber of Duncow' blurs the
distinction between the hearth of the superstitious Gordon
family and the drawing-rooms of the readers of *Fraser's
Magazine* by extending its fictional audience to include its actual
readership. But if, throughout his fiction, Hogg is concerned
with exploding the possibility of 'downright lies', he is
extremely interested in investigating lies of other sorts. His
technique is to provoke a confrontation between the assumptions of a literary readership and the organization of realism
within his tales. He does so not by accepting an absolute gulf
between the oral word and the literary readership, but by
forging a continuity. A purely internal realism is something
found more commonly in novels—hence the view that the
nineteenth-century novel was the pinnacle of realistic writing
because it does not obviously draw attention to its own
conventions.[31] Oral storytelling frequently does involve some
discussion of its own truth-status, even if this is only to elicit

[29] Henry Duncan, *The Cottage Fireside, or The Parish Schoolmaster*, 6th edn.
(Edinburgh: William Oliphant, 1862), 10.   [30] Ibid. 23.
[31] On this subject see Elizabeth Deeds Ermarth, *Realism and Consensus in the
English Novel* (Princeton: Princeton University Press, 1983).

comments such as 'really?' from the audience. Hogg exploits the way oral stories are performed by both the narrator and his or her audience; his stories challenge assumptions about both the internal structuring of realistic conventions and the external life of a story as it interacts with its audience.

Hogg's stories mix oral tropes with literary ones while making jokes about both. In 'The Mysterious Bride', the Laird of Birkendelly is heard singing one of Burns's songs, 'which like all the said bard's best songs was sung 150 years before he was born'. Birkendelly then encounters 'an uncommonly elegant and beautiful girl' and wishes he had an assignation with her, as the protagonist of the Burns song had with his sweetheart. From the situation of a traditional ballad, Birkendelly then finds himself as the subject of the psychologically omniscient narrator of nineteenth-century realism, a situation further complicated when the supernatural visitor also takes on this omniscience: 'As the laird was half thinking half speaking this to himself the enchanting creature looked back at him with a motion of intelligence that she knew what he was half saying half thinking and then vanished over the summit of the rising ground before him called the Birky Brow.'[32]

Hogg's tales dramatize not only stories themselves, but also the activity of storytelling. He circumnavigates Scott's anxiety that stories have 'a stronger influence when told than when committed to print' by pressing print circulation into the service of storytelling. The contextualized occasion of performance that Scott ascribes to the oral storytelling situation alone is used by Hogg in the stories he sent to magazines, as these stories enter into the interaction of written and spoken stories. Journals can be seen to combine characteristics associated with orality with those of a newly forged literary establishment: the anonymity and plurality of magazine articles and stories were contained by the embracing identity of the journal itself. As Jon Klancher observes, 'the journal represented itself as an institution blending writer, editor, and publisher in what could only appear to be an essentially authorless text'.[33] Furthermore, as Ina Ferris

---

[32] *Stories*, 145, 146. Mack identifies the song as a traditional one of which Burns's version is 'Let me in this ae night'.

[33] Jon Klancher, *The Making of English Reading Audiences, 1790–1832* (Madison: University of Wisconsin Press, 1987), 51.

has demonstrated, the journals of the early nineteenth century were in a state of change, their editors attempting to create for themselves the image not of 'the hacks and drudges of booksellers' but of 'liberal practitioners of the art of criticism'.[34] In this transitional condition, journals inhabited a border territory linking oral transmission to controlled literary circulation. Thus, as Ferris points out, the prestigious quarterly set out to establish 'the independence of its discourse from the merely temporal', thereby distinguishing itself from the monthly journals with their more rapid consumption and greater emphasis on timeliness.[35]

Most of Hogg's stories first appeared in the monthly Blackwood's and, after 1830, the London-based Fraser's Magazine, and he freely exploits the characteristics of magazine structures and circulation to give a printed context for the kind of narratives more usually thought of as an oral form very different from nineteenth-century literary productions. Oral narratives are particularly interesting for the nineteenth-century writer exploring the ancient relationship between lying and fiction because they lay bare the questions which were often glossed over by the ways in which nineteenth-century realist novels were read. Typically, the realist novel does not overtly encourage the reader to question the conventions of realism (though many such novels do so covertly). Oral storytelling, on the other hand, actively engages its audience in the process of establishing degrees of realism, a process rather different from

---

[34] Ina Ferris, The Achievement of Literary Authority: Gender, History and the Waverley Novels (Ithaca and London: Cornell University Press, 1991), 20.

[35] Ibid. 25. Hogg could also get away with greater 'indelicacy' in monthly magazines than when some of his stories were later reprinted and revised in book form; see Douglas Mack's introduction to Hogg's Stories, pp. vii–viii. For Hogg's dealings with journals see Gillian Hughes, 'The Importance of the Periodical Environment in Hogg's Work for Chambers's Edinburgh Journal', in Papers Given at the First Conference of the James Hogg Society, ed. Gillian Hughes (Stirling: James Hogg Society, 1983), 40–8; and 'The Spy and Literary Edinburgh', Scottish Literary Journal, 10/1 (1983), 42–53; and Mark L. Schoenfield, 'Butchering James Hogg: Romantic Identity and the Magazine Market', in At the Limits of Romanticism: Essays in Cultural, Feminist, and Materialist Criticism, ed. Mary A. Favret and Nicola J. Watson (Bloomington and Indianapolis: Indiana University Press, 1994), 207–24. For Hogg's relationship with his publishers and readership, see also Peter Garside, 'Three Perils in Publishing: Hogg and the Popular Novel', Studies in Hogg and his World, 2 (1991), 45–63.

the suspension of disbelief demanded by the realist text which thereby retains control of its own contextual realism.

Richard Bauman's study of how modern American oral narratives function within a storytelling community looks at storytelling as 'expressive lying', a term which dispenses with the truth/fiction opposition and replaces it with an exploration of how fiction is created by complex interpersonal exchanges and metanarrative elaborations. These pass through a whole set of terms: 'outright lies', 'fabrications', 'tall tales', 'creative exaggeration', 'stretching the truth'. The application of such terms often depends on the way narrators contextualize tales, passing them off as their own experience, or as stories told to them by the protagonist, or as tales they have heard from an unspecified third party. We can see this spectrum of truth-status at work in an example of 'expressive lying' from Bauman's study:

What appears to be going on is an account of actual events; what is really going on is a lie masquerading as such an account—a double lie. The man who tells such a tale in the third person is a liar; the man who tells it in the first person is a tricky liar, a con man. Thus two potential dimensions of 'lying' enter into the expressive ambience of coon hunters: outright lies and fabrications.

Oral storytelling functions within a community of listeners by means of a combination of familiarity and surprise: generic expectations are an important factor, as they are in the realist novel, but here they are cut through with the ambiguities of storytelling. They can encourage suspension of disbelief but, as Bauman points out, 'The effect is reciprocal, of course: The obvious exaggeration of the tall tale creates an aura of lying that colors the "true" stories as well.'[36] Thus while fictions are passed off as truth, supposedly true stories are at the same time experienced as fiction.

Hogg's stories employ many of the techniques that Bauman identifies in the dog-trading stories for negotiating the truth-status of stories: generic expectations, personal testimony, hearsay, and audience response. They also characteristically use the 'aura of lying' to pervade stories presented as true, and vice

---

[36] Bauman, *Story, Performance and Event*, 20.

versa, so that, although the reader's participation is invited, he or she is persuaded that any attempt to fix the story as either truth or fiction will prove futile. The title of 'The Barber of Duncow—A Real Ghost Story' plays with the word 'real': is the story authentic because it is a genuine folk narrative, or because if it is heard and not believed, a real ghost will appear? The confusion is exacerbated by the problem of deciding at what level reality is operating in the first place. Hogg's stories are events which, far from containing the presence of Romantic oral nature, tease their audience with what they leave unstated and unexplained. 'Real' characters, including Hogg himself, mingle freely with fictional ones and the fantastic is verified by personal experience. People regularly witness the supernatural and in 'Some Terrible Letters from Scotland' a correspondent to a magazine describes his own death with a chilling casualness: 'a little before daylight I died.'[37] Hogg sets up connections between his fictional narrators and the real editors of magazines, setting up the sense of collective interchange, as if the stories are circulating within a community. The three 'Terrible Letters' have been 'Communicated by the Ettrick Shepherd' to the editor of the London magazine *The Metropolitan* (the expatriate Scot, Thomas Campbell), and the various writers of the letters insist on their personal relationships and common acquaintances with Hogg or with his London associates. The first letter draws on these personal connections and the topicality of Hogg's 1832 trip to London:

As I knew you once, and think you will remember me,—I having wrought on your farm for some months with William Colins that summer that Burke was hanged,—I am going to write you on a great and trying misfortune that has befallen to myself, and hope you will publish it, before you leave London, for the benefit of all those concerned.[38]

---

[37] *Tales*, 178.

[38] Ibid. 176. The writer's 'misfortune' is the cholera epidemic of 1831–2 which had reached London from Scotland. Despite public agitation, the Cholera Acts were not passed until the disease was already established in London. In Scottish cities, the disease was surrounded by rumour and led to popular protest against the authorities' inaction. The spread of sickness in poor areas seemed like the spread of orality and the use of hearsay and plurality of narrative accounts in the 'Terrible Letters' invites a connection between the fear of orality in the period and the terror of infection that the letters describe.

Peter Murphy, describing Hogg's own appearances in his texts, writes: 'Unfortunately, he also sets himself up for manipulation and confusion, since in posturing rather too clearly, he cheerfully becomes a kind of being of print. For those willing to let it go, he remains the singing Shepherd.'[39] My own reading is that such is Hogg's own manipulation of context that no such option is available to the reader: the singing Shepherd and the being of print are never clearly distinguishable. Hogg's stories occupy the border position much frequented by orality, enacting contiguity and the transition between speech and writing, yet revealing the very different construction of literacy and orality in the nineteenth century. In his oral stories for a readership obsessively and self-consciously interested in printed material, Hogg both effects the continuation of oral techniques into print, and exposes ideologies which mark the division into a rural working class identified with the low status of orality, and an urban middle-class readership. The narrators of the stories, often 'James Hogg' or 'The Ettrick Shepherd' himself, act as intermediaries between these worlds, but never particularly reliable ones. The Hogg of the stories published in *Blackwood's* as 'The Shepherd's Calendar' adopts the role of antiquarian, helpfully offering his readers a taxonomy of the various types of story in his collection. The stories are to be classified partly according to their subject-matter, and partly according to their status as either factual, or 'traditionary', or fantastic. Yet the more the narrator attempts to categorize his tales, the more the taxonomic impulse is overtaken by a contrary movement, preventing the reader from fully grasping the rules by which veracity is to be established. As in the 'Real Ghost Story' of the barber of Duncow, it is never made clear whether stories are 'authentic' because they are really told by shepherds, or because they really happened. 'Tibby Hyslop's Dream' is announced as being indisputable because Hogg 'went and visited all those connected with it, so there is no doubt with regard to its authenticity',[40] but 'Mary Burnet' is a tale which seems to the narrator not quite to fit into his categories of 'legends ... founded on facts' or 'traditionary tales that seem originally to

---

[39] Peter T. Murphy, *Poetry as an Occupation and an Art in Britain, 1760–1830* (Cambridge: Cambridge University Press, 1993), 117.   [40] *Stories*, 50.

have been founded on facts'.[41] Nevertheless, he includes it on the grounds that it is of the 'antiquated and visionary' sort preferred by shepherds themselves.

Hogg often uses the real characters' *dis*belief to authenticate his own stories, by transmuting an opposition between true and false into a subject for discussion or a matter of opinion. 'The Mysterious Bride' opens with the suggestion that a number of people known to the narrator are doubting the existence of the supernatural: 'Even Sir Walter Scott is turned renegade and with his stories made up of half-an-half like Nathaniel Gow's toddy is trying to throw cold water on the most certain though most impalpable phenomena of human nature'.[42] The effect is not merely to imbue the stories with the status of fact, but, just as importantly, to confer upon the stories' 'factual' context the status of fiction. Conversely, characters brought on to verify stories do not always do so. The events of 'The Mysterious Bride' are authenticated by the narrator's claim that they are 'facts which happened in my own remembrance', yet by the end of the story, a witness whose testimony is ostensibly used to confirm the tale's veracity in fact opens up the opposite possibility: 'She gave the parishioners a history of the Mysterious Bride so plausibly correct, but withal so romantic, that every body said of it (as is often said of my narratives with the same narrow-minded prejudice and injustice) that it was a *made story*.'[43]

Hogg hereby invites his readers into a hall of mirrors from which they have little chance of escaping. Like the wrangles between Captain Clutterbuck and the Author of Waverley in *The Monastery*, this author and his fictional narrators engage in a mutual dependency which threatens to eliminate the credibility of both. This elimination of any hope of 'proof' returns us finally to *Confessions of a Justified Sinner* where the *Blackwood's* letter about the then anonymous corpse is reprinted in the novel and the editor describes his expedition with a number of 'real' people to dig up the remains. According to Wilson, Hogg's fictions, as the productions of a 'natural' writer, were supposed to represent nature. Yet Hogg has already seeded the ground of nature with fiction: it is impossible to say

[41] *Stories*, 71.   [42] Ibid. 145.   [43] Ibid. 156.

whether the novel is authenticated by the letter, or the letter discredited by its reappearance in the novel. All that the 'real' witnesses can conclude on the matter of the letter's status as evidence is that 'Hogg has imposed as ingenious lies on the public ere now.'[44]

Perhaps, then, 'ingenious lies' inhabit Hogg's favourite border territory between 'downright lies', which are detectable only when everybody knows the difference between truth and lying, and Bauman's 'expressive lies', which are only operable when such a distinction is no longer relevant. Hogg's ingenious lying is a way of deconstructing the truth/falsehood opposition imposed on the working class, but it is also a way of pointing out the social divisions that come about when ways of manipulating the truth-status of stories, as understood by a storytelling group, encounter a middle-class readership. While we can never decide what the truth is, neither can we ever be quite sure that it is *not* to be found in the 'disgusting oral tales' which Hogg introduces to his literary culture.

[44] James Hogg, *The Private Memoirs and Confessions of a Justified Sinner*, ed. John Carey (Oxford: Oxford University Press, 1969), 246.

5

Bookmen: Orality and Romance in the Later Nineteenth Century

SOME of the most important recent work on Scottish writing has been on the development of the romance in the first half of the nineteenth century. Ina Ferris has argued persuasively that Scott appropriated the genre from its association with women and accorded it a masculine authority. Ian Duncan has further shown how Scott reinvented the romance structure for the purposes of a public, national fiction.[1] Yet, as these books reveal, contrary movements are at work in the earlier nineteenth-century romance forms which allow in unauthorized forces connected with the sexual, the female, and the ambiguous or covert. Duncan writes: 'The romance scheme Scott takes over has a risky valence, that of the male's anxiety about being in the passive position, even as he begins to fear that this may in fact be his true relation to historical power.'[2]

By the end of the century, an increasingly emphatic masculinization of the romance and its laying claim to an imaginative authenticity came under stresses and strains which its adherents could not quite withstand. When the oral—long used to constitute the romance's myths of lost origins—encounters the Victorian obsession with the discovery of origins, these stresses become increasingly apparent as orality enters the fields of anthropology and psychology. And as orality joins forces with

---

[1] Ina Ferris, *The Achievement of Literary Authority: Gender, History and the Waverley Novels* (Ithaca and London: Cornell University Press, 1991). Ian Duncan, *Modern Romance and Transformations of the Novel: The Gothic, Scott, Dickens* (Cambridge: Cambridge University Press, 1992).

[2] Duncan, *Modern Romance*, 72. See also Judith Wilt, *Secret Leaves: The Novels of Walter Scott* (Chicago: University of Chicago Press, 1985).

the masculine adventure romance of the later nineteenth century, explorers undertaking adventures tend to discover more than they bargained for. Nevertheless, the particular problems of the later nineteenth-century oral did not hinder its enthusiastic adoption by participants in two important debates at this point: one about popular literature and the other about realism in fiction. For Andrew Lang and Robert Louis Stevenson, the romance became a way of negotiating a place in these debates, and they continued to organize their arguments along the lines of speech and writing. As in the earlier part of the century, however, the relationship between orality and literacy is a fluid one as they can exist neither together nor apart in a culture which prizes both, but loads each with contradictory values.

Stevenson explicitly attempts to isolate an idealized form of orality that was not an isolated and static lost-origin myth, but a process. He uses the idea of speech to create a poetics of romance that was to theorize much of the work carried out earlier by Hogg and Scott in their attempts to write a literature that would *perform* stories, blurring the distinction between narrator and narrated events. In his essays on the state of the novel, much of Stevenson's opposition to the thesis-novel is centred on its tendency to contain and organize narrative and he employs speech as a countering principle. Like Tristram Shandy, Stevenson protests, in 'A Gossip on Romance', that the so-called 'well-written novel' is preoccupied with homogenizing, controlling, and thus limiting experience: 'Our art is occupied, and bound to be occupied, not so much in making stories true as in making them typical; not so much in capturing the lineaments of each fact, as in marshalling all of them towards a common end.'[3]

As an alternative to the monologic authority of writing, Stevenson offers speech, and devotes two essays, both entitled 'Talk and Talkers', to the analysis of its powers. Stevenson's opening move in the first essay is to assert that the processes of conversation are only possible because we talk in speech and not in writing. Talk and talkers are juxtaposed in the titles because,

---

[3] *MP* 187. Stevenson here clearly foreshadows Virginia Woolf's famous attack on pre-modernist fiction in the essay 'Modern Fiction'.

in the essays, each is contingent upon the other: talkers converse in speech, and speech is directed to another speaker—talkers exist in the plural. Stevenson does not see the speaker as laying claim to a fully individuated and discrete self, replete with the full metaphysics of presence. The position of the speaker remains important, but implies no discrete identity for either the speaker or any meaning transmitted by him or her. First, Stevenson challenges the idea that the function of speech is to represent anything outside its own processes. Specifically, he claims that speech does not pursue 'subjects, so called' in the hope of embracing and representing any essential truth that they might yield:

There is nothing in a subject, so called, that we should regard it as an idol, or follow it beyond the promptings of desire. Indeed, there are few subjects; and so far as they are truly talkable, more than the half of them may be reduced to three; that I am I, that you are you, and that there are other people dimly understood to be not quite the same as either.[4]

The speaker's presence is not a static identity but an imaginative engagement with possible positions. Speakers define themselves by coming to a recognition of their difference from others: conversation has no subjects but only subject positions. Oppositions between the speaker and others are never absolutely determined as such differences are not finite but something which is 'dimly understood'. For Stevenson the 'subject' of speech is not that which is spoken about, but whoever does the speaking, and, importantly, who is therefore subject to the dynamics of speech. Stevenson does not attempt to disguise the importance of the speaker's presence, indeed he insists that 'that is the best kind of talk where each speaker is most fully and candidly himself'.[5] However, he argues that such a presence cannot precede speech; rather it is brought into being by the conversation. The speaker is determined by the conversation and not the other way round.

The immediacy of speech, in Stevenson's argument, does not imply the direct transmission of pre-existent meaning and

---

[4] *MP* 148.   [5] Ibid. 167.

neither can the processes of speech reach or construct any stable meanings which can then survive them. On the contrary:

Like enough, the progress is illusory, a mere cat's cradle having been wound and unwound out of words. But the sense of joint discovery is none the less giddy and inspiriting. And in the life of the talker such triumphs, though imaginary, are neither few nor far apart; they are attained with speed and pleasure, in the hour of mirth; and by the nature of the process, they are always worthily shared.[6]

This sets up an unstable identity for the talker. He or she is 'inspirited' but also made 'giddy'; that is, given a sense of self while simultaneously experiencing the disruption of it. Other disruptions fissure the possibility of completeness or totality. Already in the essay Stevenson has equated 'mirth' and 'jest' with the subversive power of speech which 'intervenes' in literature's attempts to enclose didactic truths: 'the solemn humbug is dissolved in laughter and speech runs forth out of the contemporary groove into the open fields of nature, cheery and cheering, like schoolboys out of school.'[7] Here, and throughout this essay, Stevenson consistently identifies speech with the natural, but the natural with the plural and the disruptive. Writing is associated with containment and speech with excess: 'All natural talk is a festival of ostentation'; 'talkers, once launched, begin to overflow the limits of their ordinary selves.'[8]

Stevenson thus imagines an idealized subjectivity free from all political considerations and epitomized in speech, yet the attempt to clear such a space for the oral is as problematic for the late Victorian writer as it was for the Romantics. Although orality no longer represents a static, moral human nature, as it had done earlier in the century, Stevenson still reaches back to an apparently pre-social condition to describe, in 'A Humble Remonstrance', his ideal of speech as process and performance, rather than imitation and description:

Literature, above all in its most typical mood, the mood of narrative, similarly flees the direct challenge and pursues instead an independent and creative aim. So far as it imitates at all, it imitates not life but speech: not the facts of human destiny, but the emphasis and the suppressions with which the human actor tells of them. The real art

---

[6] Ibid. 155.　　　　[7] Ibid. 145–6.　　　　[8] Ibid. 149.

that dealt with life directly was that of the first men who told their stories round the savage camp-fire.[9]

Thus far, Stevenson's theory of talk seems rather like Bakhtin's concept of speech as dialogue: the way language is generated by utterances performed in response to other actual or possible utterances. But Bakhtin also reminds us that language springs not only from responses but also from expectations; there may be endless permutations of speech, but for a speaker to use one of them he or she must select and formulate it according to learned forms or 'genres', and these genres are produced by the complex dynamics of society. In this light, talk may not be quite as free or self-sufficient as Stevenson would have it. Stevenson's attempts to characterize speech and writing as autonomous entities have to be seen in the context of other discourses which use speech and writing for ideological ends. Even the 'Talk and Talkers' essays are framed by their own cultural context as they are essays à clef, encrypted descriptions of Stevenson's friends for whom the freedom of talk comes not only from the inherent characteristics of speech but also from their position as middle-class men of letters engaging in conversations in clubs. The association of the oral with romance thus becomes complicated by the difficulty of positioning the romance itself in the late nineteenth century.

The condition of orality in the later nineteenth century grew out of the problematic relations of literacy, orality, and illiteracy which I discussed in my first chapter. Victorian society feared increasingly that the whole of Britain was in danger of sinking under a flood of 'illiterate scurrility', writing tainted by orality's low social status and characterized, like oral storytelling, by its rapid circulation and ephemeral behaviour. In this context, Stevenson's association of orality with excess becomes part of a wider anxiety about the behaviour of working-class readers. B. G. Johns, writing in the Edinburgh Review in 1887, gives a view of 'The Literature of the Streets' which expresses the late nineteenth-century fear of a popular literature which is not only out of the control of the middle-class arbiters of culture but also beyond the control of the market which calls it into being. As

---

[9] MP 283–4.

supply appears to Johns to exceed demand while nevertheless continuing to swell, the construction of popular writing again shows signs of a desire to mimic an oral storytelling which is unstructured by economic demands. Johns writes:

But the fountain head of the poisonous stream is in the great towns and cities, especially in London itself; and it is with that we now have to deal. Here the readers are to be numbered by hundreds of thousands, and the supply exceeds even the wildest demand. There is now before us such a veritable mountain of pernicious trash ... that, but for its actual presence, it would seem incredible.[10]

Johns's answer is not to censor existing literature but to colonize it with a better, more controllable version of itself which can exploit the 'craze for a tale, a story, a romance' for moral ends. Johns asks: 'why should there not be a library of Penny Romance, of wholesome, sound, and healthy fiction?'[11] Improving fiction was to be distinguished from its degenerate counterpart not only by its content, but also by its circulation; the corrupting, excessive, and unmanageable qualities of oral transmission were to be purged from written texts and these were then to be fixed as books in the controllable institutions of libraries. The romance then stood in a border position, touched on the one side by the corrupting association of illiteracy, and on the other by the redeeming value of the book. Not surprisingly, dealings with such a position were problematic for promoters of the romance like Lang and Stevenson. The 'healthy' romance for young adventurers and its corrupting *doppelgänger* were strangely alike and it was not always very easy to ascertain whether the theories Lang and Stevenson were constructing around the romance were reinforcing or subverting the ideological conformism of the day.

Among the literati of the late nineteenth century whom John Gross, using Lang's own term, has characterized as 'Bookmen', Andrew Lang stands out as a critic concerned both with defining the position of Scotland in the literary values of the later Victorian period, and with establishing those values in Britain as a whole. Lang's influence as a reviewer and cultural arbiter was

---

[10] [B. G. Johns], 'The Literature of the Streets', *ER* 165 (1887), 40–65 (pp. 42–3). [11] Ibid. 61.

considerable, and his good opinion of a text was a valuable marketing asset. But, for someone so influential in his time, Andrew Lang does not now figure greatly in accounts of the later nineteenth century. Even when he does feature he is generally regarded as a master of whimsy, the promoter of Rider Haggard's literary career, and the implacable foe of writers, especially Henry James, who would later feature in a Great Tradition of English literature. In fact James's own estimation of Lang speaks damningly of qualities which thereafter went to make up Lang's reputation. James objects to 'his *cultivation*, absolutely, of the puerile imagination and the fourth-rate opinion, the coming-round to that of the old apple-woman at the corner as after all the good and the right, as to any of the mysteries of mind or of art'.[12] James puts Lang's sorry failings down to 'his extraordinary *voulu* Scotch provincialism',[13] and indeed Lang's dedication to the romance is reinforced by his sense of himself as a citizen of Scotland's republic of letters, with its cultural life again organized round the unstable polarities of orality and literacy. John Gross, unimpressed by Lang's professional amateurism, writes that 'For newspaper readers in the 1880s, no single journalist personified Oxford—and "culture"—more strikingly than Andrew Lang'.[14] But Lang himself had seen the idea of 'culture' as something more problematic and in need of investigation. Though he was himself an Oxford don between 1868 and 1875 (when he left Merton College to become a full-time journalist), Lang counters Oxford as the seat of cultural perfection with his '*voulu* Scotch provincialism'. Far from espousing the idea of culture associated

---

[12] Henry James, *Letters*, ed. Leon Edel, iv, *1895–1916* (Cambridge, Mass. and London: Harvard University Press, 1984), 68.

[13] Ibid. 69.

[14] John Gross, *The Rise and Fall of the Man of Letters: English Literary Life Since 1800* (1969; repr. Harmondsworth: Penguin, 1991), 146. A more representative summary of Lang's importance for my purposes here can be found in Peter Keating's *The Haunted Study: A Social History of the English Novel 1875–1914* (London: Secker and Warburg, 1989). See also Roger Lancelyn Green, *Andrew Lang: A Critical Biography* (Leicester: Edmund Ward, 1946). For a more specialized study of Lang's significance in the late Victorian period see Robert Crawford, 'Pater's *Renaissance*, Andrew Lang, and Anthropological Romanticism', *ELH* 53 (1986), 849–79; and for Scottish writing and anthropology in general, Crawford's indispensable *Devolving English Literature* (Oxford: Clarendon Press, 1992).

with Oxford and with Matthew Arnold, that ineffable pursuit of human perfection, he sought alternatives to it, finding that 'sweetness and light' excluded his own particular interests: 'Culture is saddened at discovering that not only boys and illiterate people, but even critics not wholly illiterate, can be moved by a tale of adventure.'[15] Lang opposes Arnoldian culture with the spirit of adventure: where culture is refined, spiritual, and abstract, adventure is populist, physical, and practical; where culture emanates from universities, adventure has its source in illiterate people whose taste, reversing commonly held beliefs about the education of the masses, can usefully penetrate the domain of the critic.

Lang's interest in entertainment for 'boys and illiterate people' is part of his concern with preliterate societies in general, and in much of his criticism of late nineteenth-century reading habits he is furthering—not unproblematically—a wider anthropological investigation. The aspiration to return to preliterate societies is not new in the century, but whereas the Romantic quest is for an orality that speaks a pre-socialized nature, the Victorian anthropologist seeks a society in which the aesthetic is integrated into the social, in which culture is not confined to 'high art', but constitutes, in Edward Tylor's well-known definition, of 1871: 'knowledge, belief, art, morals, law, custom, and any other capabilities and habits acquired by man as a member of society.'[16] Lang's primitivism constructs a past in which art functions both as social ritual and also for purely pragmatic purposes. In his various excursions into the super-natural, Lang complained that modern ghosts were without a sense of purpose, whereas the old-fashioned variety 'knew what they wanted, asked for it, and saw that they got it'.[17] In an essay

---

[15] Andrew Lang, 'Realism and Romance', *Contemporary Review*, 52 (1887), 683–93.

[16] E. B. Tylor, *Primitive Culture: Researches, into the Development of Mythology, Philosophy, Religion, Art, and Custom* (2 vols., London: John Murray, 1871), i. 1. Competing definitions of 'culture' and their relation to popular literature in the late Victorian period are also discussed by Joseph Bristow in *Empire Boys: Adventures in a Man's World* (London: Harper Collins, 1991), 4–38, and this work has been generally informative for my discussion here.

[17] Andrew Lang, *The Book of Dreams and Ghosts* (London: Longman's, Green and Co., 1897), 110.

on 'The Art of Savages', Lang locates the concept of 'useful' art in early societies, echoing Stevenson's conception of the primitive artist as performer rather than imitator: 'His dances are magical dances, his images are made for a magical purpose, his songs are incantations. Thus the theory that art is a disinterested expression of the imitative faculty is scarcely warranted by the little we know of art's beginning.'[18]

However, although the genre of adventure fiction as it looks back to 'primitive' society is intended to offer an alternative to Arnoldian culture, its position as preliterate performance is a vulnerable one. If romance was not to be, in Lang's terms, the 'disinterested expression of the imitative faculty', it was certainly required to be disinterested in other ways, particularly in its claim to be free of political value, and eventually it begins to take on the characteristics of the 'culture' it was intended to oppose: Arnold's disinterested pursuit of perfection. The problem with Lang's oral societies is that they are constructed in opposition to things which are themselves not very clearly established. Orality is simply defined as the absence of literacy, the 'Folk' are the people 'of the classes which have least been altered by education',[19] but literacy and education, both highly problematic and disputed areas in the nineteenth century, remain as unequivocal givens. Ultimately, and despite his interest in the sociological inquiry of anthropology, Lang allows orality to stand for the undefinable, the asocial, and the natural, thereby creating a vacuum into which various ideological concepts could, and did, rush.

Lang's dogged opposition to realism and naturalism in the novel stems from a now familiar bifurcation of orality and literacy. When separated out into their polarities of a preliterate society and a self-consciously literary one, Lang advocates the former, frequently asserting that realism is less 'true', and naturalism less 'natural', than romance. Modern society has become impoverished by its apparent separation of the aesthetic from the practical, a split which Lang consistently claims to go against nature: 'The Coming Man may be bald, toothless, highly "cultured," and addicted to tales of introspective analysis.'[20]

---

[18] CM 276.   [19] 'The Method of Folklore', CM 11.
[20] 'Realism and Romance', 689.

Romances, however, in Stevenson's opinion, are the expression of their readers' natural desires: 'their true mark is to satisfy the nameless longings of the reader.'[21] Just as it had in the earlier part of the century, this idealization of the oral turns out to be a graphocentric construction through which the social superiority of writing reveals itself. Lang's organization of cultural life is in fact as dependent on books as it is on orality, and his anthropological interest in preliterate societies must be set against his cultivation of the persona of the 'bookman' concerned with acquiring or collecting books for their own sake. Lang appears to sanction his activities as a bookman by identifying his own 'bookishness' (a word he frequently uses) with the orality of romance; he explores books as if encountering them on an expedition into an unknown continent, in which the excitement of new discovery is modified by the naturalness of his being there. His relationship with written texts constitutes 'Adventures Among Books', and his *autobiographia literaria* of that title describes his early explorations as he goes 'rummaging' among books, collecting assorted chap-books and cheap periodicals.

The appeal by the written to the oral, however, can be reversed in Lang's case. As well as his celebration of preliterate art, Lang is interested in books for their own sake or for their purely aesthetic attraction, as he is unable to resist the privileging of the book as the symbol of cultural élitism. As a collector of books, he engaged in an activity which reinforces the notion of 'mere reading', that is, of literacy as an absolute cultural good whose value needs no explanation. In fact, Lang went out of his way to keep bookishness free from vulgar economic value (moving rather closer to Arnold than he may have intended), by observing that 'In England publishers are men of business; in France they aspire to be artists'.[22] Lang's aphoristic pronouncements thus leave the book as a symbol of indeterminate but unquestionable status. In 'A Bookman's Purgatory', bookmen themselves are warned of dabbling in the economics of books by the example of Blinton, a collector who buys cheaply and sells on at a profit. He is accosted by the devil (who resembles most of the 'mysterious characters of history

---

[21] MP 255. [22] 'Bibliomania in France', BB 90.

and fiction') and is forced to buy up worthless multi-volume sets and to auction off his own collection in order to pay for them.[23]

Thus, rather than allowing the written to take on the characteristics of the oral, Lang can be said to value covertly the authorizing power of the book. There is a parallel here with the association of adventure fiction with imperialism (Lang energetically promoted the literary career of Rider Haggard) and with anthropology's part in the representation of 'savages'. Lang writes of 'our mixed condition, civilized at top with the old barbarian under our clothes';[24] for him, culture was not necessarily synonymous with civilization, and civilized barbarians were generally preferable to savage ones, just as written romances, though themselves exhibiting a 'mixed condition', are not about to give way to the performances of actual preliterate societies. Furthermore, the civilized reader's access to savagery in the romance is an exclusive one: after praising the merits of 'a *true* Zulu love story', Lang comments that 'If one were all savage, all Zulu, "Through One Administration" would leave one a little uninterested.'[25] The European as civilized savage, engaging in some perfectly natural selection, was, of course, a common justification for imperial conquest, and imperialism is one of the last ideologies in the nineteenth century that orality is used to underpin.[26]

Scotland's role in British imperialism and colonialism is a complex one, as it is for any country which can occupy the position of both colonizer and colonized. For Lang, as for J. G. Frazer, Scotland maintained traces 'of a stage of thought, which is dying out in Europe, but which still exists in many parts of the world', and he gave prominence to Scottish folklore in his studies of myth.[27] Scottish readers are characterized as the best audience for ghost stories because of their primitive racial inheritance, and Lang comments of Stevenson's 'Thrawn Janet': 'we have enough of the old blood in us to be thrilled by that

---

[23] BB 125.   [24] 'Realism and Romance', 690.
[25] Ibid. 689–90.
[26] For anthropology and popular literature, see Brian V. Street, *The Savage in Literature: Representations of 'Primitive' Society in English Fiction 1858–1920* (London and Boston: Routledge and Kegan Paul, 1975).
[27] CM 13.

masterpiece of the described supernatural.'[28] On the other hand, Scots who left Scotland throughout the eighteenth and nineteenth centuries were epitomized as explorers (among them Mungo Park, David Livingstone, and John Rae) as well as colonial adventurers. R. M. Ballantyne, author of *The Coral Island*, left Edinburgh at 16 to become a fur trader in Canada, and, in his public lectures, would dramatically enact his early career by shooting a stuffed eagle on stage.[29] Scots abroad, then, were seen to be exploiting their native hardiness to make their fortunes in the Empire, a cogent imperialist myth which set their own barbarous origins both against and in sympathy with the barbarity they encountered. The adventure romance celebrated absolutely by Lang, and much more equivocally by Stevenson, is predicated on this structure of belief.

One of the characteristics of adventure fiction was its outdoor associations. The novel-reader might physically degenerate indoors, but the reader of romance could, at least vicariously, engage in some healthy exercise. (As romance-reading is deemed essentially an unselfconscious process, the distinction between lived experience and reading is in any case continually blurred.) This offered a chance for Scottish orality to be promoted as a cure for late Victorian fears of racial degeneracy and morbid introspection. Scotland was already celebrated for the outdoor productions of the Kailyard school. These idealized rural stories about the moral peasantry of the past took precedence in the Anglo-American market over the fund of Scottish newspaper fiction, now revealed for us by William Donaldson, which concerned itself more with life in cities.[30] Scottish ballads, with their open-air ethos, formed a natural site for romance: in 'A Gossip on Romance', Stevenson selects the scene from *Guy Mannering* (reproduced in a cropped form, as Stevenson thought Scott had written it carelessly) in which Harry Bertram

---

[28] 'The Supernatural in Fiction', *AB* 278.

[29] For a valuable survey of writing on this subject, see Allan MacGillivray, 'Exile and Empire', in *The History of Scottish Literature*, iii. *The Nineteenth Century*, ed. Douglas Gifford (Aberdeen: Aberdeen University Press, 1988), 411–27. See also *The Enterprising Scot: Scottish Adventure and Achievement*, ed. Jenni Calder (Edinburgh: Royal Museum of Scotland, 1986).

[30] William Donaldson, *Popular Literature in Victorian Scotland: Language, Fiction and the Press* (Aberdeen: Aberdeen University Press, 1986).

hears the half-remembered ballad, as 'a model instance of romantic method'. The heroes of Scottish legend make up a mythology enacted by the militaristic, masculine, hardy characters who made an early impression on Andrew Lang:

The first books which vividly impressed me were, naturally, fairy tales, and chap-books about Robert Bruce, William Wallace, and Rob Roy. At that time these little tracts could be bought for a penny apiece. I can still see Bruce in full armour, and Wallace in a kilt, discoursing across a burn, and Rob Roy slipping from the soldier's horse into the stream.[31]

The scene makes clearly visible the important features of Lang's Scottish popular tradition: kilted, armoured, and slipping into a cold bath, these figures synthesize the traditional hero as Scottish, warlike, and out of doors. And such texts are also 'natural' reading for Scottish boys who feel able to participate through them in the definition of national culture. The whole ballad world seemed to encapsulate the outdoor scene of adventure, in part simply because it *was* out of doors. In keeping with Lang's polarization of the oral as wholesome and healthy, while too much introspection makes the reading public bald and toothless, John Geddie, promoting Border ballads in the 'Famous Scots' series, makes the opposition between healthy orality and decadent reading clear:

As soon as the ballad is written down—at least as soon as it is fixed in print—the elements of natural growth it possesses are arrested. It is removed from its natural environment and means of healthy sub-sistence and development; and from a hardy outdoor plant it is in danger of becoming a plant of the closet—a potted thing, watered with printer's ink and trimmed with the editorial shears.[32]

Even more explicitly, Scotland's oral past, exhibited in its 'fresh' and 'clear' scene, was prescribed by John Veitch, Professor of Moral Philosophy and Rhetoric at Glasgow, as a healthy alternative to the morbid tendencies of the late nineteenth century:

As a distinctive form of poetry, Border Song has a permanent place in our national literature. It is simple, outward, direct, not without art,

[31] AB 5.
[32] John Geddie, *The Balladists* (Edinburgh and London: Oliphant, Anderson and Ferrier, n.d.), 141.

especially in its later forms, yet powerful mainly because it is true to feelings of the human heart, which are as universal and permanent as they are pure; and because it is as fresh as the sights and sounds of the varied land of hill and dale, of purple moorland and clear sparkling streams, which it loves so well. It is a form of poetry with which we can at no time dispense, if we are to keep our literature healthy; and it is especially needed in these times. For we have abounding morbid introspection and self-analysis; we have greatly too much for the close hot atmosphere of our own fancies and feelings.[33]

Stevenson, although his relationship with the ideology of the healthy body is very equivocal, can advocate the beneficial and health-giving effects of romance in a passage that would not be out of place in *Scouting for Boys*: 'the interest turns, not upon what a man shall choose to do, but on how he manages to do it; not on the passionate slips and hesitations of the conscience but on the problems of the body and of the practical intelligence, in clean, open-air adventure, the shock of arms or the diplomacy of life.'[34]

In general, however, the case of Stevenson reveals the fissures which appeared in the promotion of romance as the literature of imperialism and its concomitant ideologies. The late nineteenth-century construction of romance is a strange hybrid, grafting Boy's Own adventure on to what, earlier in the century, had been seen as a female genre, and the masculine romance was never quite able to shake off the psychological and sexual associations which it attempted to repress.

In a culture basing its imperial goals on personal hygiene and mental healthiness, Stevenson was oddly placed.[35] He was the author both of the Boy's Own adventure *Treasure Island* and of *The Strange Case of Dr Jekyll and Mr Hyde*, a narrative exposing the consequences of the sexual repression that late Victorian mental health required. On the one hand, Stevenson

---

[33] John Veitch, *The History and Poetry of the Scottish Border: Their Main Features and Relations* (Glasgow: James Maclehose, 1878), 555.

[34] *MP* 251.

[35] For imperialism and late Victorian constructions of healthiness see William Greenslade, 'Fitness and the Fin de Siècle', in *Fin de Siècle/Fin du Globe: Fears and Fantasies of the Late Nineteenth Century*, ed. John Stokes (Basingstoke: Macmillan, 1992), 37–51.

could be applauded in an early notice for having 'treated a well-worn theme with freshness',[36] while on the other, William Robertson Nicoll (Kailyard author and editor of the popular literary journal *Bookmen*) privately detected the whiff of corruption in his writing: 'Don't you think there is something sickly about R.L.S.—perfume at best, opium at worst? He is not *fresh* in the right way, is he?'[37] Even on what was arguably his freshest book, *Treasure Island*, opinion was divided as to its suitability for young minds. *Treasure Island* is both a romance and an adventure, genres which combined commonly but uneasily in the later Victorian period. Most commentators praised its bracing qualities ·(it was among the 'wholesome, sound and healthy fiction' recommended by Johns),[38] and agreed with the reviewer in the *Mall Gazette* who stated that 'Our opinion of boys will fall considerably if "Treasure Island" is not their perennial favourite.' But the reviewer in the American *Dial* was less convinced of the healthiness of such a choice: 'It will be relished by adventure-loving boys, but whether it will be wholesome reading for them is more than doubtful.'[39]

Furthermore, the fervour with which the supporters of romance proclaim its superiority over realism tends to let slip the romance's historical associations with the irrational and with repressed desire. Stevenson's account of the romance evokes a kind of sensuous pleasure which leaves the mind lost in a strange psychedelic confusion: 'In anything fit to be called by the name of reading, the process itself should be absorbing and voluptuous; we should gloat over a book, be rapt clean out of ourselves, and rise from the perusal, our minds filled with the busiest, kaleidoscopic dance of images, incapable of sleep or of

---

[36] Review of *Treasure Island* in the *Academy*, in *Robert Louis Stevenson: The Critical Heritage*, ed. Paul Maixner (London: Routledge and Kegan Paul, 1981), 128.

[37] T. H. Darlow, *William Robertson Nicoll: His Life and Letters* (London: Hodder and Stoughton, 1925), 76.

[38] Stevenson's own response to mass publication was ambivalent. See Patrick Brantlinger and Richard Boyle, 'The Education of Edward Hyde: Stevenson's "Gothic Gnome" and the Mass Readership of Late-Victorian England', in *'Dr Jekyll and Mr Hyde' After One Hundred Years*, ed. William Veeder and Gordon Hirsch (Chicago and London: Chicago University Press, 1988), 265–82.

[39] *The Critical Heritage*, ed. Maixner, 138, 142.

continuous thought.'[40] Yet the essay is ostensibly praising the virtues of adventure; Stevenson's readers are required simultaneously to gloat over their books in absorbed and uninhibited voluptuousness, while experiencing vicariously the 'brute incident' of clean, open-air romance—a bizarre combination. Lang's account of reading locates the experience even more explicitly in a drug-induced haze as he argues himself, almost by accident, into the association of bookmen with opium. His odyssey among books threatens to end perilously close to the land of the Lotus-Eaters:

The habit of reading has been praised as a virtue, and has been denounced as a vice. In no case, if we except the perpetual study of newspapers (which cannot fairly be called reading), is the vice, or the virtue, common. It is more innocent than opium-eating, though, like opium-eating, it unlocks to us artificial paradises. I try to say what I have found in books, what distractions from the world, what teaching (not much), and what consolations.[41]

Stevenson's novels sometimes trace the attempt, usually unsuccessful, to evade the category of 'not *fresh* in the right way': in *Weir of Hermiston*, the introspective Archie is sent to the bracing atmosphere of the moors where he fails to be cured of his hypersensitivity. The romance as the expression of natural desire may take on less healthy characteristics. The buried-treasure romance of *The Master of Ballantrae* is overtaken by insalubrious threats of miscegenation and the disruption of gender roles—the adventure hero's worst nightmares.[42] The outdoor adventure in 'the stringent cold of the Canadian border'[43] is not at all beneficial for James Durie who dies at the same moment he is restored to the open air after his burial alive. Lang, otherwise an admirer of the book, found this incident hard to take, proclaiming himself 'staggered by the ghastly attempt to reanimate the buried Master', and he particularly objected to the improbability of the strangely delicate Secundra

---

[40] *MP* 247.   [41] *AB* 3.

[42] For the homoerotics of the late nineteenth-century romance, see Wayne Koestenbaum, *Double Talk: The Erotics of Male Literary Collaboration* (New York and London: Routledge, 1989).

[43] 'The Genesis of *The Master of Ballantrae*', in *Robert Louis Stevenson: Selected Essays and Poems*, ed. Claire Harman (London: Dent, 1992), 217.

Dass who blows into James's mouth in the attempt to revive him.[44]

Lang also extended the masculine agenda of the adventure romance to his activities as a bookman. Bookmen are also members of the 'brotherhood' of book hunters, whose activities are redolent of a Scottish masculinity: 'I often think that the pleasure of collecting is like that of sport. People talk of "book-hunting," and the old Latin motto says "one never wearies of the chase in this forest." But the analogy to angling seems even stronger. A collector walks in the London or Paris streets, as he does by Tweed or Spey.'[45]

After a spot of bibliographical hunting, shooting, and fishing, the bookman can retire to his study, 'remote from the interruption of servants, wife, and children'.[46] Despite Lang's attempts to associate desirable reading with childhood by making it a natural experience innocent of economic or social values, or with working-class readers for whom chap-books and popular literature were produced, Lang here shuts out these people from the study, the space reserved for male middle-class reading. The old social categories of the demoted oral—women, children, and servants—are again observed. In Lang's opinion, women could not be bookmen, and even in their honorary position of 'Lady book-lovers' they completely failed to grasp the basic requirements of bookmanship: 'a studious girl or matron says, "This is a book," and reads it, if read she does, without caring about the date, or the state, or the publisher's name, or even very often about the author's.'[47] But this ethic did not go uncontested. Margaret Oliphant took issue with the misogyny of bookmanship in a *Blackwood's* review of Lang's *Life and Letters* of Lockhart. Oliphant, a *Blackwood's* writer, is partly defending the magazine itself, and partly striking back at Lang's bookman-like gendering of reading. Lang's weighty tome is pictured as a hero of romance, aggressively imposing its physical presence:

---

[44] Andrew Lang, 'Mr. Stevenson's Works', *Essays in Little* (London: Henry and Co., 1891), 33.
[45] Andrew Lang, *The Library* (London: Macmillan, 1881), 8.
[46] Ibid. 34.   [47] BB 136.

It comes to us from the press, imposing, with its blazoned shield, like a knight into the lists, thanking God that it is not as other books, but fit for any drawing-room or dignified library—a separate kind of production altogether from those vulgar volumes which are meant only to be read. We do not desire to imply that Mr Lang's beautiful volumes are not meant to be read, though we confess we look for the day when a cheap edition will provide us with something easier to hold and study.[48]

In Lang's manly text, the less physically imposing monthly *Blackwood's Magazine*, touched by the accelerated circulation of orality, is a *belle dame sans merci* (though not very beautiful in this case), who has ensnared the unfortunate knight Lockhart. Lang has written: 'One really begins to think of "Maga" as of a cankered witch, who has spellbound the young man' and Oliphant protests not only at the defamation of *Blackwood's*, but also at the misogyny that underpins Lang's feminization of the magazine, and she fills in for Lang the implied ending of his gynophobic romance plot:

Has 'Maga' been unkind to Mr Lang? All feminine creatures, we are aware, are apt to give rise to prejudice in this way. In some womanish mood they fail to smile, at a critical moment they look coldly upon a suitor's offering; and lo! the enchanting heroine becomes a cankered witch and her graces charm no more—notwithstanding that she is just as fair as before the untoward accident occurred.[49]

Oliphant's encounter with Lang marked an attempt, bounded by her conservatism, to wrest orality from the bookmen. Earlier, Oliphant had staked a claim for a female orality which could empower the speaking subject. Scottish history offers such a condition, which has evidently been made less available by a literary climate fostering the 'little effusions of criticism' in which Lang himself later specialized:

Nobody is *blasé*, few dispirited—life, strong, wilful, and not to be discouraged, overflows everywhere. Nobody reads, but everybody thinks. The mild adoption of some one else's opinions, and the calm stagnation of mind which makes it desirable to have one's opinions made for one, is a state unknown to the energetic soul of these stout

---

[48] [Margaret Oliphant], 'John Gibson Lockhart', *BM* 160 (1896), 607–25 (p. 607).   [49] Ibid. 610.

generations. . . . Literature and literary talk, discussions of books, and little effusions of criticism, were happily unknown to these times.[50]

Oliphant's nostalgia employs the 'clear, sharp air' of out-of-door Scottishness to draw on the myth of Scottish democracy. Alarmed by the failure of mass literacy to sustain stable class relations within the democratic ethos (she maintained a conservative stance on the subject of popular literature, and the notorious preference of the working class for 'trash'),[51] Oliphant turns to orality to shore up the myth. The oral thus allows a space for the fearless exchange of views between classes, but locates such a dialogue within a stable class structure existing before the advent of popular literacy:

Looking back through the clear, sharp air, we see the frugal country, with all its primitive thrifts and managements, its homespun coats and manners, its energy of speech; the leisurely ploughman pausing in his furrow to hold his own against his master; the faithful servant caustically critical upon the affairs of his 'family'; the quaint dialogue maintained with equal freedom on both sides between my lord and the passing beggar or trespasser; while at home women spin and talk, and bring up sturdy children.[52]

But Oliphant's association of speech with women sets up an important alternative structure for the figuring of the oral throughout the rest of the century as she identifies 'a scattering of solitary independent personages, principally ladies, sometimes men in the same circumstances; a class of talkers unrivalled, and thinkers not to be despised'.[53] Oliphant's oral women are not entirely confined to spinning and talking at home; they also make themselves heard in history, as she reinstates orality to a position from which Scott, in the Border Minstrelsy, had nervously debarred it: 'this class of celibates behaved themselves with great energy and emphasis in the world, and have worked themselves into the history of their time with a force and clearness not to be surpassed'; the vocabulary of masculine orality—'energy', 'force', 'clearness'—is here established as female.

[50] 'Scottish National Character', BM 87 (1860), 715–31 (p. 720).
[51] See Oliphant's 'The Byways of Literature: Reading for the Million', BM 84 (1858), 200–16.   [52] 'Scottish National Character', 720.
[53] Ibid. 721.

Later nineteenth-century writers absorbed the older association of women with orality and experimented with it. In their
fiction of the 1880s and 1890s, Oliphant and Stevenson
explored further the oral as a bearer not only of social, but also
of psychological meaning. Or rather, the oral starts to become
a means of evading signification altogether as it becomes
identified with inarticulacy and non-meaning. In Stevenson's
1881 story, 'Thrawn Janet', the Reverend Mr Soulis is strongly
identified with the authority of the book: he is 'fu' o' book-
learnin'' and is 'writin' a book himsel', which was surely no'
fittin' for ane o' his years an' sma' experience'.⁵⁴ According to
the popular (oral) interpretation of events, a local woman, Janet
M'Lour, despite renouncing Satan on the advice of Mr Soulis, in
fact becomes possessed by the devil. It is believed that Janet is
really dead but that her body is animated by the devil who has
taken up residence in it. Mr Soulis tries to talk to her, but can
make no sense of what she says: 'Whiles she sang louder, but
there was nae man born of woman that could tell the words o'
her song' (p. 147); as in Guy Mannering's attempts to 'master'
Meg Merrilies's ballad, the female oral escapes patriarchal
authority. Eventually Soulis manages to exorcize the devil,
whereupon 'the auld, deid, desecrated corp o' the witch-wife,
sae lang keepit frae the grave and hirsled round by de'ils, lowed
up like a brunstane spunk and fell in ashes to the grund'
(p. 151).

In the terms of psychoanalysis, the scene being played out
here seems to enact the necessary absence of the mother's body
in order that language may take place: the bookish Soulis
triumphs over Janet's wordless voice. This seems at first to be
backed up by a highly misogynist ideology about child-bearing
and the female body: Janet's body, having evacuated the life it
was sustaining, is now all consumed and crumbles to useless
dust.⁵⁵ Yet inarticulate orality somehow manages to survive the

⁵⁴ Robert Louis Stevenson, 'Thrawn Janet', in *The Merry Men and Other Tales
and Fables* (London: Chatto and Windus, 1887), 139, 140. Further references
appear in the text.
⁵⁵ Margaret Homans, in her psycho-social study of the relationship between
women and writing in the nineteenth century, points to parallels between Lacanian
theory and Victorian hostility to the mother's body (*Bearing the Word: Language
and Female Experience in Nineteenth-Century Women's Writing* (Chicago and
London: Chicago University Press, 1986), see esp. pp. 153–88).

disintegration of the woman's body, to render Soulis as unintelligible as Janet herself: 'lang, lang he lay raving in his bed' (p. 151), observes the narrator, commenting that thereafter he became the sadly diminished character that he remains to this day. Soulis, himself a bookman, is unable to control this female orality and becomes engulfed by it, reversing the normal order of events in which speech is supposed to be contained in writing. These activities of a subversive orality challenging the security of literacy set the scene for the problematics of writing throughout the fiction of the second half of the century.

6
Documentary Disclosure:
The Master of Ballantrae

STEVENSON'S *The Master of Ballantrae* occupies a pivotal position in a study of speech and writing in Scottish culture. It looks back at the social incarnations of the oral in the earlier part of the nineteenth century, as well as examining its later reappearance in the imperialist romance. The novel is also important in a second way in that it goes directly to the heart of the opposition between speech and writing and asks if such a distinction, freed from socially determinating factors, can ever be sustained. *The Master of Ballantrae* announces its retrospective activity by presenting its inner story in the favourite device of nineteenth-century Scottish literature: the manuscript handed from writer to—eventually—publisher. Stevenson had originally rejected the device on the grounds that it was 'a little too like Scott',[1] and the parallels are interesting. *Rob Roy*, for instance, raises some now familiar questions about the status of texts in Scottish literature. The novel was advertised in the first edition with the statement that the Author had 'received a parcel of papers, containing the outlines of this narrative'.[2] In his introduction added in 1829 Scott further supplies some history of the MacGregors: 'The history of the tribe is briefly as follows. But we must premise that the tale depends in some degree on tradition; therefore, excepting when written documents are quoted, it must be considered as in some degree dubious' (pp. xxviii–xxix).

---

[1] *R. L. S.: Stevenson's Letters to Charles Baxter*, ed. DeLancey Ferguson and Marshall Waingrow (New Haven: Yale University Press, 1956), 355.

[2] *Rob Roy*, Border, pp. xxv–xxvi. Further references appear in the text.

What, then, is the status of *Rob Roy*? By announcing its origin in a 'parcel of papers' does it aspire to the authenticity of a written history, as opposed to the dubious oral variety? Or are such claims rendered impossible by the Author's later caveat warning against both spoken and written testimony: 'Clannish partialities were very apt to guide the tongue and pen' (p. xcix)? Other familiar questions about the nature of stories begin to arise. How, for example, are the 'outlines' of a narrative to be characterized in a theory of stories? How are the Author's contributions to be identified, and are they too claiming authenticity because they are written down? As in *The Monastery*, the authenticity of antiquarian evidence is undercut by the play of fiction.[3]

Rob Roy is unusual among Scott's novels in being throughout a first-person narration. Although many of the Waverley Novels' introductory epistles discuss the provenance of the story, few sustain the voice of the 'original' author which becomes subsumed by the protean voice of the Author of Waverley. Frank Osbaldistone's narration, conscious of the time lapse between writer and reader, begins by speculating on the relative functions of speech and writing in the transmission of texts. His view is that while 'the tale told by one friend, and listened to by another, loses half its charms when committed to paper', writing can nevertheless represent 'a faithful transcript of my thoughts and feelings' (p. 2). That is, he separates the performative qualities possessed only by speech from the assumed ability of writing to transcribe and contain ideas which pre-exist it.

Stevenson's *Master of Ballantrae* returns us to this situation, but with a difference. Whereas the Author of Waverley and Frank Osbaldistone speculate within *Rob Roy* on the relative merits of speech and writing in the creation of histories, *The Master of Ballantrae* is *itself* a speculation on the subject. The novel starts at the point at which the manuscript, dormant for a hundred years, is about to be read. Despite Stevenson's opinion that this state of affairs was 'too like Scott', his decision

---

[3] Diana Elam productively uses Scott's notes and introductions in *Rob Roy* to discuss the play of history and romance in Scott's novels (*Romancing the Postmodern* (London and New York: Routledge, 1992), 51–79).

to include it for the Edinburgh edition may in fact remind us of his difference from Scott in this respect. The author of *Rob Roy* does not explain how he came by the parcel of papers, indeed, in the Magnum Edition he seems tired of the whole game, admitting 'that the communication alluded to is entirely imaginary' (p. xxvi). The fate of the manuscript which makes up the central narrative of *The Master of Ballantrae*, on the other hand, is controlled, as far as possible, by its fictional narrator.

Ephraim Mackellar is both historical figure and historian, attempting to assume the positions of both Scott, in arbitrating between authentic and dubious ways of recording history, and Frank, in writing down his own part in history. *The Master of Ballantrae* investigates the nature and functions of a historical document, in that it examines in what sense a document can be said to be historical, while simultaneously exploring what a written document is. Histories are the result not only of interpretations of events, but also of the way such interpretations are themselves conditioned by evaluations of the means by which events have become recorded. To modify Marshall McLuhan's famous formula, it is not so much the medium *itself* that constitutes the message, but the way that medium is valued.

As *The Master of Ballantrae* investigates further the authority of writing, it strips away some of the surrounding layers of its mystique. In the partially literate societies represented in *The Three Perils of Man* and *The Monastery*, written texts laid claim to an emergent authority, powerful but threatening, concealing its socialized power with magical mystique: grammar as glamour. In *The Master of Ballantrae*, whose narrator identifies himself as an advocate and skilled practitioner of the written word, writing has become the accepted norm, and it is now speech which, from the cultural margins, threatens writing's dominance. The grammar of Mackellar's book learning is here distinct from, and pitched against, the dangerous and persuasive speech of his enemy, James Durie, and it is James's speech which has the power to 'cast a glamour' over his auditors.[4] In its

---

[4] *The Master Of Ballantrae*, ed. Emma Letley (Oxford: Oxford University Press, 1983), 164. Further references appear in the text.

exploration of attitudes to speech held by a representative of a literate and literary culture, the novel interrogates some of the assumptions about orality which lie behind Scott's endeavours in the *Border Minstrelsy* to make ballads from the oral fringes of a literate culture eligible for inclusion in the canon of literary texts. Unease about the social status of orality is masked by a frustrated attempt to posit essential differences between speech and writing themselves. But where Scott is overtly welcoming towards oral forms, the fictional Mackellar is openly suspicious of speech. That is, Mackellar sees the desired clarity and authority of logocentrism as a quality specific to writing. *The Master of Ballantrae* is another of those texts in which speech is seen by some of the characters as subversive, dangerous and, rather than acting as the bearer of meaning, tending to generate multiple meanings.

In the graphocentric world of Mackellar's narration, the privileging of authoritative presence is projected on to writing. The author's intention is believed to be locked into the text and is guarded by the meaning of that text in the author's physical absence. Speech, by contrast, is seen to distort or multiply potential meanings. Oral transmission encourages a plurality of versions so that the presence of the speaker and the text exist in a series of fluid, indeterminate relationships. Even when only one speaker can be identified, speech can take up the position formerly occupied by magic language in, for example, *The Three Perils of Man*: it engages in no referential process at all, yet has the ability to influence events. However, despite his apparent confidence as a narrator, Mackellar struggles repeatedly with the contradictions that arise whenever speech and writing are subjected to value judgements. The very grounds for making such judgements shift beneath him, and he is unable to sustain any coherent opposition between the oral and the written.

The events of this story are thus told from the point of view of a writer self-consciously creating a historical document. Mackellar tries to ensure that it will be received as such, trusting to the apparent objectivity of the historical perspective which will guarantee that his account is read as it was written. To this end, he annexes a view of historical record which ascribes certain qualities to writing. Like the editor of the *Minstrelsy of the Scottish Border*, Mackellar does not himself openly admit differences between speech and writing to be socially determined. Rather, he expresses such differences as if they were inherent qualities, valuing his literate education because it equips him to deal in facts and to press language, more specifically written language, into the service of their transmission. He offers the reader his own written account because of two valuable properties which are often assumed to be inseparable from written language: its supposed lack of context and its ability to endure through time. In the papers handed down to Mr Thomson, Mackellar specifies that they are not to be opened for a hundred years. The possible reasons for such an act are crucial to our understanding of Mackellar's position as a narrator. The length of time specified cannot be merely to protect the participants who clearly will not live so long (and indeed it is made clear by the editor that the longest surviving character, Henry's daughter Katherine, died sixty-two years before the opening of the manuscript). Not only does this hundred year postponement appear to demonstrate the lasting quality of writing, but it is also used by Mackellar to underpin the objectivity of his account.

Mackellar introduces his narrative with the comment: 'The full truth of this odd matter is what the world has long been looking for, and public curiosity is sure to welcome' (p. 9). His account will be the complete, objective truth and he can confidently predict that it will also be accepted as such by an anonymous reading public universalized as 'the world'. This achievement will be assisted by the potential qualities of a written account which has survived a hundred years. First, the author will by this time be long dead and thus not available for questioning, so that his 'meaning' will have to be taken on trust. This is an opinion about writing sometimes articulated in the twentieth century. Walter Ong explains the theory of writing as 'context-free language' or 'autonomous discourse':

Like the oracle or the prophet, the book relays an utterance from a source, the one who really 'said' or wrote the book. The author might be challenged if only he or she could be reached, but the author cannot be reached in any book. There is no way directly to refute a text. After absolutely total and devastating refutation, it says exactly the same thing as before. This is one reason why 'the book says' is popularly tantamount to 'it is true'.[5]

Written language is said to be autonomous because it is free of the context of an audience at the moment of its production. This not only guarantees the integrity of the author's input, but also projects all responsibility for protecting the author's interests on to the text itself, which is then seen to exist in splendid isolation. The supposedly context-free existence of writing appears therefore to have a number of advantages in the communication of information. It gives the impression of a pure source, uncorrupted by the shared narration associated, by Benjamin and others, with oral transmission. It is on these conditions, as Lynette Hunter points out in an essay challenging such assumptions, that writing becomes associated with authority: 'the absence of audience becomes the key factor in recent criticism that, because of this absence, writing has to become authoritative, imposing its point upon the reader or audience.'[6]

The second quality that Mackellar identifies in writing is its durability. The hundred years during which Mackellar intends the manuscript to lie unopened are representative of the action of writing itself, which (despite numerous exceptions) is not usually read at the same time as it is produced. This effect is to be amplified by the process of printing to which Stevenson-as-editor is invited to subject the manuscript. Writing, therefore, seems to hold out promises additional to the survival of the author's meaning. Like printing, writing can be seen as a technology which provides the necessary temporal distance and physical space for a cool and rational assessment of material.[7] It can be seen to address itself to an abstract generality; the removal of writing from any immediate context seems to prevent prejudiced reading. Mackellar's papers are destined by

---

[5] Walter J. Ong, *Orality and Literacy: the Technologizing of the Word* (London and New York: Methuen, 1982), 78–9.

[6] Lynette Hunter, 'A Rhetoric of Mass Communication: Collective or Corporate Public Discourse', in *Oral and Written Communication: Historical Approaches*, ed. Richard Leo Enos (Newbury Park, Calif.: Sage Publications, 1990), 216–61. I am indebted throughout this chapter to Hunter's incisive critique of the oral/literate debate.

[7] For writing as technology see Ong, *Orality and Literacy*, 81–3.

him for 'the world' and 'the public', which, together with the temporal gap, emphasize a sense of shared impartiality and objectivity. They will become print, which allows the author to communicate to a large number of people at the same time, thereby removing any interpersonal context.

Mackellar's concept of writing, then, neatly combines the control of the single author with the authenticity of the absent-author text. He claims the privileged status of the best possible single author with immediate access to the events described: 'I was intimately mingled with the last years and history of the house; and there does not live one man so able as myself to make these matters plain, or so desirous to narrate them faithfully' (p. 9). Conveniently, this approach is the one most desired by an imagined readership who can apparently show an interest in the events, while remaining disinterested. In brief, the nature of writing seems to be to guarantee historical truth over time and space and to encourage its objective reception. Stevenson, however, undermines his narrator's aspirations, by including the 1894 preface, in which a fairly anonymous version of himself is handed Mackellar's papers. We are reminded that we are reading not one, but two historical contexts and if we examine these two contexts, it becomes apparent that writing has manifestly failed in its prescribed duties.

Mackellar's story commences with the political choices made by members of the Durie family during the 1745 Jacobite rebellion, as the family strives to protect its future. Lacking a Michael Scott to predict the outcome of the rebellion, the family decides to play safe: the elder son, James, joins the Stewart cause and the younger, Henry, affirms allegiance to the British Crown. After Culloden, James escapes abroad, but later returns incognito. Mackellar suspects him of being an agent for the British government. These actions have complex implications for Scotland's status in the Union, and Mackellar's document does seem at first to focus on a critical moment in Scotland's national history, turning on 'that memorable year 1745, when the foundations of this tragedy were laid' (p. 10). But the novel's ability to play out the dramas of history foils Mackellar's privileging of the logocentric historical document. A narrative written in 1789 and read in 1889 is likely to offer more than one historical perspective. Mackellar cannot be both Frank

Osbaldistone and the Author of Waverley; he must relinquish control of his writing to his readers. The editor, receiving the story in 1889, is himself one in a line of people and things who return or reappear to find themselves other than they were, culminating in the grim circumstances of James's burial alive and re-emergence dead. Rather than seeing himself as a constant, the editor admits that he exists in a series of differing selves in past, present, and future, 'smitten with an equal regret for what he once was and for what he once hoped to be' (p. 5). The manuscript that Mackellar seals up in 1789 will not be quite the same if it is read in 1889.

A reading of Mackellar's tale from the perspective of 1889 might, for example, focus not so much on the divisions of the Jacobite rising, but on Britain's activities in its colonies and Scotland's part in imperialism.[8] The representation of Scots leaving Scotland carries echoes of the destruction of the clan system, of emigration and the clearances, but also of colonialism. Cast out of Scotland, James profits by piracy. Other rootless Scots—Pinkerton and Hastie—appear among the 'dregs of colonial rascality' (p. 225) in America. In a novel full of doublings, the ironically named Hastie, with his education from Edinburgh College and his humourless disposition, can be seen as Mackellar's own dark double. It is hard to say who are the dispossessed and who the dispossessors. For John Flory, the anti-hero of Orwell's *Burmese Days*, the Scots have, forty years on, become an insidious threat, profiting from the imperial endeavour while remaining marginalized from its nationalist centre: 'The British Empire is simply a device for giving trade monopolies to the English—or rather to gangs of Jews and Scotchmen.'[9] Thus Orwell's novel about colonialism locates

[8] In suggesting the significance of historical conditions at the novel's publication, I do not underestimate its important engagement with eighteenth-century Scottish history. Mary Lascelles points out, for example, that the brothers' dual allegiance was a circumstance 'well attested in the history of the successive Jacobite risings' (*The Story-Teller Retrieves the Past: Historical Fiction and Fictitious History in the Art of Scott, Stevenson, Kipling, and Some Others* (Oxford: Clarendon Press, 1980), 68).
[9] George Orwell, *Burmese Days* (London: Secker and Warburg, 1986), 39. The narrator of *Burmese Days* looks back towards Stevenson as an apologist for imperialism, supplying the novel's Britanophile Dr Veraswami with phrases 'that probably came from Stevenson' (p. 41).

Scots in the uncertain position which we find them occupying in *The Master of Ballantrae*. Cast out of his homeland James wanders through Europe, India, and America until he becomes cast out of societies altogether.

Read from this perspective of its dramatized reception in 1889, the novel plays on prevalent late nineteenth-century fears about socialism, national identity, and racial degeneracy. Pirates are not always the working-class types defeated in *Treasure Island*, but members of the House of Durrisdeer.[10] Servants are described as 'decayed gentlemen'. The class axis itself becomes overtaken by the problem of defining nationalities in a novel in which characters can rarely be identified by national concerns. Scots, Irish, English, British, French, and Americans form temporary alliances which are dependent on contingent circumstances. National characteristics are only ascertainable when they are self-inflicted parodies like Burke's adoption of his 'Crowding Pat' guise. To be European is to lose any hope of clear social identity and to become part of an assortment of colonists rather like that which populates Polynesia in *The Ebb-Tide*: 'Throughout the island world of the Pacific, scattered men of many European races and from almost every grade of society carry activity and disseminate disease.'[11]

Not only class and nationality, but also race becomes confused as both Indians from India and Red Indians appear in the American wilderness: 'There was now no danger of an Indian onslaught' (p. 224), remarks Mackellar in a sentence that describes the (not Red) Indian Secundra Dass crawling around in the bushes. Furthermore, Indians can also be strangely European. Amid a narration that strives to stress the superior, gentlemanly and 'polite' qualities of the French/English/Scots/Irish, Burke, James's Irish companion, lets slip a telling question

---

[10] Christopher Harvie observes that 'There is a sense in which *Treasure Island* could be seen as a sort of social parable: an embattled microcosm of civil society . . . being menaced by the lower orders under brutal and materialistic leadership' ('The Politics of Stevenson', in *Stevenson and Victorian Scotland*, ed Jenni Calder (Edinburgh: Edinburgh University Press, 1981), 107–25 (p. 120)). See also Joseph Bristow, *Empire Boys: Adventures in a Man's World* (London: Harper Collins, 1991), 109–23.

[11] *The Ebb-Tide*, in *Dr Jekyll and Mr Hyde and Other Stories*, ed. Jenni Calder (Harmondsworth: Penguin, 1979), 173.

as to whether a war-party 'were French or English Indians' (p. 68). Mountain's party, 'the dregs of colonial rascality', can hardly object to finding their companions killed in the night by natives when this is the very fate they were hoping to inflict on James. When Stevenson wrote that the novel was to be about 'savagery and civilisation' he omitted to specify which was which.[12] The novel also uses doublings to disrupt any sense of stable identity and James's relationship with Secundra Dass plays on race. When he discovers James in India, Burke makes clear racial distinctions ('The place was soaking with the dew, which, in that country, is exceedingly unwholesome, above all to whites', p. 148) while James blurs the contours of racial identity. A character always associated with speech, he refuses now to speak himself, rather communicating through Secundra Dass's 'Hindustanee'. James perversely insists in undermining the imperialist romance's clear-cut (though vulnerable) distinctions of class, race, gender, and sexuality. Mackellar himself exposes the genre's suppressed homoeroticism in his love for Henry, his jealousy of Alison, and his open dislike of women in general. He is uncertain about the application of the codes appropriate to servant/master and masculine/feminine behaviour as he tries to read James's relationship with Secundra Dass: 'I saw he was a kind friend or a good master (whichever it was) to his Secundra Dass—seeing to his comfort; mending the fire with his own hand, for the Indian complained of cold; inquiring as to the rice on which the stranger made his diet; talking with him pleasantly in the Hindustanee' (p. 165).

Looked at in these ways, *The Master of Ballantrae* has as much in common with novels set in the period of its publication as it does with Stevenson's more nostalgic eighteenth-century Scottish fiction, *Kidnapped* and *Catriona*. Particularly, the novel has an interesting relationship with Conrad's *Heart of Darkness*, to which I shall return. Thus Mackellar's narrative is already framed by a split historical context which at all points challenges assumptions about the status of writing as context-free. Not surprisingly, Mackellar's distinctions between speech and writing cannot be sustained by him; the story he tells is

[12] 'The Genesis of *The Master of Ballantrae*', in *Robert Louis Stevenson: Selected Essays and Poems*, ed. Claire Harman (London: Dent, 1992), 217.

Stevenson's cautionary tale of a Scot who valued writing over speech. Mackellar's narration traces a move from a faith in the essential realities of speech and writing to a position where all language becomes unstable and spoken and written texts begin to reverse the roles previously assigned to them.

All judgements about speech and writing depend to some extent upon a social context. Mackellar is much influenced by the relative social merits of speech and writing in the eighteenth century, although his own social status is equivocal; like Malvolio's, his standing as a steward is fraught with difficulty. He attempts to evade the issue, describing himself as a 'loving servant of the house of Durrisdeer', his involvement in the economy of the estate apparently transcended by his emotional links with the family. Yet he is dogged throughout his narrative by the question of whether he is, or is not, a servant. A 'loving servant' may be a servant nevertheless, and James Durie does his best to keep Mackellar in such a position. On James's first return to Durrisdeer, Henry feels obliged to protect Mackellar from James's orders, commenting politely to Mackellar, ' "We are constantly troubling you: will you be so good as to send one of the servants?"—with an accent on the word' (p. 85). Later, after Henry and his family have left for New York, James and Mackellar jostle pointlessly for position at the head of a dining table now set for only three people.

Despite his dedication to the interests of the aristocratic Ballantrae family, Mackellar seems to have fallen prey to the middle-class moral ideology that saw servants as notorious bearers of orality. In reaction, and as if in compensation for the ambiguity of his position, Mackellar emphasizes his status as a literate, indeed highly educated steward. He loses no time in informing the reader that he has received a mastership of arts from Edinburgh University and that he can be observed 'quoting Horace . . . like a young man fresh from college' (p. 23). Writing is his preferred medium and a guarantee of status in a graphocentric society. Removed into a rural society which relies on oral transmission, Mackellar's tactic is to emphasize the social status of writing. He has to recount events which took place before his arrival at Durrisdeer, and he investigates the proliferation of oral reports which have grown round the Durie family, long a focal point for discussion and storytelling in the neighbourhood. Yet he is notably unhappy at being forced to rely on the evidence of orality, and frets anxiously about its authorship and authority. The Duries appear in a ballad 'which common report attributes to Thomas of Ercildoune himself—I cannot say how truly, and which some have applied—I dare not say with how much justice—to the events of this narration' (pp. 9–10). He hastily moves on to the more reliable source of 'Authentic history', as opposed to the inauthenticity of the oral ballad.

At the start of his narrative, Mackellar is somewhat confounded by the oral activity around him. At first he does his best to follow the spread of oral information, and to trace rumours through their transmitters, while simultaneously assessing the likelihood of their being true. But this kind of oral transmission always seems to be one step ahead of him. He feels it to be something alien to himself and claims he can never become accustomed to it: 'News came to Durrisdeer of course, by the common report, as it goes travelling through a country, a thing always wonderful to me' (p. 15). Furthermore, Mackellar considers the oral spread of news to be dangerous and unreliable. Local information is equated with distorting and possible malicious gossip, the truth can easily become so corrupted that it is inappropriate for a written narrative: 'so defaced by legends . . . that I scruple to set it down' (p. 11). Mackellar thus tends to locate oral transmission in a lower class whose unchecked circulating of disinformation threatens the stability of the aristocracy (despite evidence that the representative family in the novel is busy splitting its own stability down the middle).

At first, then, Mackellar will always prefer a written narrative to an oral one, an opposition which he defines in terms of the relationship between the writer and the absent audience. His distrust of speech continually returns to its association with the performative, which he believes to effect its unreliability. When he has a choice between the two, his preference for writing overrides other considerations. He would rather relinquish narrative control to Burke's written report than retell an oral one in his own terms. Mackellar's inclusion of Burke's narrative might seem at first to argue against his belief in the authority of the single author. But his motives for using Burke do not include a desire for narrative plurality. In 'Wandering Willie's Tale', such plurality was dependent on the impossibility of voices being traced back to their precise sources; here the opposite is the case, reminding us of the ability of the oral to stand for completely opposed cultural ideas, and its consequent lack of an essential nature. Mackellar complains of the oral's tendency to obscure the traces of its origins: overhearing James's voice he is reminded of an old story of a fairy visitant who spoke 'often in a tongue that signified nothing to the hearers; and went again, as she had come, under cloud of night, leaving not so much as a name behind her' (pp. 152–3). James—the focal point of Mackellar's anxieties—is here associated with an irrational, female, and subversive orality which threatens the male romance.

Mackellar's belief in the singularity of authorship is absolute and it is dependent on a theory of writing. He privileges Burke's written account, believing it factual and reliable, over Burke's 'varnished' spoken report of the same events:

In this way my readers will have a detailed and, I believe, a very genuine account of some essential matters; and if any publisher should take a fancy to the Chevalier's manner of narration, he knows where to apply for the rest, of which there is plenty at his service. I put in my first extract here, so that it may stand in place of what the Chevalier told us over our wine in the hall of Durrisdeer; but you are to suppose that it was not the brutal fact, but a very varnished version that he offered to my lord. (p. 37)

Mackellar's objections to oral performance lie not only in its susceptibility to influence by an audience; he also fears its perceived secretive, subjective behaviour, the significance of which can escape him just as he was unable to keep control of the circulation of oral rumours. Performance is a threat because it can involve elements not recorded in words. The presence of a speaker can open up discourse to a number of extraverbal or paralinguistic features: changes in tone, gestures, physical expressions, and so on. Speech also has the capacity to draw attention to things which then need not be further spoken about because of the shared context between speaker and audience. Further, speech lends itself to phatic discourse, here described by Deborah Tannen: 'In face to face spontaneous conversation such as that which occurs at a dinner table, the fact of speaking to each other is often more important than the information or messages conveyed.'[13] Language can be used to send various interpersonal signals and to establish the relationship between the speakers, no matter what the topic of conversation.

Mackellar hopes to protect his readers from such discourse. Not surprisingly, for someone who believes his words to be directly conveying a message which represents 'the full truth', Mackellar is very suspicious of performance and phatic discourse, to which he refers respectively as 'the story of looks' and 'the message of voices when they are saying no great matter'. Not only will his account be free of such dangerous concepts, but he claims that he cannot even represent them in writing: 'My pen is clear enough to tell a plain tale; but not to render the effect of an infinity of small things, not one great enough in itself to be narrated; and to translate the story of looks, and the message of voices when they are saying no great matter' (pp. 29–30). Yet the novel does seem curiously unable to tell 'a plain tale' without its context. Mackellar, despite his faith in the truthfulness of the written narrative with its absent author cannot, in fact, resist an attempt to fill in the gaps which such an absence must open up. Immediately after he has denied being able to 'render the effect of ... small things' and to 'translate the story of looks', Mackellar undermines his argument by doing precisely these things. First he describes in detail the ways in which Alison expresses her increasingly distant attitude to Henry shortly after their marriage:

She held him at the staff's end; forgot and then remembered and unbent to him, as we do to children; burthened him with cold kindness; reproved him with a change of colour and a bitten lip, like one shamed by his disgrace: ordered him with a look of the eye, when she was off her guard; when she was on the watch, pleaded with him

[13] Deborah Tannen, 'Relative Involvement in Oral and Written Discourse', in *Literacy, Language and Learning: The Nature and Consequences of Reading and Writing*, ed. David R. Olson, Nancy Torrance, and Angela Hildyard (Cambridge: Cambridge University Press, 1985), 124–47 (p. 128). Tannen argues that no communication is context-free, and that the argument that writing is inherently less contextualized than speech stems from erroneously ascribing usages of speech and writing to orality and literacy *per se*.

for the most natural attentions, as though they were unheard-of favours. (pp. 31–2)

Similarly, Mackellar is eager to interpret the 'message of voices', hinting at the dark implications of a brief exchange between Henry and Alison after she has accepted James's letter:

'O, read it and be done!' he had cried.
'Spare me that,' said she.
And by these two speeches, to my way of thinking, each undid a great part of what they had previously done well. (p. 36)

Mackellar's choice of verbs here underlines a central opposition in his theory of speech and writing: speech, as here, does things—it is an action—whereas the function of writing is to report. Such a distinction is undercut at the very start of his narrative, which, he accidently lets slip, aspires to an overall performance. The 'full truth' is not only that objective account which the world will read to find out what happened, it is also Mackellar's final act of service to Henry: 'The truth is a debt I owe my lord's memory' (p. 9). The repayment of a debt is an act and when it takes the form of a story, that story becomes a verbal act, like the tales in the storytelling competition of *The Three Perils of Man*. Nevertheless, Mackellar, at least in the first part of the story, loads his narrative with examples to support his case.

James's story of the Count and the Baron, as reported by Mackellar, is doubly illustrative of the active powers of speech. Mackellar explicitly identifies the narration of this story as itself performative: James 'must tell me a tale, and show me at the same time how clever he was, and how wicked' (p. 183). The tale too is an example of how storytelling can not only relate the past (or purport to do so) but also influence events. A count (whom Mackellar suspects of being James himself), after narrowly escaping a fall down an old well shaft, replaces the broken railing so that it will collapse under the weight of anyone else who looks down into the well. The count is secretly nursing a grievance against a German baron to whom he describes a fictitious dream in which he watches the baron being drawn to the site of the well. Needless to say, the count arranges to pass by the well in the company of the baron and announces that this was the very place in his dream. The baron, intrigued, goes to

investigate and is never seen again. The innermost layer in the
Chinese box of narrators at this point is the count himself,
telling the story of his supposed dream to the baron. This story
hints, with a sort of demonic irony, at its own dangerous lack of
referentiality. The well down which the baron is presumed to
plunge is not mentioned in the narrative of the dream: there is
nothing at the centre of the story which the narrative describes;
the story refers to nothing, but its effects are nevertheless fatal to
its audience.

In Mackellar's view of language, writing is inherently
authoritative, but speech can establish a kind of spurious local
authority for the speaker. This again is founded in his belief in
the objective and decontextualized nature of writing. Writing is
simply a transparent medium for conveying accurate information, but orality allows speakers to influence interpersonal
relationships in 'the message of voices when they are saying no
great matter'. Mackellar takes the view that speakers may have
an agenda which goes beyond the imparting of information and
that consequently they are very likely to exert a dangerous
influence over their audience.

Mackellar identifies the main practitioner of this kind of
speech as James Durie, who openly admits that 'speech is
very easy, and sometimes very deceptive' (p. 161), but an
earlier example in Mackellar's narrative is the case of Tam
Macmorland, a local man who has fought in the 'Forty-five and
who brings back reports of the fighting, which has not been
going well for the Jacobites. Tam claims that the cause has
been betrayed by Henry Durie's apparent desertion of it.
Mackellar is instantly suspicious of Tam's oratory: 'There was
not much harm in Tam; but he had that grievous weakness, a
long tongue; and as the only man in that country who had been
out—or, rather, who had come in again—he was sure of
listeners' (p. 17). Mackellar imputes the effectiveness of Tam's
speech not to any particular qualities of individual speakers, but
to the inherently surreptitious and persuasive force of speaking
itself in his dictum: 'Let any one speak long enough, he will get
believers' (p. 18). Speech is dangerous because of the presence of
a speaker who will be able to exploit context. Mackellar
comments of James's persuasive abilities, 'It is one of the worst
things of sentiment, that the voice grows to be more important

than the words, and the speaker than that which is spoken' (p. 102). Later, Henry tries to limit James's authority by insisting, 'He will have no voice ... and, I hope, no influence' (p. 161).

Mackellar has personal reasons for privileging writing as a more neutral medium than speech. Speaking can be dangerous for the speaker who becomes too prominent in the relationship between the voice and the words. Traditionally, speakers are rarely identified as a neutral transmitter of words. The exchange between Mackellar and old Lord Durrisdeer, after the duel between James and Henry, foregrounds the perilous nature of the spoken, rather than the written word. Mackellar, believing James to be dead, finds it very difficult to communicate this to James's father, but drops substantial hints that all is not well. Lord Durrisdeer reacts by warning Mackellar that his spoken words are unacceptable: 'These are dangerous words' and 'Here is too much speech' (p. 118). In instances like these, the glamour of speech can rebound upon the speaker, giving Mackellar grounds for his distrust of the oral.

Opposed to the personal and performative nature of speech, in Mackellar's theory, is writing's faithful referentiality. Mackellar equates writing with reporting—the exact recounting of events after they have taken place, thereby drawing apart the idea of an event and a narration, a distinction blurred for him by speech. He puts considerable trust in writing, which he believes to be more reliable than speech, and more likely to convey the truth. Having resolved to warn Alison of the pernicious influence of James, Mackellar wonders how best to approach her: 'Finding no occasion of free speech, I bethought me at last of a kind of documentary disclosure' (p. 128). He presents Alison with a collection of paper testifying to James's draining of the estate and his sinister dealings with the British government. Again, writing is seen as a reliable medium as it is in Mackellar's overall policy in creating a historical document: documents 'disclose' things which existed before them, they are the transparent bearers of information.

Writing can seem to claim this authenticity because it appears to be context-free; Mackellar might find the opportunity to speak to Alison, but he fears that his words would be compromised by the circumstances, as they were in his attempts to communicate with Lord Durrisdeer. Mackellar relies on 'documentary' evidence in a double sense of the word: he respects it because it is both composed of written documents and supposed to be factual rather than fictional. A document is thus by its very nature more accurate than an oral communication. As if to prove this point, he comments that 'the best will be to reproduce a letter of my own' (p. 129), allowing us to see exactly what Alison reads. Mackellar trusts writing over speech because it has this facility of being accurately reproduced. He can fearlessly disclose documents to Alison—as he hopes to do to his unknown readers—and they will in turn disclose the truth.

Yet Mackellar's documentary disclosure is also very vulnerable in a way which strikes at the heart of his privileging of writing by dispatching it to futurity as the bearer of truth. Although Mackellar's hundred-year plan for his manuscript presents the written word as something more durable than the spoken, it is not necessarily true to say that writing is always more permanent than speech. Speech is an immediate utterance; there is no transitional period before speaking and hearing in which words can be altered or erased. Words once spoken are not easily taken back, even if they cannot be said to represent what the speaker intended. Frank Smith makes the point that 'speech is permanent and writing provisional, because anything spoken can never be altered or erased'.[14] Mackellar narrates an example of this endurance of the spoken word early on in the story during the argument about which of the brothers should join Prince Charlie. Henry, in the hearing of his father, becomes heated, and Mackellar reports that 'a little after he had another expression, plainer perhaps than he intended. "It is your duty to be here with my father," said he. "You know well enough that you are the favourite" ' (p. 13). This remark remains with Lord Durrisdeer for some time and he brings it up again after James has been presumed dead at Culloden, telling Henry that of his two sons he has been left the kinder. Mackellar draws attention to the enduring power of Henry's earlier remark: 'It was a strange thing to say in such a moment; but my lord had never forgotten Mr Henry's speech' (p. 16).

---

[14] Frank Smith, 'A Metaphor for Literacy: Creating Worlds or Shunting Information?', ibid. 195–213 (p. 207).

While speech can be unexpectedly durable, writing, on the other hand, is vulnerable precisely for the reasons that make it potentially durable. Writing is a physical entity that can easily be changed or destroyed. Alison's response to Mackellar's 'documentary disclosure' is simple, but effective: she burns the evidence against James, calling his attempts to impose his authority by writing 'a sword of paper' (p. 131). Mackellar comments, 'the correspondence with the Secretary of State, on which I had reckoned so much against the future, was nowhere to be found' (p. 130). The 'sword of paper' metaphor works in two contradictory ways: paper can be an effective weapon in influencing the future, but that effectiveness is subject to paper's material vulnerability. Mackellar is only partially successful in his hopes that writing can survive into the future: his manuscript survives a hundred years, but his earlier 'documentary disclosure' suffers the physical fate to which writing is liable.

Mackellar's privileging of writing, already vulnerable in the context of the novel as a whole, becomes increasingly unstable as the action shifts to America. The confusions of race, social identity, and national interest, the accelerated doublings between James and Henry, undermine any clear-cut distinctions, and the opposition between speech and writing is an inevitable casualty. The journey away from Scotland prefigures that of Marlow in Conrad's *Heart of Darkness*, another novel whose narrators cannot be confident about speech and writing, and again reminds us that Mackellar's tale of the eighteenth century is also a novel of the late nineteenth century. Like Marlow, Mackellar finds the familiar authority of writing not all as at first appears. In the Cyrillic 'ciphers' which make the familiar reality of *Points of Seamanship* cryptic and alien, Marlow discovers that what should be a manual of instruction has become the site of mystery and competing languages. Mackellar too finds that writing does not guarantee absolute meanings.

In New York Mackellar runs up against a problem which often occurs in attempts to ascribe different characteristics to written and oral texts: ephemeral writing. Henry has become obsessed by a Whig pamphlet which has fallen into his hands. The pamphlet proclaims James's restoration to the title, makes some disparaging remarks about him, and further alleges that

Henry is himself 'bred up in the most detestable Principles' (p. 211). Suddenly writing has taken the place of speech as a dangerous medium, creating its own fictive realities. Again, Mackellar's attitude rests on an unacknowledged political distinction which distrusts any popular voices including those characterized as hack writers. (We might remember that his narrative is dated 1789, the year which saw the symbolic start of a revolution famously said by Hazlitt to be the result of the widespread dissemination of print.) For Mackellar, this marks a significant threat to his earlier belief in the trustworthiness of writing, which, now fallen in his estimation, begins to take on the 'characteristics' of speech: 'it was reserved for some poor devil in Grub Street, scribbling for his dinner and not caring what he scribbled, to cast a spell across four thousand miles of the salt sea' (p. 207). It is now writing that can cast a 'glamour', or spell: a use of language promoting the performative at the expense of the referential; the writer of the pamphlet, 'not caring what he scribbled', has relinquished his authorial responsibility of documentary disclosure.

Mackellar still clings to the hope that his own account will be the self-evident truth when all around him are voices indistinguishable in kind from written texts. These voices are like Marlow's narration which, heard in the growing darkness, becomes to Heart of Darkness's frame narrator 'no more to us than a voice', unable to yield up the clue to its origin.[15] Even at the very start of the long journey that eventually ends in the American wilderness, Mackellar becomes afflicted by the sourceless voices, the 'bits of absurd sentences'[16] that trouble Marlow: 'I would overhear the voices from within, talking in that tropical tongue which was to me as inarticulate as the piping of the fowls' (p. 176). It is at this point that Mackellar has his 'vision' of the despairing Henry which, defeating documentary disclosure, can only be described, in an impossible contradiction, as a 'true illusion' (p. 176). The true illusion

---

[15] Joseph Conrad, 'Heart of Darkness' and Other Tales, ed. Cedric Watts (Oxford: Oxford University Press, 1990), 173. For the relationship between Heart of Darkness and oral storytelling see John Lyon, 'Half-Written Tales: Kipling and Conrad', in Kipling Considered, ed. Phillip Mallett (Basingstoke: Macmillan, 1989), 115–34.   [16] Heart of Darkness, 179.

returns, not only in his mind, but in writing. Mackellar reports seeing Henry in a scene corresponding in some, but not all parts to his vision. This incident has, mysteriously, become public knowledge, apparently in the same untraceable way that rumours were spread orally 'by the common report' in Scotland. But now it is print that disseminates information, taking on those qualities previously assigned to speech but, with a frustrating irony for Mackellar, still claiming the authority he believes writing self-evidently to possess: 'I must say a word upon this, for the story has gone abroad with great exaggeration, and I have even seen it printed, and my own name referred to for particulars' (p. 208). It is Mackellar's name which is used to authenticate other stories, just as he uses it to authenticate his own account—a version which is by now looking increasingly provisional. Looking back over his story, we notice how unreliable Mackellar in fact is as a narrator: his prejudices, his misogyny, his uncertainty about the events surrounding the duel, the telling gaps in his account in which he appears to have edited out the decline of his relationship with Henry's son.[17]

In the wilderness, all the characters are edgy and suspicious of each other. The proliferation of both oral and written accounts accelerates as the travellers find it increasingly difficult to make sense of their experiences. Any communication, oral or written, is either frustrated or ambiguous, and distinctions between speech and writing are subsumed in the general breakdown of language itself.[18] James loses his powers of speech and Mackellar loses his faith in writing. James's previous success with performative stories deserts him. With a misplaced confidence reminiscent of Mackellar's promise to deliver 'the full truth', James tries to win over the party with a camp-fire rendition of 'the whole truth' (p. 230) but his narrative first

---

[17] For Mackellar's unreliability see James F. Kilroy, 'Narrative Techniques in The Master of Ballantrae', Studies in Scottish Literature, 5 (1967–8), 98–106; and Douglas Gifford, 'Stevenson and Scottish Fiction', in Stevenson and Victorian Scotland, ed. Calder, 61–87.

[18] For the novel's narrative multiplicity, see Alison Lumsden, 'Postmodern Thought and the Fiction of R. L. Stevenson', in Of Lion and of Unicorn: Essays on Anglo-Scottish Relations in Honour of Professor John MacQueen, ed. R. D. S. Jack and Kevin McGinley (Edinburgh: Quadriga Publishing, 1993), 115–38.

descends into silence, and then turns into a fierce argument with other members of the party. Like Kurtz, with his 'ability to talk',[19] James is 'so apt a speaker' (p. 164) but his oral facility—formerly seen by Mackellar as absolute—is now much more precarious. Significantly, Secundra Dass's abortive technique for suspended animation involves swallowing the tongue; James's death is coterminous with the failure of speech.

Mackellar begins to lose confidence in the security of writing. His earlier devotion to 'the truth' shows signs of a growing anxiety in which he distrusts the written information of others and jealously guards their spoken confidences. His privileging of writing over speech undergoes a reversal which undermines distinctions between them. Writing now becomes a matter for suspicion, and precisely because of that property which Mackellar had previously regarded as a strength—its suitability as a medium for making things public. We may remember his opening sentence, 'the full truth of this odd matter is what the world has long been looking for, and public curiosity is sure to welcome.' Now he pieces together his narrative which he has 'compiled out of three sources, not very consistent in all points'. He gives reasons for this lack of consistency as follows:

First, a written statement by Mountain, in which everything criminal is cleverly smuggled out of view;
Second, two conversations with Secundra Dass; and
Third, many conversations with Mountain himself, in which he was pleased to be entirely plain; for the truth was he regarded me as an accomplice. (p. 223)

Leaving aside the unlikelihood of the evidently untrustworthy Mountain's regarding the strait-laced Mackellar as an accomplice, this is an unusual position for Mackellar to adopt and just what he had hoped to avoid in his handling of Burke's contributions to the narrative. Writing has now become a medium for deceitful manipulation and suppression; far from disclosing a pre-existent truth, it opens up gaps from which truth has mysteriously gone missing, being 'cleverly smuggled out of view'. Such, however, is exactly what Mackellar is himself engaged in at this point in the events. Sending letters

[19] *Heart of Darkness*, 203.

back to Alison, and thereby faced with a similar dilemma to that which confronts Marlow in his lie to Kurtz's Intended, Mackellar wonders about how much he should himself smuggle out of view.

Any utterance is now potentially dangerous, and 'disclosure' is now something to be discouraged. As Henry becomes increasingly paranoid, talking obsessively about his brother, Mackellar hints to Sir William that Henry is not quite right in the head: 'I touched my head and shook it; quite rejoiced to prepare a little testimony against possible disclosures' (p. 221). Mackellar is not very specific as to what might be disclosed; he is evidently willing to sacrifice Henry's reputation in the interests of an unspecified secrecy. The term 'disclosure' has altered in meaning. As James is dug up, his eyes open, with fatal results for Henry: 'For at that first disclosure of the dead man's eyes my Lord Durrisdeer fell to the ground, and when I raised him up he was a corpse' (p. 251). Life has already left James's eyes; what should be here 'disclosed' is already absent. The act of disclosure starts to signify that there is nothing to be disclosed, the opposite of Mackellar's earlier intended meaning.

In an attempt to shore up his now damaged confidence in writing, Mackellar turns back to it at the end of his account by having a rudimentary tombstone engraved for James and Henry who have both been buried in the wilderness. On the one hand, this brings the novel's end round to its beginning, allowing Mackellar to reassure himself about the security of documentary disclosure and to send his papers off to futurity. He isolates writing, with its ability to be accurately copied, as an appropriate mark not only of the brothers' end but also of the closure of his story: 'I had chiselled on a boulder this inscription, with a copy of which I may fitly bring my narrative to a close' (p. 252). We are reminded of his confidence in the transition of his writing to print, of the fact that we also hold 'a copy' of *The Master of Ballantrae*, and of writing's ability to disseminate the same information to multiple readers. Yet we are simultaneously made aware of writing's ability to relocate itself in new environments, and reminded of the different readings offered by the novel's dual historical contexts. Mackellar may intend his copy of the inscription as another example of documentary disclosure, but, by insisting on the capacity of writing to be copied, he inadvertently draws attention to another way of looking at texts.

Because writing is copiable it must also be self-identical. It therefore cannot represent the author's intention or indeed any specific interpretation; it can only be itself. Ontologically, writing is made up of marks which can be reproduced in any situation, and which therefore exist wholly independently of the writer. Like Hogg's games with reading and magic language, Stevenson plays with the problematics of speech acts, later to be illuminated by the encounters between speech act theory and deconstruction. Derrida, who calls the capacity of writing to be repeated 'iterability', points out that 'To write is to produce a mark that will constitute a kind of machine that is in turn productive, that my future disappearance in principle will not prevent from functioning'.[20] Derrida used this argument against J. L. Austin's tendency, in *How to Do Things with Words*, to associate speech with the performative, leaving writing to represent 'constative' language (Austin's word for language which says something, rather than doing something). As this distinction is, in general terms, rather like that operated by Mackellar in his narration, it may be helpful to use Derrida's concept of iterability to explore what is going on at the end of *The Master of Ballantrae*.[21]

The inscription on the boulder self-referentially enacts this state of affairs. James's epigraph reads that he 'lies here forgotten', a phrase that effectively does away with the author who claims to have erected the stone in the brothers' memory.

[20] Jacques Derrida, 'Signature Event Context', in *Margins of Philosophy*, trans. Alan Bass (Brighton: Harvester Press, 1982), 316.

[21] Derrida's main arguments with speech act theory are: first, with Austin's dismissal of literature as parasitic on 'real life' speech acts and, secondly, with the idea that for a speech act to be performative its meaning must be inextricably bound up in its utterance. In Derrida's view this would make speech acts as impossible as the magic language discussed in this book. Recent accounts of the encounter between Derrida and Austin, however, tend to emphasize the similarities between their approaches to language. See Stanley Fish, 'With the Compliments of the Author: Reflections on Austin and Derrida', in *Doing What Comes Naturally: Change, Rhetoric, and the Practice of Theory in Literary and Legal Studies* (Oxford: Clarendon Press, 1989), 37–67; and Sandy Petrey, *Speech Acts and Literary Theory* (New York and London: Routledge, 1990).

The words exist alone in the wilderness, remaining the same marks in the radical absence of author or reader. The inscription acts metaphorically in another way: if the message 'lies here forgotten' had any intrinsic meaning it would not be readable, or, to put it the other way round, James cannot be forgotten if someone is reading about him. Yet James will not exactly be remembered, but will be constructed by each new reading of the inscription and, by extension, of the novel. The act of reading, in Derrida's terms, links repetition with alterity; when the inscription is repeated in the act of reading it cannot mean what Mackellar intends, but it can signify all sorts of other things. The rest of the writing on the graves invites the reader into such a play of possible, but indeterminable, meanings. In addition to the brother's epigraphs, Mackellar copies the puzzling inscription that follows them: 'THE PIETY OF HIS WIFE AND ONE OLD SERVANT RAISED THIS STONE TO BOTH'. These words explicitly claim Mackellar's and Alison's piety both as their meaning and the agency of that meaning, yet such a situation cannot obtain. Alison's wishes cannot be consulted by Mackellar, the intention to which the inscription bears witness is absent, mirroring the general condition of writing itself. The inscription is extremely cryptic: the description of James is at odds with Mackellar's estimation of him elsewhere, neither is there much evidence of Alison's piety in the novel. Writing does indeed, as Mackellar had earlier suspected, draw our attention to gaps, contradictions, and things 'smuggled out of view'. Furthermore, the language of the inscription is itself impossible to pin down with exact meanings. Henry's epigraph says that he sleeps 'with his fraternal enemy', a phrase as enigmatic as the earlier 'true illusion'. Does this mean that James and Henry were brothers who were enemies, or that they were brotherly, in the sense of friendly, enemies? Or, given the repeated doublings between the brothers, should Mackellar's frequent associations of James with the devil be extended to Henry? The inscription would then suggest that the brothers were alike in enmity, not of each other, but of humanity.

Finally, then, the novel offers us a re-examination of the relationships between speech, writing, and context. Derrida argues that Austin's associations of speech with the performative 'permanently demand a value of *context*, and even of an exhaustively determinable context'.[22] In *The Master of Ballantrae*, writing does indeed turn out to be context-free, though not quite in the way Mackellar had intended: while it endlessly escapes determination by any single context, it cannot, if it is to be readable, transcend context itself.

[22] Derrida, 'Signature Event Context', 322.

7
Words in Themselves: Weir of Hermiston

IN the preface to *The Master of Ballantrae*, the editor and Mr Thomson discuss how, if at all, Mackellar's manuscript should be altered for publication. Their conversation reviews the dialogue which Stevenson had entered into with Henry James, in 'A Humble Remonstrance', about realism, romance, and kinds of narrative fiction: the novel of adventure, the novel of character, and the dramatic novel. Mr Thomson suggests the novel of character as the most appropriate: 'all you have to do is work up the scenery, develop the characters, and improve the style'. The editor, however, resists, preferring to leave Mackellar's text in its 'purely narrative character', an impression which, at first glance, the text itself seems to confirm by Mackellar's habit of calling chapters 'A Summary of Events'. Mr Thomson, however, ends the discussion about narrative by commenting 'Well, we shall see',[1] and, as we *have* seen, identifying a narrative by its events does not guarantee it as a healthy adventure story of 'brute incident'. The nature of 'incident', however, continued as a focus for Stevenson's attention in his last work, *Weir of Hermiston*. The book returns us to some of the formal questions about stories, their plots, and their narrations which were important to Hogg and Scott, and, as in these writers' texts, such problems become involved in questions of realism and its relativity. *Weir of Hermiston*, however, goes further, in extending the debate about the ontology of stories into Stevenson's continuing investigation of language itself and the relationship of words with the unconscious.

Like *The Master of Ballantrae*, *Weir of Hermiston* is both

---

[1] *The Master of Ballantrae*, ed. Emma Letley (Oxford: Oxford University Press, 1983), 8, 7.

retrospective, aware of its place in Scottish literature, and of its time, attentive to new developments in the social construction of orality and literacy. At one level, the novel acts as a critique of some late nineteenth-century Scots' tendency to turn to the ballad as an invigorating antidote to the unhealthy self-analysis of novel-reading and novel-writing: Archie's removal to the bracing moors of Hermiston does not succeed in making him any less introspective. Despite Archie's introduction to a branch of his family who specialize in 'brute incident', there is even here a hint that other of the natives of Hermiston may not quite be the stuff of adventure romance. The modern peasants are 'degenerate moorsmen'[2] who are apparently in decline from a heroic barbarism to the less healthy savagery that haunted the later nineteenth century with fears of racial regression.

Yet *Weir of Hermiston* does discriminate between the readers of novels (always conscious that it is one) and the audience of ballads, holding the two in a tension which, far from offering the reader a healthy alternative to the deleterious experience of novel-reading, disturbs even further by emphasizing the cultural relativity of different modes of storytelling. Appropriately enough for an unfinished novel, *Weir of Hermiston* insists on the extreme difficulty of storytelling when neither the ballad nor the realist novel seems able to provide adequate realization of fictional subjectivity.

On a level different from, but consonant with, the social construction of orality, the novel returns to the problematic relations of grammar and glamour. *Weir of Hermiston* enacts a struggle between those two representative figures in nineteenth-century Scottish texts, Old Mortality and Michael Scott, and thus between grammar and glamour, the inherent and referential powers of language. In this novel, the emphasis is not only on the social status of writing but also on the nature of words themselves, an exploration which takes Stevenson from the descriptive powers of narrative to the symbolic functions of language. This, Stevenson's uneasy last work, is about language as power and the attempt to acquire that power which takes the form of a competition. Language is thus bleakly evolutionary, a

---

[2] *Weir of Hermiston*, in *'Dr Jekyll and Mr Hyde' and 'Weir of Hermiston'*, ed. Emma Letley (Oxford: Oxford University Press, 1987), 136. Further references appear in the text.

weapon (and this novel is also about the violence of language) in the struggle for existence—a struggle in which Archie, the linguistically unhappy central character, does not do very well. And, as in many late nineteenth-century texts, there are things in this novel which interrupt or reverse the progress of evolution: the movement of the plot is from sophistication to primitivism, and the narration experiments with accessing earlier forms of narrative. Despite its eighteenth-century setting, the world of the novel is one of anxious modernity, seeking to shake off the burdens of complexity and even of signification itself, but, in this case, the oral worlds of language and narrative do not offer much consolation.

The novel starts, as *The Master of Ballantrae* ends, with a gravestone, yet this time the memorial enacts not the formal durability of signs, but their fragility. *Weir of Hermiston* opens with a scene in which the function of language as record is under attack, as it depicts the work of Old Mortality whose self-appointed task was to keep legible the inscriptions on the graves of his fellow Covenanters, as they become eroded:

In the wild end of a moorland parish, far out of the sight of any house, there stands a cairn among the heather, and a little by east of it, in the going down of the braeside, a monument with some verses half defaced. It was here that Claverhouse shot with his own hand the Praying Weaver of Balweary, and the chisel of Old Mortality has clinked on that lonely gravestone. (p. 83)

This descent into non-signification recalls the opening of Scott's *Old Mortality* in which neither glamour nor grammar seems able to constitute a history able to resist the effects of time. Peter Pattieson, one of that novel's frame narrators, comments of Old Mortality that 'The common people still regard his memory with great respect; and many are of the opinion that the stones which he repaired will not again require the assistance of the chisel.' But the magical power of writing is no more effective than any other attempt to record history, as Pattieson observes that the inscriptions 'are hastening, like all earthly memorials, into ruin or decay'.[3] For Archie Weir, the

---

[3] *Old Mortality*, ed. Angus Calder (Harmondsworth: Penguin, 1975), 64. This novel has been the subject of some important work on the nature and different uses of language. See Peter Garside, '*Old Mortality*'s Silent Minority', *Scottish Literary*

protagonist of *Weir of Hermiston*, language is no more reliable, and in Archie's career Stevenson explores the desire to avoid the necessary decay of referential signs by escaping referential language altogether.

Like *The Three Perils of Man*, *Weir of Hermiston* addresses the relationship of stories and their narrations, although it is somewhat less hopeful than is Hogg's novel about their peaceful coexistence. Appropriately enough, the novel has itself been subject to some discussion concerning this matter by virtue of its being unfinished at the time of Stevenson's death in 1894. Some readers are dissatisfied at discovering that the plot does not 'come to an end', or that Stevenson's intended continuation of the story, as recorded in the first edition by his literary executor Sidney Colvin, does not seem to be a suitable one.[4] Such readers protest that the novel has been leading towards an unhappy ending and that it is inappropriate for Archie to be rescued from prison at the last moment. Of course, we cannot speculate on *how* Stevenson might have finished his last work, particularly as the section of the novel that we do have contains more than one idiom.[5] If we do decide to include Colvin's account of the continuation of the plot in an analysis of the novel, we are assuming that the plot of any story can have an existence independent of the way, or ways, in which it is told. Whatever the reader makes of the story's 'continuation', its existence may alert her or him to the novel's own exploration of the unstable relationship between the events of stories and their narration.

Early in the novel, the narrator holds out the possibility that a narrative voice is not always needed for stories to exist. In the brief introduction, describing the moorland landscape of Hermiston, it seems the events which have a bearing on the

Journal, 7/1 (1980), 127–44; and, an article which also has a bearing on the authority of books discussed in my second chapter, Daniel Whitmore, 'Bibliolatory and the Rule of the Word: A Study of Scott's *Old Mortality*', *Philological Quarterly*, 65 (1986), 243–62.

[4] In the projected ending Archie kills his rival Frank Innes and is tried by his own father. Archie is sentenced to death, but later escapes with Christina to America.

[5] The question of *why* Stevenson apparently planned a happy ending is addressed by Mary Lascelles in *The Story-Teller Retrieves the Past: Historical Fiction and Fictitious History in the Art of Scott, Stevenson, Kipling and Some Others* (Oxford: Clarendon Press, 1980), 103–11.

place have no need of verbal record; history itself seems to have transmitted its presence without the need for a verbal intermediary: 'Public and domestic history have thus marked with a bloody finger this hollow among the hills' (p. 83). Hermiston is a rich source for local stories, and the narrator details how 'it was told' that a ghost walked at Francie's Cairn, but then suggests that 'the facts' of stories themselves can have an existence apart from their telling: 'But the age is one of incredulity; these superstitious decorations speedily fell off; and the facts of the story itself, like the bones of a giant buried there and half dug up, survived, naked and imperfect, in the memory of the scattered neighbours' (p. 83).

Peter Zeninger notes how this, the 'late nineteenth-century insistence on facts deprives the story of its decorations and leaves the narrator with a fleshless and imperfect story',[6] but the narrator's stance faces in more than one direction. The loss of traditional narrations in a modern age is set against the survival of 'the story itself'; in this ballad landscape, stories escape identification with individual tellings, a condition which the ballad itself is sometimes thought to enact. The possibility that events can be known without narration is an imaginary state which links conceptions about the ballad to the relationship between the human subject and language itself, and this correspondence can take different forms. Stevenson complicates the late nineteenth-century anthropological association of 'primitive' states of society with the unconscious. The Scottish ballad had been useful to Lang and others because it had provided a link between a primitive society—the material for anthropological investigation—and language.[7] The ballad was commonly seen as the unconscious expression of the people, and this also establishes a connection between the collective unconscious and speech, leaving writing as a means of *conscious* expression:

[6] Peter Zeninger, 'The Ballad Spirit and the Modern Mind: Narrative Perspective in Stevenson's *Weir of Hermiston*', in *Studies in Scottish Literature: Nineteenth Century*, ed. Horst W. Drescher and Joachim Schwend (Frankfurt am Main: Peter Lang, 1987), 233–51 (p. 239).

[7] For Stevenson's interest in the folktales of 'primitive' cultures, see Robert I. Hillier, 'Folklore and Oral Tradition in Stevenson's South Seas Narrative Poems and Short Stories', *Scottish Literary Journal*, 14/2 (1987), 32–47.

But this process of purging and refining the ballad, so that it shall become—like the language, the proverbs, the folklore and nursery tales, and the traditional music of a nation—the reflection of the race itself, if it is to be genuine, must go on unconsciously. As soon as the ballad is written down—at least as soon as it is fixed in print—the elements of growth it possesses are arrested.[8]

Stevenson's more complex dealings with the unconscious did not confine it to the ballad world, and other of his texts, most clearly *The Strange Case of Dr Jekyll and Mr Hyde*, investigate the way the irrational can be played out in cities. But Stevenson, like Oliphant, was interested in the oral as a site in which the unconscious exerts a pressure on the conscious. The novel plots Archie's experiences as a child and young man through his acquisition of language and his troubled transition to the power of words as signs. The novel consistently locates Archie's problems as both psychological and linguistic, so that he experiences his Oedipal desires in terms of speaking as he complains of his father, 'You know the way he talks? . . . My soul is sick when he begins with it; I could smite him in the mouth' (p. 119). Archie's father's first name is Adam, the biblical giver of names,[9] and Lord Hermiston imposes his law upon his son, condemning everyone of Archie's sensitive disposition by naming them: 'He had a word of contempt for the whole crowd of poets, painters, fiddlers, and their admirers, the bastard race of amateurs, which was continually on his lips. "Signor Feedle-eerie!" he would say, "O, for Goad's sake, no more of the Signor!" (p. 99).

Though Archie aspires to acquire the power of language for himself, he initially experiences his father's speech in a different way: Archie is brought up in a world in which words themselves, regardless of what they signify, have power. His early distaste at his father's swearing is described in a way that alerts the reader to such a use of language: 'The man was mostly silent; when he spoke at all, it was to speak of the things of

---

[8] John Geddie, *The Balladists* (Edinburgh and London: Oliphant, Anderson and Ferrier, n.d.), 10.

[9] For the significance of Adam Weir's name, see Edwin M. Eigner, *Robert Louis Stevenson and Romantic Tradition* (Princeton: Princeton University Press, 1966), 222–3.

the world, always in a worldly spirit, often in language that the child had been schooled to think coarse, and sometimes with *words that he knew to be sins in themselves*' (p. 91, emphasis mine).

Archie's earliest encounters with language come through his mother. Mrs Weir uses language in a pre-symbolic way, as a sensory presence which evades the task of representation. In her discourse, a wedge is driven between her firm conviction that moral absolutes really do exist in the world, and her complete lack of interest in establishing the relation they bear to the words she uses to describe them. Mrs Weir is far more concerned with the way words feel subjectively to her than with any things or concepts which they might signal. She has a limited repertoire of 'texts' or fragments which fail to make complete sense: 'Are not two sparrows', or 'Whosoever shall smite thee' (p. 90). Rather, these words have a glamour-like presence in themselves: 'they haunted her like a favourite air, they clung about her like a favourite perfume' (p. 90). Words for Mrs Weir are active in their own right, particularly her favourite word—'*Persecutor* was a word that knocked upon the woman's heart'—and in his early relationship with his mother Archie derives from her articulation of this word a pleasure which gratifies him physically: 'she had a voice for that name of *persecutor* that thrilled in the child's marrow' (p. 89).

Not surprisingly, into this pleasurable dyadic relationship enters Archie's father with devastating results for the boy. Things begin to go wrong when Archie discovers that the word 'persecutor' represents more than the pleasurable exchange between himself and his mother alone. When the Weir family's carriage is surrounded by a mob shouting 'Down with the persecutor! down with Hanging Hermiston' (p. 89), Archie is confused and asks why the familiar word should be applied to his father. Mrs Weir refuses an explanation on the typically vague grounds that 'this is poleetical. Ye must never ask me anything poleetical', and Archie is left with a word fixed in his mind by 'an obscure but ineradicable sense of something wrong' (p. 89). Soon, however, Archie wants to try out the function of words in a symbolic order and his first attempt to assert power through language is announced in the text as an important event: 'the day came when Archie spoke' (p. 92). At this point,

Archie is beginning to expect more from language than the simple power of articulated speech: he now expects that words will point to something more substantial outside themselves, that they will have precise objects of reference, and that they can be used to contain logical sequences of thought. Archie has absorbed all his mother's emotive doctrines and tests them, much to her agitation, to see if they amount to logical discourse. He has already gathered together a selection of his mother's random epithets for people she thinks evil—'reprobates, goats, God's enemies, brands for the burning' (p. 92)—and has used them with a specificity never intended by his mother, concluding privately that his father must be 'the chief of sinners' (p. 92). Now, on the day when he 'speaks', he tries to move on from impressions to logical inferences, asking his mother, 'If judging were sinful and forbidden, how came papa to be a judge?' (p. 92). Archie is no longer content with the physical presence of words in themselves; now he wants to know about the relationship between words and things: 'Were not babes and innocents the type of the kingdom of heaven? Were not honour and greatness the badges of the world?' (p. 92). His demands for types and badges mark his desire for the paternal authority of the symbolic order and not surprisingly, these new demands upon words lead him into a crisis of Oedipal proportions. As he tries to come to terms with the concept of naming, Archie manœuvres himself into a position whereby his attempt to transform the disembodied texts he has learned from his mother into signifying words threatens the death of his father. What Hermiston 'is called' by the external world suddenly becomes very important to Archie:

'It's all very fine,' he concluded, 'but in my opinion, papa has no right to be it. And it seems that's not the worst yet of it. It seems he's called "the Hanging Judge"—it seems he's crooool. I'll tell you what it is, mamma, there's a tex' borne in upon me: It were better for that man if a milestone were bound upon his back and him flung into the deepmost parts of the sea. (p. 92)

Archie is unable to come to terms with a process of naming which represents the pronouncements of society, what 'it seems' that his father is called, and social discourse remains difficult for him as his own subjectivity cannot be accommodated within it:

'He flew his private signal, and none heeded it' (p. 100). Not surprisingly, resistant to words as the tokens of taboo, he seeks substitutes for his early linguistic relationship with his mother. As he struggles to adjust to the problem of naming, Archie turns to his father's friend, Lord Glenalmond, a sexually ambiguous character to whom Archie is attracted, 'his eyes dwelling on those of his old friend, like a lover's on his mistress's' (pp. 99–100). Glenalmond seems a substitute for Archie's mother, offering a kind of language which speaks directly to the heart, thereby circumventing the problem of figurative words: 'The beautiful gentleness and grace of the old judge, and the delicacy of his person, thoughts, and language, spoke to Archie's heart in its own tongue' (p. 99). But when Archie broaches the subject of his father, Glenalmond puts an end to this kind of communication, by using language in a way already identified with Lord Hermiston: 'no doubt your father (if he were here) would say, "Signor Feedle-eerie!" ' (p. 100). The absent mother is suddenly replaced by the figure of the father, a multiple sign as Glenalmond represents not only Lord Hermiston, but also Hermiston's symbolic language.

As Archie grows older, he tries, unsuccessfully, to confront his father on his own terms. In his tortuous exchange with Lord Hermiston, Archie attempts to move beyond his mother's verbal realm into his father's, by using words to represent himself. Before their interview, the anxious Archie seems locked into his pre-symbolic realm in which his father's omniscience precedes language: 'Words were needless; he knew all—perhaps more than all—and the hour of judgment was at hand' (p. 111). But Hermiston is more interested in an external order imposed by language on its subject, intruding upon Archie both physically and linguistically as he 'discloses' his authority:

For a moment Hermiston warmed his hands at the fire, presenting his back to Archie; then suddenly disclosed on him the terrors of his Hanging Face.
'What's this I hear of ye?' he asked.
There was no answer possible to Archie. (p. 112)

Appropriately, in an unfinished text, Archie has no answer as his desire will never come to an end. Yet he struggles to find something to say, in the hope that symbolic language will work for him if he can find words that will correspond to an objective truth but will still remain 'his' words, an expression of his self. He protests at his father's version of his outburst in court:

> 'No, sir, these were not my words,' cried Archie.
> 'What were yer words' then?' asked the Judge.
> 'I believe I said, "I denounce it as a murder," ' said the son. 'I beg your pardon—a God-defying murder. I have no wish to conceal the truth'. (p. 112)

Needless to say, Lord Hermiston remains unimpressed by Archie's efforts and threatens not only Archie's recourse to language but also his masculinity. Archie's own suggestion that he join the army elicits the response, 'Ye auld wife, the sodgers would bray at ye like cuddies!' (p. 114) and Hermiston's biblical metaphors crush any sexual threat that Archie might attempt to rehearse: 'Ye've been reading some of my cases, ye say. But it was not for the law in them, it was to spy out your faither's nakedness, a fine employment in a son' (p. 113). This marks the end of Archie's opposition to his father, though not his admiration of him, as the source and embodiment of external authority and social judgement: 'Archie was now dominated. Lord Hermiston was coarse and cruel; and yet the son was aware of a bloomless nobility, an ungracious abnegation of the man's self in the man's office' (p. 115).

Stevenson's identification of the suppression of Archie's subjectivity in language extends itself beyond these immediate exchanges between Archie and his father. The text as a whole is an investigation of the relationship between language and the subject, the place of Archie's father being occupied, in complex ways, by the figure of the narrator who takes up the position of author. As the text engages in debates about the relative functions of narrators in realism and romance, the relationship between character and author comes to re-enact Archie's Oedipal experience with his father, as Archie is never given the opportunity to express himself, but is always written by the narrator.

The novel looks back over the development of fiction in nineteenth-century Scotland and draws attention to the radical separation of nature and writing, putting an end to the possibility, often articulated in the century, that Scottish writers might annexe the voice of nature, or that a literary mode of writing might successfully combine with a communal or popular voice. This perspective is bound up in Archie's individual problems with language. At Hermiston, Archie momentarily seems able to gain access to nature itself, 'the essential beauty of the old earth', a nature that recalls his mother's pre-symbolic relationship with words that 'clung about her like a favourite perfume': 'Vagrant scents of the earth arrested Archie by the way with moments of ethereal intoxication.' He tries to figure this bodily experience in writing which the narrator identifies as specifically Scottish, but Archie's aspiration to write poetry is no more successful than his attempt to 'take his place' in language itself.

He surprised himself by a sudden impulse to write poetry—he did so sometimes, loose, galloping octosyllables in the vein of Scott—and when he had taken his place on a boulder, near some fairy falls and shaded by a whip of a tree that was already radiant with new leaves, it still more surprised him that he should find nothing to write. (p. 147)

Archie cannot write himself because he is already written; fiction is not something which Archie can do himself, but something which is done to him. Dr Gregory tells Archie a story about his childhood in which Lord Hermiston evinced concern for his son when he had the measles. Archie is moved by this information which seems to be personal to him, yet his response slips from his own control: 'The anecdote might be called infinitely little, and yet its meaning for Archie was immense. "I did not know the old man had so much blood in him" ' (p. 110). It is not made clear in the text whether it is Archie or the narrator who is quoting this line from *Macbeth*; Archie might intend the line to refer to an unexpected quality of warmth and affection in his father, but its original literary context produces contrary connotations, unapparent to Archie, though available to the reader here (and elsewhere when Archie thinks of his father), of death and murder.

Writing, in this text, is the sign of an authority to which Archie can never quite lay claim, but which is nevertheless available to others. Archie is not only caught between grammar and glamour, figurative language and words in themselves, but also between different conceptions of a narrative text, mediated by a not very reliable narrator. *Weir of Hermiston*, like *The Three Perils of Man* as well as Hogg's shorter tales, uses narratological approaches to stories as a means of assessing how notions of realism interact with the conditioning factor of audiences. But where Hogg's ludic confusion of the boundaries between events and narration and between 'popular' and 'sophisticated' audiences and readerships is designed to further the continuation of storytelling, Stevenson's novel is imbued with more gloomy suggestions about the incommunicability of experience in a modern world. Ballad stories, the novel implies, seem to have an extraverbal existence because of their location in the convictions of a community, albeit a denuded one, of storytellers. Thus the 'facts' of this story survive 'in the memory of the scattered neighbours'. Novels, however, are seemingly directed to a dispersed readership, whose values will have to be assumed (or manufactured) as they cannot be consulted. Stevenson locates his narrator in the isolated position in which Walter Benjamin saw the novelist:

The storyteller takes what he tells from experience—his own or that reported by others. And he in turn makes it the experience of those who are listening to his tale. The novelist has isolated himself. The birthplace of the novel is the solitary individual, who is no longer able to express himself by giving examples of his most important concerns, is himself uncounseled, and cannot counsel others.[10]

Stevenson's narrator, standing between the outward confidence of the nineteenth-century realist narrator, and the uncertain narrative voices of the early twentieth century, exploits the certainty of realism for more doubtful ends. As Elizabeth Ermarth has indicated, 'The genial consensus of realistic narration implies a unity in human experience which assures us that we all inhabit the same world and that the same meanings are available to everyone.'[11] The narrator of *Weir of Hermiston* takes up such a position, masking the subjectivity of any narration behind a claim to be articulating collective values, yet, committing himself further to the path of an

[10] S 87.
[11] Elizabeth Deeds Ermarth, *Realism and Consensus in the English Novel* (Princeton: Princeton University Press, 1983), 65.

absolute realism, he extends an assumed consensus to include realities known apparently only to *him*. In his realist mode, the narrator underwrites his contextual realism with an implied documentary realism, implying that the characters exist in an extraverbal realm lying just outside the reader's consciousness: 'And if you could have caught Frank off his guard, he would have confessed with a smirk that, if he resembled any one, it was the Marquis de Talleyrand-Périgord' (p. 176). Thus, however inadequate his attempts to describe characters or their supposed experiences to the reader, the narrator apparently has an exclusive recourse to the truth of these matters.

Because of the close identification of Archie's experience with language, his own 'living and life-like' status within the novel is problematic. The narrator, and a number of the other characters, exhibit a much greater facility than does Archie with the power of words and of narration, negotiating with ease the tricky relationship between words and things. Archie is not just a tragic character in a novel; his tragedy is that he *is* in a novel and, among the other participants, both actants and narrators, in this novel, he is uniquely unable to deal with it.

The narrator grants to other characters the completed self which Archie is never able to establish. He has an unerring ability to identify things and people as they 'really' are, and he always has the right name for these identities. This ability is usually signalled by his claim to understand fundamental or 'essential' natures: Hob Elliott is 'essentially a decent man' (p. 136); Clem, 'an eminently solid man at bottom' (p. 139); Kirstie is known to the narrator by her 'essential self' (p. 157) which is her 'passionate and irritable nature' (p. 183), and Frank Innes is 'by nature a thin, jeering creature' (p. 106) and 'essentially glib ... essentially careless of the truth' (p. 175). Yet, despite his tones of confident omniscience, the narrator hovers uneasily between his absolute pronouncements on character and value, and the sense that his whole narration is a construct. The 'truth' about characters is often elsewhere in this novel, unavailable either to narrator, who from time to time apologizes for the inadequacy of his raids on the inarticulate— 'Every lineament that appears is too precise, almost every word used too strong' (p. 157)—or to us, who, because 'we are all grown up and have forgotten the days of our youth' (p. 101), will be unable to appreciate Archie's dilemmas. The narrator's omniscience is itself under the scrutiny of the novel as Stevenson explores his own ambivalence towards late nineteenth-century realism. On the one hand, the narrator is the determiner of values and a repository of knowledge about people's essential natures. On the other, the narrator obliquely suggests his own role to be something more sinister.[12]

The Glenalmond/Hermiston point of view on literary narration is that it is not very good at communicating thoughts and that the reader is dislocated from the author's intentions. In his discussion with Archie about Lord Hermiston, 'literary and decorative' language is described as being highly unreliable: 'Before you are done you will find some of these expressions rise on you like a remorse. They are merely literary and decorative; they do not aptly express your thought, nor is your thought clearly apprehended, and no doubt your father (if he were here) would say, "Signor Feedle-eerie!" ' (p. 100).

'Literary' language here has its own destructive autonomy, threatening to rise up and consume anyone who uses it, and this passage shares the character of the late nineteenth-century attack on realism as something morbid and corrupting which investigates the 'close hot atmosphere of our own fancies and feelings'.[13] Thus Archie seems to be a victim of the kind of realism which Lang, and sometimes Stevenson, insisted was *un*real, though *Weir of Hermiston* offers a more sophisticated exploration of the subject than the simple opposition of realism to adventure romance. The narrator is ambivalent about his narrative position, suggesting that his own realist fiction preys on the psychological processes of its characters, yet giving such processes as the reason for the novel's very existence. Archie too has a projected existence just outside the novel, as the reader is invited to consider Archie's life had events taken a different course. But it is precisely because the reader is given a fleeting glimpse of his separate existence that Archie becomes not so much a construct but a victim of the predatory nature of the

[12] See Kenneth Simpson, 'Author and Narrator in *Weir of Hermiston*', in *Robert Louis Stevenson*, ed. Andrew Noble (London: Vision, 1983), 202–27.

[13] John Veitch, *The History and Poetry of the Scottish Border: Their Main Features and Relations* (Glasgow: James Maclehose, 1878), 555.

realist novel: 'With the infinite delicate sense of youth, Archie avoided the subject from that hour. It was perhaps a pity. Had he but talked—talked freely—let himself gush out in words (the way youth loves to do and should), there might have been no tale to write upon the Weirs of Hermiston' (p. 100). Talking and writing are again in conflict, taking up the relationship that Derrida detects in Rousseau: a natural expression of 'that interior spontaneity which is speech' opposed to its distant representation in writing.[14] Here the opposition is couched in the terms of Stevenson's continuing debate about romance and realism. Archie's imagined speech is the naturalness of romance in which no narrative voices intrude between text and reader. But in *Weir of Hermiston* this natural expression is no longer available and the realist narrator enters to write in the gaps opened up by Archie's silence. The oral romance of free speech has been overtaken by the written novel with connotations of the morbid speculations of a predatory realist fiction that can only exist because of Archie's linguistic defeat: had Archie talked 'there might have been no tale to write'.

Yet because the novel exists as writing there cannot be an equal opposition between the oral romance and the written text. The narrator's 'perhaps' here seems to indicate both his need for and his suspicions of the slippage between experience and text that writing necessarily represents. *Weir of Hermiston* complicates its own narration, somewhat in the same manner as 'The Highland Widow', by proffering one model of storytelling and then proceeding down a different route and, again like 'The Highland Widow', uses its characters to enact its narrative puzzles. Dr Gregory suffers from none of Archie's linguistic problems. He is equally at home with verbal and non-verbal communication; he can read any system of signs with equal fluency and, for him, these signs always correspond to a psychological truth. Simply by looking at Archie, Dr Gregory can read his state of mind, and he can also produce the words which accord exactly with what he intends them to describe: 'The doctor turned about and looked him all over with a clinical eye. ... He knew the father well; in that white face of

---

[14] Jacques Derrida, *Of Grammatology*, trans. Gayatri Chakravorty Spivak (Baltimore and London: Johns Hopkins University Press, 1976), 170.

intelligence and suffering, he divined something of the son; and he told, without apology or adornment, the plain truth' (p. 110).

But the narrator is not quite straightforward with the reader here. In the little tale that follows this passage, Dr Gregory *does* apologize for his choice of words and he *does* adorn his story with numerous narrative devices. In fact, his account of Archie's childhood illness is a highly self-conscious piece of rhetoric: he uses metaphor and the verbal tropes of storytelling, he dramatizes his little narrative with the imagined response of Archie, and times it for optimum effect on his audience ('The doctor left no opportunity for anticlimax', p. 110).

The contradictions in the narrator's position are strangely echoed in the novel's villain, Frank Innes. Frank practises the absolute character judgements of the narrator: Archie is, in Frank's opinion, 'a hunks at heart, incapable of true generosity and consideration' (p. 178). But Frank's narration is also an overtly fictional construct. Like the narrator's predatory re-creation of Archie's suffering, the pleasure Frank takes in his texts has no regard for its subject. When Innes happily spreads a rumour that Archie has suffered an 'access of insanity', the narrator remarks: 'I doubt if Innes had the least belief in his prediction; I think it followed rather from a wish to make the story as good and the scandal as great as possible; not from any ill-will to Archie—from the mere pleasure of beholding interested faces' (p. 107).

Storytelling here takes on dark and oppressive connotations as Archie becomes constructed by the local people *as* a fictional character, whose exploits appear to occur for them in serial form:

And by thus milling air out of his mouth, he had presently built up a presentation of Archie which was known and talked of in all corners of the county. . . . Archie began to be regarded in the light of a dark, perhaps a vicious mystery, and the future developments of his career to be looked for with uneasiness and confidential whispering. (p. 175)

Poor Archie is again suffering the fate of being written by others as Frank assumes the role of narrator. Like the novel's narrator he writes not only Archie's characterization in the neighbourhood, but also extracts words from Archie's silence. Archie's wincing when the subject of his evenings with Christina is brought up elicits Frank's response: 'Thank you. That was all I wanted, an articulate confession' (p. 180). In this context even Innes's casual remark to Archie, offered as concern for his future, takes on a sinister meaning: 'All I wish is to keep you quiet.' In filling the neighbourhood with his own narrative Frank excludes Archie's.

Archie, however, is not quite alone in being discomforted by the novel. Stevenson also manœuvres the reader into a position in which the experience of reading disrupts any easy relationship with the text. As is often remarked upon, *Weir of Hermiston* divides into different narrative modes, and these emphasize the relativity of the conventions of each. Archie's tortuous presence in the novel presents the reader with a set of problems which the later characterization of the Elliott brothers, in the Hermiston section, evades. The Elliotts seem able to negotiate stable identities for themselves within a community, indeed they are known by names which identify their social functions. Unlike Archie, who suffers from the effects of being named by others, the brothers apparently have the power to name themselves: 'Clement was Mr Elliott, as upon his door-plate, the earlier Dafty having been discarded as no longer applicable, and indeed only a reminder of misjudgment and the imbecility of the public; and the youngest, in honour of his perpetual wanderings, was known by the sobriquet of Randy Dand, (p. 142).

Like Archie, however, the Elliotts are subject to a process of textualization—in their case that of oral narrative. The narrator retells the story of the brothers' revenging the death of their father in Kirstie's idiom. The narrative pronouncements of absolute facts are not presented as scientific truths about essential nature, but as consciously formulaic observations whose status comes from their being often repeated: 'It is ill to catch an Elliott', for example. In the Elliott brothers' case, their story, like their social identity, is not told by the predatory exclusivity of realism, but by the shared narration of storytelling and the congruence of 'all tales':

Come to the ford, and there was Dickieson. By all tales, he was not dead, but breathed and reared upon upon his elbow, and cried out to them for help. It was at a graceless face that he asked mercy. As soon as Hob saw, by the glint of the lantern, the eyes shining and the whiteness of the teeth in the man's face, 'Damn you!' says he; 'ye hae your teeth,

hae ye?' and rode his horse to and fro upon that human remnant.
(p. 135)

In this, his last work, Stevenson reveals the dangers and
problems inherent in storytelling when it encounters nineteenth-
century realism. Located uneasily between two traditions, *Weir
of Hermiston* reveals tensions created by their incompatibility.
The different responses they require each seem inadequate in the
proximity of the other. This confrontation is thrown into relief
by the two executions in the completed part of the story, those
of Duncan Jopp, sentenced to death by Lord Hermiston, and
Dickieson, the victim of the Elliott brothers.

Jopp and Dickieson are described in similar terms; Jopp is 'a
rag of a man' (p. 104), Dickieson a 'human remnant' (p. 103)
but the reader is manœuvred into a position of responding to
them very differently. The reader is asked to share Archie's pity
for Duncan Jopp in a complex psychological way:

> There was pinned about his throat a piece of dingy flannel; and that
> it was perhaps that turned the scale in Archie's mind between disgust
> and pity. The creature stood in a vanishing point; yet a little while, and
> he was still a man, and had eyes and apprehension; yet a little longer,
> and with a last sordid piece of pageantry, he would cease to be. And
> here, in the meantime, with a trait of human nature that caught at the
> beholder's breath, he was tending a sore throat. (p. 103)

But where Jopp's death seems calculated to inspire pity,
Dickieson's is marked by the narrator's evident enthusiasm
and excitement. The two events inhabit different kinds of
narrative—one of the novel of psychological realism and the
other of the ballad story. In their separate idioms they create no
problems, but juxtaposed they may. We are required to react in
one way to Jopp's sore throat, and in another to the gruesome
trampling to death of Dickieson. As each exists within the novel
in the context of the other the Dickieson story seems callous and
inhuman, and the detail of the soon-to-be-hanged Jopp's sore
throat, an example of black humour in questionable taste. Thus
the reader is cut off from Archie, whose experiences seem
increasingly less narratable.

Weir of Hermiston looks both at nineteenth-century psychological realism and at a much older tradition of oral narrative.
The novel's unstable narrative voice sometimes accords stories a

reality that is not dependent on any fixed form, but in fact *Weir* is highly equivocal on the issue of whether this facility can really be extended into the narratives of late nineteenth-century Scotland. Archie cannot be, to use Tam Craik's narrative position again, both living and lifelike, yet the novel offers contradictory evidence that he is both an independent agent who creates the story, and a character trapped inside a predatory mode of fiction. Narrative in *Weir of Hermiston* becomes cast dangerously loose from *any* experience, and Archie's extraordinary sensibility can find no corresponding narrative.

8

Beyond Words: Orality and the Unconscious

THE opening of *Weir of Hermiston*, with its vision of eroded inscriptions on a gravestone, seems to locate its oral society not so much in a preliterate world as in a post-literate one. The decay of writing points to a deepening anxiety, towards the end of the nineteenth century, about culture in general and the status of fiction in particular. In the crumbling gravestone inscription, the usual idea of the progress of a civilized society from orality to literacy is reversed, and a number of later nineteenth-century Scottish texts are caught up in a general dissatisfaction with Victorian progress in which the decay of writing is prominent. Literacy, in any case, was no longer the guarantee of civilization as the degenerate masses in the cities had apparently already subjected themselves to the corrupting influence of popular reading. The evolutionary course of literacy seemed to have been thrown into reverse, or at least into confusion, as, while literacy was seen to be statistically on the increase, it was believed to be morally on the decline. The masculine romance, with its similarity to the degenerate reading matter for which it was supposed to be the antidote, is precariously poised at the turning-point of this contrary movement, enacting both an impulse forward, in its quest structure and associations with exploration and conquest, and a backward one, in its promotion of barbarism and promise of a return to childhood. And childhood itself stands in turn in a border position between, on the one hand, the embodiment of healthy imperialist values and, on the other, a site in which the operations of unconscious fears and desires are more clearly visible than in later life. Thus the concept of regression involves orality not only in the imperialist adventure story, but also in the late nineteenth-century fantastic with its dangerous yet desirable attraction to the deathly, the sexual, the irrational, and the seemingly abnormal.

Stevenson's elaboration of the nature of romance offers readers of 'A Gossip on Romance' the chance to regress to their childhoods, but even as he formulates the child's search for adventure as digging 'blithely after a certain sort of incident, like a pig for truffles',[1] Stevenson's text inadvertently discovers things other than truffles which lie buried in the ground and which the act of reading may bring to the surface:

> It is not only pleasurable things that we imagine in our day-dreams; there are lights in which we are willing to contemplate even the idea of our own death; ways in which it seems as if it would amuse us to be cheated, wounded or calumniated. It is thus possible to construct a story, even of tragic import, in which every incident, detail and trick of circumstance shall be welcome to the reader's thoughts. Fiction is to the grown man what play is to the child; it is there that he changes the atmosphere and tenor of his life; and when the game so chimes with his fancy that he can join in it with all his heart, when it pleases him with every turn, when he loves to recall it and dwells upon its recollection with entire delight, fiction is called romance.[2]

Here the regression to the pure experience of childhood is also a pleasurable imagining of 'the idea of our own death'. The act of reading is a loss of consciousness, a total immersion in the life of the imagination which opens up another world, underlying normal experience and in which the whole 'atmosphere and tenor' of the reader's life undergoes a change. In this altered state, differentiations are not clearly apparent: details become blurred in a general feeling of enjoyment in which life and death, pleasure and pain are not easily separable.

The long social and anthropological division between speech and writing is now recast in symbolic roles: the oral as sensation, and writing as representation. But the experiences that constitute the oral cannot be represented in writing which finds that speech slips away to obscure the traces of its presence. Romance is the kind of writing that aspires to be most *unlike* writing in writing's compulsion to represent and differentiate. Stevenson's concept of romance marks the attempt to fill in the gap between words and things by calling up the absences that

---

[1] MP 248. [2] Ibid. 268–9.

words betoken, but, because this attempt must always be carried out *in* words, the non-verbal, however desirable, always remains elsewhere. The continual references to childhood by Stevenson and Lang in their writing on (and of) romance play out the need to recapture a lived past which, because it can never quite be represented in writing, must be returned to again and again. In the texts that form the subject of this chapter, speech and writing function as points of connection and transition, never very permanent, between the conscious and the unconscious, the living and the dead, the seen and the unseen, and between representation and what might be represented.

In these texts the oral lies just to the side of the non-verbal or pre-verbal.[3] We have already seen this process at work in *Weir of Hermiston* in Archie's relationship with his mother and her apparently non-symbolic use of language. Later in the novel, Archie's attraction to Christina marks an attempt to recapture the pre-symbolic sound-world of his childhood, but this time the oral world of his mother has slipped into an experience which is altogether non-verbal and which re-creates a child's sense-world with a suggestion of the child's identification with the mother by eye-contact and the mutual gaze: 'Archie was attracted by the bright thing like a child. He looked at her again and yet again, and their looks crossed. The lip was lifted from her little teeth. He saw the red blood work vividly under her tawny skin. Her eye, which was great as a stag's, struck and held his gaze.'[4] The regression to childhood is both seductive and perilous for the male romance hero, as Archie discovers that what had appeared under his control is in fact controlled by the gaze of a dangerously toothed woman who links emergent sexuality with death. This pattern, the attraction to the oral/non-verbal with the concomitant thought that it is probably better avoided, tends to characterize the appearances of the oral in the Scottish supernatural stories under discussion in this chapter, texts in

---

[3] A link suggests itself here between oral sound and Freudian oral gratification. William Veeder identifies Stevenson's concern with the latter in 'Dr Jekyll and Mr Hyde: Children of the Night: Stevenson and Patriarchy', in 'Dr Jekyll and Mr Hyde' After One Hundred Years, ed. William Veeder and Gordon Hirsch (Chicago and London: Chicago University Press, 1988), 128–9.

[4] Weir of Hermiston, in 'Dr Jekyll and Mr Hyde' and 'Weir of Hermiston', ed. Emma Letley (Oxford: Oxford University Press, 1987), 151.

which the authority of writing is established only at the cost of the repression of speech.

Reading the Runes: 'The Merry Men'

Stevenson's 'Gossip on Romance' explicitly connects the romance with sound: written words 'should run . . . in our ears like the noise of breakers'.[5] The noise of breakers had already been the subject of a short story (the breakers are the Merry Men of the title) and in that context they are associated with madness, death, and transgression in a story whose metaphors for the unconscious combine the geographic with the linguistic. The narrator, Charles Darnaway, visits his Uncle Gordon and cousin Mary, and becomes engaged to the latter, on the isolated island of Aros off the west coast of Scotland, a very dangerous area for ships. He is interested in shipwrecks off the island and hopes to find the wreck of the *Espirito Santo*, possibly a ship of the Spanish Armada. While on the island Charles discovers traces of a much more recent ship, the *Christ-Anna* (or *Christiania*, or *Christiana*), which had gone down the previous February, and he witnesses the wreck of a third which may be that of Spanish treasure-hunters. He also discovers that his uncle, who collects goods from the wrecks, is prone to fits of drinking and madness, and Charles suspects him, although there is no conclusive evidence, of the murder of a survivor from the *Christ-Anna* whose grave he discovers. The unexplained appearance of a mysterious black man, presumed to be a survivor of the most recent wreck, pushes Gordon into insanity until he is pursued into the sea by the black man where both drown.

The island of Aros is the dark double of the Treasure Island, and the treasure-hunting romance plot is subject to gaps and uncertainties where names, identities, and even events are unclear. Charles commences the story as the embodiment of institutional rationality; he has undertaken some historical research into the Armada wrecks under the instructions of 'our then Principal in Edinburgh College, the famous writer,

---

[5] MP 247.

Dr Robertson'.[6] Dr Robertson has commissioned Charles to 'rearrange and sift of what was worthless' (p. 10) from a collection of old historical documents. Charles's status as literary figure is therefore associated with ordering, authority, and judgement, yet historians in this story are not all they may appear. Dr Robertson had gathered the papers together for a man claiming to be a Spanish historian, but Charles, on hearing of the visit to Aros of a foreign-looking person, concludes, or rather 'fancies', that this treasure-hunter is 'the same with Dr. Robertson's historian from Madrid' (p. 26). After the wreck of the ship Charles believes to be that of the treasure-hunters, he laments:

I had thus been right in my conjecture; the pretended historical inquiry had been but a cloak for treasure-hunting; the man who had played on Dr. Robertson was the same as the foreigner who visited Grisapol in spring, and now, with many others, lay dead under the Roost of Aros: there had their greed brought them, there should their bones be tossed for evermore. (pp. 61–2)

The authority of writing thus proves to have been taken over by a dark romance of deception and death, and this is repeated throughout the story as the impulse 'to rearrange and sift of what was worthless' is set against the lure of the irrational. The treasure-hunting romance ends in a decidedly anti-romantic move, as the plundering, possibly murderous Gordon Darnaway is driven to his death by the black man conjectured by Charles to be a slave. However, 'The Merry Men' is not only about the return of the oppressed, but also about the return of the repressed, in this case rather like the Freudian 'primitive' fear of revenants: 'the old belief that the dead man becomes the enemy of his survivor and seeks to carry him off to share his new life with him.'[7] Charles's narrative, with its uncertainties about what 'really' happened, is a doomed attempt to piece together a cohesive account of a memory which has become flooded with the irrational.

---

[6] *The Merry Men and Other Tales and Fables* (London: Chatto and Windus, 1887). Further references appear in the text.

[7] 'The Uncanny', in *The Standard Edition of the Complete Psychological Works of Sigmund Freud,* trans. and ed. James Strachey (24 vols., London: Hogarth Press and the Institute for Psychoanalysis, 1953–72), xvii. 217–56 (p. 242).

'The Merry Men' explores a fractured border in the interactions between the island's land-based and sea-based residents. The sea in the story is a world like, but not quite the same as, the land: Gordon Darnaway remarks, 'If there's folk ashore, there's folk in the sea—deid they may be, but they're folk whatever' (p. 19). Whatever is cast away into the sea (the black man is called a 'castaway') has an uncanny habit of returning, first in fragments (Charles finds a bone of one drowned sailor), and then in the form of the black man. The story is scattered with the tropes of the fantastic and their psychological implications. The Darnaways' name carries suggestions of their encounters with the unconscious: 'Dern' or 'Darn' in Scots means either 'secret, hidden', or 'to hide, to conceal', so 'Darnaway' carries the possible meanings of both to hide away, and to do away with concealment, to bring to light. Thus it has the same connotations as Freud's 'Unheimliche', or uncanny: that which reverses both the familiar (homely) and the strange (secretive) through the return of the repressed. Charles's identification of the possibly bogus historian from Madrid with the treasure-hunter who turns up at Aros carries echoes of Nathaniel's confusion of Coppelius/Coppola in Hoffmann's 'classic' uncanny text, 'The Sandman'. Other distinctions are blurred between living and dead, and, in the story's denouement, both black and white and pursuer and pursued become involved in a *Frankenstein*-like mutual dependency as Gordon Darnaway and the black man perish together.

Among these collapsed distinctions is one between speech and writing. Charles Darnaway, a castaway from the bookish world of literary Edinburgh, finds himself overwhelmed by the island's 'constant mass of sound' and associates this sound-world of the breakers with death and madness: 'As when savage men have drunk away their reason, and, discarding speech, bawl together in their madness by the hour; so, to my ears, these deadly breakers shouted by Aros in the night' (p. 49). The oral continues to be identified with a wordless or unintelligible or non-symbolic language. In Aros, the literary Charles encounters a storytelling society and he informs us that 'The country people had many a story about Aros, as I used to hear from my uncle's man, Rorie'. Rorie's oral discourse, however, resists the kind of doubts and questions which the Darnaways put to them, and they take a different position as regards language and its symbolic functions. The following conversation concerns a story Gordon Darnaway has heard about a boat being attacked by a sea creature:

> 'It will have been a merman,' Rorie said.
> 'A merman!' screamed my uncle, with immeasurable scorn. 'Auld wives' clavers! There's nae sic things as mermen.'
> 'But what was the creature like?' I asked.
> 'What like was it? Gude forbid that we suld ken what like it was! It had a kind of heid upon it—man could say nae mair.'
> Then Rorie, smarting under the affront, told several tales of mermen, mermaids, and sea-horses that had come ashore upon these islands and attacked the crews of boats upon the sea; and my uncle, in spite of his incredulity, listened with uneasy interest.
> 'Aweel, aweel,' he said, 'it may be sae; I may be wrang; but I find nae word o' mermen in the Scriptures.'
> 'And you will find nae word of Aros Roost, maybe,' objected Rorie, and his argument appeared to carry weight. (pp. 21–2)

Gordon's first move is to dismiss Rorie's merman to the world of female/oral improbability: 'Auld wives' clavers!' Charles then tries a more rational approach—'what was the creature like?'— but this is exactly what Gordon *cannot* explain. In the oral storytelling mode, words resist metaphorical status, they cannot say what things are 'like'. Pressed towards the completed explanation that his narrative opposes, Gordon can only come up with the unformed, fragmentary, nightmarish image, 'it had a kind of heid upon it', and the repetition of stories which cannot be contained, or made whole, by explanation. Gordon next tries to reassert the symbolic order of language as represented by *written* texts which appear to authorize the real by representing and containing it, and by consigning anything not found there to the realm of the unreal or imaginary. Rorie, however, points out that there may be things which do not depend on the order of writing for their existence, allowing the oral to slip the control of the written. Writing thus becomes a pre-existent symbolic order, to which the imaginary beasts of the unconscious/oral world will not accommodate themselves. Gordon Darnaway, between his bouts of madness, is, like Archie Weir, both attracted and repelled as he listens 'with uneasy interest'.

Just as Rorie's oral stories have the last word here, so writing becomes much less conclusive than Charles had first imagined. Writing on Aros is incomplete and unstable. When Charles discovers the wreck of the ship his uncle calls the *Christ-Anna* he finds that 'Her name was much defaced, and I could not make out clearly whether she was called *Christiania*, after the Norwegian city, or *Christiana* ... in that old book the "Pilgrim's Progress" ' (p. 30). Despite his appeal to historical and literary sources, Charles finds that writing's cultural power of naming has become eroded and it is as difficult to say what things are called as it is to say what they are like. In fact, the two difficulties are really the same, as to name something is an attempt at representing it in language, and, as things emerge from the sea, Charles finds it increasingly problematic to represent them in his narrative.

The fractured division between the oral unconscious and the written conscious is even more apparent in Charles's dealing with the 'sea-runes' which appear on the surface of the water in Aros Bay. These 'strange, undecipherable marks' (p. 22) seem to take the form of letters which the spectator is compulsively driven to make up into words. Charles sees an 'M' which he first thinks stands for 'Mary', his cousin with whom he is in love, and then for a host of other associations: 'as I mentally ran over the different words which might be represented by the letter M— misery, mercy, marriage, money, and the like—I was arrested with a sort of start by the word murder' (p. 24). These apparently free-floating signifiers make up a metonymic chain which falls into place only when Charles comes to retell the story of 'The Merry Men': Gordon Darnaway's misery, his lack of mercy to the survivor, his greed for salvaged goods, Charles's hopes to marry Mary and his status as Gordon's heir, and so on. The word 'murder', which seems to Charles to arise uncannily as if from the unconscious, acts as the projected end to the sequence and the link in the chain which will give it a narrative completeness. If Charles can establish that his uncle *did* murder a survivor from the *Christ-Anna*, then the subsequent events will follow in a sequence of cause and effect, and Gordon's own death, as he is driven into the sea by the black castaway, can become a symbolic act of atonement for his murder of the earlier sailor (Charles explicitly exhorts his uncle to show 'mercy'—one of the potential rune-words—to the castaway on his first appearance). Of course, this symbolic ordering of events cannot be said to be consonant with what *did* happen, a state of affairs to which neither we nor Charles have any direct access; we never find out what Gordon's relation to the grave is, or whether the black man is trying to rescue or to kill him. But in order for Charles's narrative to make sense, this is how he fills up the empty signs on the surface of the water. Charles associates this narrative completion in the conscious mind with writing as a predetermined ordering of events which will explain the final scene of Gordon's death: 'Turn where he would, he was still forestalled, still driven toward the scene of his crime. Suddenly he began to shriek aloud, so that the coast re-echoed; and now both I and Rorie were calling on the black to stop. But all was vain, for it was written otherwise' (p. 69).

However, the conscious ordering process of writing and its estrangement of the oral do not make up the full story, and, as always in their long history, speech and writing cannot exist entirely apart. The fragmentary writing on the surface of the water joins as well as separates the elements, and the sea-runes act like Lacan's example of the Möbius strip which links the conscious and unconscious, the Symbolic and the Imaginary— and in this case speech and writing—at an unidentifiable point. The 'M' rune and its readings allow Charles consciously to construct a narrative of sin and redemption and Christian significance,[8] but the meaning 'murder' which takes Charles by surprise also points to an unconscious determining pressure: a fascination with death and compulsion to end his narrative with it.[9]

As Gordon Darnaway is driven towards what Charles imagines to be 'the scene of his crime', we are reminded of the association of murder with primal repression and a crime for which the sea, in this story representing the unconscious, is the scene. Charles in fact *causes* the death that is necessary for the completion of his narrative by cutting off Gordon's escape.[10]

[8] For the Christian significance of the story see Edwin M. Eigner, *Robert Louis Stevenson and Romantic Tradition* (Princeton: Princeton University Press, 1966), 133–42.

[9] On Freud's death-wish principle and the ends of narrative see Peter Brooks, *Reading For the Plot: Design and Intention in Narrative* (Oxford: Clarendon Press, 1984), 90–112.

[10] Eigner, *Robert Louis Stevenson and Romantic Tradition*, 141.

After this, Gordon himself returns to 'the full horror of the charnel ocean' which gives up its secrets only in fragments or in incomprehensible figures (the black man speaks a language no one else can understand). Thus writing acts both as a staving off of the oral/unconscious and a point of access to it. Charles's own writing, with its Christian allegory, attempts to explain his own narrative, though hesitantly with its gaps and inconsistencies, but the incomplete writing of the sea-runes also signals an opening up of the unconscious, a territory in which the alternative to narrative ordering is the dissolution of the subject in fragmentation and death.

Ventriloquism: Oliphant's Supernatural Stories

Margaret Oliphant's stories of 'The Seen and the Unseen' take the history of speech and writing further into an exploration of their symbolic roles in the construction of the conscious and unconscious. Like Stevenson, Oliphant is interested in speech and writing as a way of looking at the processes of signification itself, but she breaks up Stevenson's cluster of ideas surrounding the oral as a pre-verbal site of phobia, corruption, dangerous sexuality, and toothed, predatory women. Oliphant's fantastic writing moves towards the reclamation of the oral as a site not for the construction of the female, but for its expression.

Oliphant's most protracted exploration of the oral is the short novel *A Beleaguered City* which concerns the inhabitants of the French town of Semur as it is visited by the unseen, but frequently heard, ghosts of its former inhabitants. The dead, evidently unhappy with the rampant materialism in Semur, drive the residents through the city gates and lock them out. A number of the characters who succeed in re-entering the city then have either inconclusive or transient encounters with these spirits, and their written reports form a narrative of which the framing narrator is Martin Dupin, the Mayor of Semur. After a while, the dead leave the city and everyone goes home; the seemingly momentous impression made by the ghosts is quickly forgotten by most of the citizens.

A Beleaguered City is about death and how it can be controlled through writing and, although it is relevant to language in general, this inquiry also has a particular bearing on the 1870s. Historically, the novel is placed in the aftermath of the Franco-Prussian war and describes the after-effects of military conflict on a confused and demoralized populace. Although the war is explicitly referred to, the analysis of its consequences takes place, as the title suggests, largely in the imagery which creeps into characters' discussions. The citizens are 'houseless exiles';[11] they see themselves as 'like an army suddenly formed, but without arms, without any knowledge of how to fight' (p. 37); they call each other 'deserters' and the dead 'enemies' and 'tyrants' (p. 47); the principal narrator describes his own thoughts as 'like weary men on a march' (p. 68). This metaphoric representation of war suggests the need to come to terms with, or to control, loss by re-enacting it in symbolic form—the 'Fort!/Da!' game Freud witnesses as an example of his grandson's attempt to control his mother's absence by throwing away and reclaiming a toy. This war, in particular, is relevant to the control of painful absence by representation. Philippe Ariès points out that it was France's disastrous war with Prussia in 1870, the historical background to *A Beleaguered City*, that radically altered the official treatment of the war dead:

it was in France after 1870 that the memory of the dead came to be more precisely preserved and the dead venerated. Everyone knows how traumatic this period was for all of French society. ... In the beginning, of course, this did not prevent the French from burying the slain soldiers without much respect, although they were not proud of the way it was done. But they also had the new idea of drawing up honor rolls on stone or metal, as at Quiberon, and posting them, usually in the church but sometimes in the cemetery.[12]

When Oliphant visited Semur in 1871, she passed through a Paris visibly suffering the effects of the war, and she was herself engaged in creating a written record and memorial of a dead person's life as she researched her biography of the Comte de

---

[11] Margaret Oliphant, *A Beleaguered City and Other Stories*, ed. Merryn Williams (Oxford: Oxford University Press, 1988), 33. All the Oliphant stories discussed in this chapter are in this edition and further references appear in the text.

[12] Philippe Ariès, *The Hour of Our Death*, trans. Helen Weaver (Harmondsworth: Penguin, 1983), 594.

Montalembert who had died earlier that year.[13] Memorial writing thus becomes a way of managing loss, called into being, like the general condition of language itself, by the radical absence of the referent. Ten years after the publication of *A Beleaguered City*, this relationship between writing and death manifested itself in Oliphant's own life. Watching over her dying son Cyril, she witnessed him experience the hallucination of seeing his name written in front of him: as Cyril dies his name comes into being.[14] *A Beleaguered City* explores these functions of writing in the representation of death. To take one example occurring early in the novel, the Dupins own a pleasure-boat named after, perhaps in memory of, their dead child, Marie, and the presence of the name of the boat and child, inscribed on the prow, convinces Martin of the physical presence of his dead daughter: 'The sight of it made my heart beat; for what could it mean but that some one who was dear to me, some one in whom I took an interest, was there? . . . Perhaps it was my little Marie that was in the boat' (p. 40). The written name stands as a representative of its lost referent, which, as Martin recognizes, occasions its meaning. But the word and the child cannot coexist, and Marie never appears.

Though set in France, the novel is highly relevant to the Scottish obsession with speech and writing. Dupin makes an early distinction between the two that draws on the late nineteenth-century Scottish promotion of healthy orality: 'The river ran softly, reflecting the blue sky. How black it had been, deep and dark as a stream of ink, when I had looked down upon it from the Mont St. Lambert! and now it ran as clear and free as the voice of a little child' (p. 33). This touches on the childlike orality of the boys' romance promoted by Lang and Stevenson, but Oliphant's novel in fact challenges male authority as she had done in her *Blackwood's* essays where she identifies independent women as a 'class of talkers unrivalled, and thinkers not to be despised' who 'have worked their opinions and reminiscences into the history of their time with a force and clearness not to be

[13] See Merryn Williams, *Margaret Oliphant: A Critical Biography* (Basingstoke: Macmillan, 1986), 97–8.
[14] *The Autobiography of Margaret Oliphant*, ed. Elisabeth Jay (Oxford: Oxford University Press, 1990), 49.

surpassed'. To talk is to become a speaking subject, and not the object of received opinion, whereas 'reading does not always encourage thinking; perhaps on the contrary, rather stifles it, and substitutes its own ready-made conclusions for the unnecessary exertion'.[15] Oliphant thus uses speech not so much to make women visible in history as to make them heard. Speech, then, represents not the acceptance of a process of socialization which already exists and already privileges sight, but something like an alternative.

Oliphant's work recasts Stevenson's definition of romances— 'their true mark is to satisfy the nameless longings of the reader'—in a context which we would now recognize as the territory of psychoanalysis, and indeed some of her texts are strikingly close to Freudian analyses of the operations of repression and its consequences.[16] The romance as described by Lang and Stevenson, with emphasis on the natural, the oral, and the lack of narratorial presence, prompts the equation of 'nameless desires' with the unconscious and the quest for pre-Oedipal oneness, and the phrase itself also raises Lacanian questions about language and its enactment of the conscious/ unconscious division in which the object of desire can never be fully named. These are ideas which Oliphant's work addresses, but her texts are particularly interested in the place of the female in the process of signification. Oliphant raises questions put most compellingly in this century by Margaret Homans:

But why should language and culture depend on the death or absence of the mother and on the quest for substitutes for her, substitutes that transfer her power to something that men's minds can more readily control? And—most important for the question of women's writing— what does it mean to women writers that the dominant myths of our culture, as embodied in these and other founding texts, present language and culture as constructed in this way?[17]

---

[15] 'Scottish National Character', *BM* 87 (1860), 715–31 (p. 721).

[16] *MP* 255. Stevenson evidently found *A Beleaguered City* powerful, and wrote to its author that after reading it 'I have cried heartily; I feel the better for my tears; and I want to thank you.' (MLS MS 23210).

[17] Margaret Homans, *Bearing the Word: Language and Female Experience in Nineteenth-Century Women's Writing* (Chicago and London: University of Chicago Press, 1986), 4.

Homans's study of the relationship between women writers and the absent mother on whom signification depends, investigates the often ambiguous use of the literal by female novelists, and *A Beleaguered City* describes one such encounter. The citizens of Semur face the literal itself in the form of ghosts who fail to respect any differentiating principle of time or space which might supply the necessary absences against which identities might be formed, and whose voices avoid signification.

The Curé suspects women of operating a performative system which circumvents signification, and is therefore antagonistic to the patriarchal law of naming: 'Women do not discriminate the lawful from the unlawful: so long as they produce an effect, it does not matter to them' (p. 27). This is really another manifestation of glamour, set against the grammar of the Law of the Father and deemed to be outside it. As in *Weir of Hermiston*, glamour is seen as a female discourse which has to give way to the superior power of grammar, but *A Beleaguered City* investigates what happens when glamour returns to challenge the authority of the sign.

Semur is a city in which women are denied full subjectivity by being prevented from speaking, and are encouraged to respect the ideal of Victorian domesticity by becoming silent angels in the home.[18] Dupin remarks of his anagrammatically named wife, Agnès/*Anges*:

I love one woman more than all the world; I count her the best thing that God has made; yet would I not be as Agnès for all that life could give me. It was her part to be silent, and she was so, like the angel she is, while even Jacques Richard had the right to speak. *Mon Dieu!* but it is hard, I allow it; they have need to be angels. (pp. 49–50)

Dupin 'allows' the suppression of women's speech in both senses of the word: he admits that it happens, but permits it *to* happen as it is what patriarchal authority is founded upon. Although the men of the city tend to assume that the dead— 'Messieurs les Morts'—are male, those who have contact with

---

[18] Diana Basham reads Oliphant's supernatural stories as narratives of women's exclusion from society, dating from her public acknowledgement of political feminism: *The Trial of Woman: Feminism and the Occult Sciences in Victorian Literature and Society* (Basingstoke: Macmillan, 1992), 163–73.

them believe them to be of both genders. But in another way, the dead are related to the female and to the search for female expression: both the ghosts and the women in the story are associated with sound (the story starts with complaints that the local nuns are too noisy) and, as in Oliphant's *Blackwood's* article, women's voices represent the ideal of freedom from cultural predetermination.

In contrast to, or in Lacanian terms because of, the silent women's lack of subjectivity, the male citizens of Semur claim the authority of writing in a way which uses writing's materiality to reinforce the importance of signs. The whole economic and social structure of Semur is founded on the presence of writing and other material signs. The city's agriculture is regulated by both: Dupin's vines 'were in perfectly good condition, and none of the many signs which point to the arrival of the insect were apparent' (p. 4); the period of darkness which precedes the ghosts' arrival is believed to be 'caused by clouds of animalculæ coming, as is described in ancient writings, to destroy the crops' (p. 11). Dupin, in his role as Mayor, uses visual signs as indicators of the public authority, on which he is very dependent. Attempting to impose order on the panicking outcast citizens, he remembers that his scarf of office is still in his pocket and puts it on: 'That was something. There was thus a representative of order and law in the midst of the exiles' (p. 34). Later, persuading a fellow citizen to submit his written report, Dupin says, 'You will see by the emblems of my office that it is to me you must address yourself' (p. 54). So dependent are people on visual signs to order experience that Dupin is unable to understand why the dead themselves have left no mark or sign of their presence:

Had I not been myself so closely involved, it would have appeared to me certain, that the streets, trod once by such inhabitants as those who for three nights and days abode within Semur, would have always retained some trace of their presence . . . and that those families for whose advantage the dead had risen out of their graves, would have henceforward carried about with them some sign of that interposition. It will seem almost incredible when I now add that nothing of this kind has happened at Semur. (pp. 108–9)

Similarly, when Dupin re-enters the library of his house after the 'occupation' he searches eagerly for written material which might supply some lasting record of the dead's occupation: 'Some of the old drawers were open, full of old papers. I glanced over them in my agitation, to see if there might be any writing, any message addressed to me; but there was nothing' (p. 70).

However, although Dupin proposes the separation of speech and writing, it could be said that writing in this novel occupies the same position as the sea-runes in 'The Merry Men': not an absolute difference from speech but a point of transition at which writing as a secure referential system breaks down. In another sense, this can be seen as the search of the pre-gendered female to find a place in language: the ghosts who 'have not been sent of the father' are returning 'to the house of our fathers' (p. 62). The dead try a number of different ways of communication with the citizens, ranging from pure sound—which no one can understand—to a very fundamental sign which is immediately meaningful to the male narrator. Those who venture into the city after its occupation experience 'a world full of sound' (p. 62), and even those who remain outside hear something of the dead's sound-world in the bells of the Cathedral. Dupin reports, 'I do not know what it sounded like. It was a clamour of notes all run together, tone upon tone, without time or measure' (p. 34). Like Gordon's oral storytelling in 'The Merry Men' in which he cannot tell what the merman is 'like', the sound of the bells evades representation in language; the bells are not a sign of anything else, nothing has been made absent in order to call them into existence and thus they cannot be understood by the citizens who depend on absence (represented by the women of Semur) for signification. The sound of the bells precedes all ways of making sense by differentiating one thing from another as the notes are inseparable and appear not to exist in time.

At the opposite extreme from the radical absence of signs is the most famous sign of all, the phallus. The dead offer Dupin a sight of this primary signifier, causing him to experience deeply pleasurable sensations as he re-enacts his birth into the symbolic order and the accession of the patriarchal authority of naming bound up in this 'first sign':

These were the towers that could be seen leagues off, the first sign of Semur; our towers, which we had been born to love like our father's name. I have had joys in my life, deep and great. I have loved, I have won honours, I have conquered difficulty; but never had I felt as now. It was as if one had been born again. (p. 49)

Between these two extremes, the dead try to make themselves understood by using a kind of writing that imitates speech by pulling away not only from writing's material nature, but also from its status as sign. Writing, like the sea-runes in 'The Merry Men', thus becomes a point at which the signification process is interrupted and fractured. The dead's writing imitates speech in the form of an extraordinary sign or placard which they exhibit on the front of the church. This sign appears to address all the citizens individually, although it is clearly not bound by the usual laws of space as Dupin mentions that the whole façade of the Cathedral would not have held all the names. Words appear one by one upon the placard and then fade away, imitating the actions of speech in time and obliterating the traces of their own origins:

NOUS AUTRES MORTS—these were the words which blazed out oftenest of all, so that every one saw them. And 'Go!' this terrible placard said—'Go! leave this place to us who know the true signification of life.' These words I remember, but not the rest; and even at this moment it struck me that there was no explanation, nothing but this *vraie signification de la vie*. I felt like one in a dream: the light coming and going before me; one word, then another, appearing—sometimes a phrase like that I have quoted, blazing out, then dropping into darkness. (p. 25)

The sign which imitates speech is offered as a system of meaning complete in itself and entirely self-referential, it is a sign which signifies nothing other than itself. *Vraie* can be translated as both 'true' and 'real', and *signification* as both 'significance', or meaning, and 'signification' or sign system. '*Vraie signification*' here implies not only that the dead know the 'true meaning of life' but that that meaning resides in their privileged access to a system of signs. But, paradoxically, the dead use signs which are not signs at all as they cannot call up anything outside themselves. The text of this sign cannot have any kind of relationship with other texts: Dupin points out that 'there was no explanation' of the placard's text. It is therefore 'real' because it resists representation, it is the 'real thing' rather than an account of it. Any attempt to interpret the sign's meaning by explaining it, for example by offering a paraphrase, would result only in a circular argument, as its meaning is antithetical to an interpretative act of this kind. 'Signification' as meaning is identical with 'signification' as sign system; the action of the sign is its meaning and it is thus glamour rather than grammar.

The fractured writing of *A Beleaguered City*, like that of 'The Merry Men', thus marks a point of transition between speech and writing, and between the imaginary and the symbolic. Yet such a transition is very hard to achieve as all but one of the citizens are locked into the either/or pattern which rejects non-meaning. The Curé, hitherto seen as a mediator between the living and the dead, can only reproduce the signs that depend upon absence as while crossing himself he falls into the silence associated with the women of Semur:

He had been the teacher of the Unseen among us, till the moment when the Unseen was thus, as it were, brought within our reach; but with the revelation he had nothing to do; and it filled him with pain and wonder. It made him silent; he said little about his religion, but signed himself, and his lips moved. (p. 39)

More successful in the transition between the living and the dead is Paul Lecamus, an isolated, less socialized character with no living family. Lecamus undergoes an experience which is like Freud's 'uncanny', but also different from it, as he encounters not images from a subconscious created by division, but something approaching a pre-conscious state. On their placard, the ghosts of Semur insist that they are 'Nous autres morts', 'we other dead'. The dead are 'other' in two senses of the word. They are other because they are not the same as the living persons they address, and because they, like the women of Semur, are the Others which language seeks futilely to capture. But, paradoxically, they are also the other dead ones, more of the same thing, like the dead of 'The Merry Men' of whom Gordon Darnaway comments, 'If there's folk ashore, there's folk in the sea—deid they may be, but they're folk whatever' (p. 19). Thus, by their own account, the dead are not essentially different from the living, yet they are apprehended by the living characters as something quite other than themselves. They are the spectral doubles who inhabit the homes of the city's present residents and who involve them in experiences reminiscent of Freud's analysis of the 'uncanny'. Terry Castle has identified a phenomenon in the writing of Ann Radcliffe which she calls 'the supernaturalization of everyday life'.[19] For Oliphant's work, we might reverse this concept and read *A Beleaguered City* in terms of the domestication of the supernatural. The ghosts take up residence in the houses of the inhabitants of Semur and those who encounter the dead are reminded by them of themselves: Lecamus insists, 'They hope like us, and desire, and are mistaken' (p. 63) and he sees his own bewilderment reflected in theirs: 'they did not understand it any more than we understand' (p. 63).

The simultaneous sameness and difference of the dead and the living mirror the sense the living characters have of themselves. During the period of confusion immediately before they are expelled from the city, the citizens of Semur begin to have knowledge of things at one remove from themselves. Martin Dupin finds his confidence in himself as a discrete whole, the illusion of his subjectivity which he refers to as 'my perfect self-possession' (p. 17), is under attack. It is only by hearing himself, by positing the self as other, both familiar and strange, that Dupin can contemplate this new experience and he begins to recognize himself as divided: 'It was only as I walked away, hearing my own steps and those of Lecamus ringing upon the pavement, that I began to realize what had happened' (p. 19). On his return to the city in the company of the Curé, Dupin again draws attention to the sense of hearing himself as something apart; what appears at first to be 'natural', a quality of the integrated self, is immediately afterwards revealed to be dislocated, revealing the self as split: 'We spoke in our natural voices as we came out, scarcely knowing how great was the difference between them and the whispers which had been all we dared at first to employ. Yet the sound of these louder tones scared us when we heard them for we were still trembling' (p. 71). The process of experiencing the self as other even

---

[19] Terry Castle, 'The Spectralization of the Other in *The Mysteries of Udolpho*', in *The New Eighteenth Century*, ed. Felicity Nussbaum and Laura Brown (London and New York: Methuen, 1987), 231–53 (p. 234).

undermines the citizens' dependence on sight. After the dead's second summons to them, by means of music, Dupin comments, 'our very eyes seemed to be drawn out of their sockets, fluttering like things with a separate life' (p. 53).

The dead of Semur function as lost elements of the living. From one perspective, they can be seen as enacting the Freudian drama of the separation from the mother and the creation of the unconscious. The dead are apparently different from the living principally because they *are* dead, thereby positing a point in the past at which they must have been the same as the current inhabitants who now experience their loss. Looked at in this way, they enact the human subject's sense of a lost sameness: the pre-Oedipal child's unity with the mother. A rather paradigmatic instance of this occurs when Lecamus, while visiting the city during the dead's occupation of it, re-enters his home and goes into the room of his dead wife where he has a sense of union with her. Momentarily, he experiences the joining of the two parts of the divided self.

It was beyond speech. Neither did I need to see her face, nor to touch her hand. She was more near to me, more near than when I held her in my arms. How long it was so, I cannot tell; it was as long as love, yet short as the drawing of a breath. I knew nothing, felt nothing but Her, alone; all my wonder and desire to know departed from me. We said to each other everything without words—heart overflowing into heart. It was beyond knowledge or speech. (p. 59)

In Lacanian terms, Lecamus's sense that 'all my wonder and desire to know departed from me' achieves the impossible: the end of desire and of lack. His sense, when struggling with meaning, of unsatisfied longing here vanishes: 'the thing which had happened to me was that which I had desired all my life' (p. 60). He requires no object of his knowledge because he need not seek external substitutes for something that was once part of him. In fact, representation itself is no longer necessary as the experience is beyond language altogether. Even speech is finally revealed to be relevant chiefly as an alternative to writing; in the completion of Lecamus's desire, a return to a state before the recognition of discrete concepts or identities, *any* distinction becomes inapplicable.

Lecamus recognizes that his privileged experience, beyond

speech and unaffected by time, is not subject to the usual laws
that structure human consciousness. But in the world of visual
signs such a moment, like speech itself, cannot last. Lecamus
perceives that such an experience cannot coexist with a world
which requires 'public signification' (p. 59). From a Freudian
perspective, desire is again repressed in order that the subject
may function in society. Lecamus submits to Dupin's insistence
that he attempt to represent his encounter with the dead in
writing because it is his only recourse. Only the dead, by means
of their placard, are able to construct public signs which do not
attempt to signify anything beyond themselves. Yet the placard
cannot be understood as such by the citizens who associate it
with the representing function of signs in society: to them
it 'looked like a great official placard' (p. 25).

Lecamus does not long survive the difficult experience of
writing and dies 'with his papers fluttering at his feet',
abandoning the now painful process of human signification for
good. His death marks the renunciation of writing and its
associated ideas—signs and patriarchal authority. It marks also
the willing submission to castration, in its guise as blinding,
rather than Freudian terror of it. Lecamus's scattered papers
recall the moment at which 'our very eyes seemed to be drawn
out of their sockets, fluttering like things with a separate life'
(p. 53). The end of signification here implies the desire not to
possess the mother, but to become her. The gap between the
dead's orality and the living's need for writing can be crossed
only by death itself. Lecamus gains permanent 'happiness
of hearing' in the 'world full of sound', while his friends
commemorate him with an inscribed tombstone. The novel ends
with an acceptance of the writing and figurative language of
which it is itself composed.

However desirable orality might be, and however antagonistic
writing to the interests of women, the book nevertheless accepts
that it is upon writing that its intelligibility depends. Lecamus's
death, and the subsequent gravestone writing, draw attention to
death as a point looking forward into non-meaning and
backward into the retrospective construction of meaning, the
death of the narrative from which point all stories are narrated.
In Benjamin's phrase, 'not only a man's knowledge or wisdom,
but above all his real life . . . first assumes transmissible form at

the moment of his death.'[20] In *A Beleaguered City*, there is a
tension between the failure of narrative to call up experience,
and a sense that narrative is the only possible means of
transmitting that experience.

Lecamus is much less resistant to the dead than are most
of the other residents of Semur, but even he is restricted by the
fact that he has been asked by Dupin to 'draw up an account of
my residence in the town, to be placed with his own narrative'.
Lecamus struggles to transmit to the reader, in a written
narrative, the voices of the dead. Writing is here described as
something which encloses experience, yet the attempt to 'place'
Lecamus's narrative is likely to be difficult when it is an account
of something which is 'without time or measure'. Even the word
'account' here puns in the same way as it does in Hogg's
Confessions of a Justified Sinner in which both the editor and
Robert discover that their narrative accounts in fact account for
very little.

Lecamus is aware that writing, itself a sign system, is subject
to the processes of socialization that the dead resist, and after
the passage in which he tries to express his experience 'beyond
knowledge or speech', he admits that it might not *be* appropriate for the written narrative which has been commissioned from
him: 'But this is not of *public signification* that I should occupy
with it the time of M. le Maire' (p. 59, emphasis mine). Because
of the mission of his writing, Lecamus tries to reproduce the
language of the dead, but admits, 'Do not think that these were
the words they sang; but it was like this' (p. 62), an attempt
already doomed as we know that the dead's 'language' is not
like anything. Even when the dead attempt to enter into the
language world of the people of Semur via the placard,
the results are less than satisfactory as communication and their
endeavours are deemed trickery by the inhabitants. Through the
admittedly imperfect medium of Lecamus's narrative we are
told that the dead despair of being understood by the living due
to the latter's dependence on visual signs. The living are 'capable
of understanding only that which was palpable' (p. 42).
Lecamus reports: 'There went a sighing over all the city: "They
cannot hear us, our voices are not as their voices; they cannot

[20] S 24.

see us" ' (p. 64). These juxtapositions imply a causal connection: the living cannot hear the dead *because* they cannot see them in a patriarchal, sight-dependent culture. We can, more specifically, see this phenomenon as characteristic of a society which considers writing as a visible medium of communication which is more authoritative than speech (as in the phrase 'put it in writing'), and which constitutes the social authority of writing.[21] In the society of *A Beleaguered City*, the characters are both socially and psychologically dependent on visual signs.

What is true of writing itself is equally true of narrative. Both Lecamus and Dupin admit that their narrative accounts are very imperfect equivalents of their experiences, yet they can only come to terms with those experiences in retrospect, the point at which their narratives become transmissible. Lecamus is caught in this dilemma. At first he is replete with what he calls 'the happiness of hearing' (p. 61) but, like speech itself, such a state cannot be permanent—at least for the living. He has the sense of a barrier rising and confining him to the realm of afterthought in which meaning and signification must be sought. Although it is precisely by means of discovering meaning that Lecamus can 'make out' the dead's speech, he finds it a profoundly unsatisfying substitute for the direct experience of hearing without understanding:

M. le Maire will, however, be good enough to remark that I did not understand all that I heard. In the middle of a phrase, in a word half breathed, a sudden barrier would rise. For a time I laboured after their meaning, trying hard and vainly to understand; but afterwards I perceived that only when they spoke of Semur, of you who were gone forth, and of what was being done, could I make it out. At first this made me only more eager to hear; but when thought came, then I perceived that of all my longing nothing was satisfied. (p. 62)

Dupin also goes through this process. He shares with the editor of *Confessions of a Justified Sinner* a misplaced confidence in his objective narration. Both offer the reader accounts

[21] Shirley Brice Heath points out how written documents exist not always solely to be read, but also to authorize oral transactions. She observes that 'The having of something in writing is often a ritualistic practice, and more often than not, those who hold the written piece are not expected to read what they have' ('Protean Shapes in Literacy Events: Ever-shifting Oral and Literary Traditions', in *Spoken and Written Language: Exploring Orality and Literacy*, ed. Deborah Tannen (Norwood, NJ: Ablex, 1982), 91–117 (p. 94).

constructed from a variety of sources, the *Confessions* editor from the 'powerful monitors' of historical and traditional records, Dupin from the reports of Lecamus and de Bois-Sombre. Despite what prove to be the highly subjective and empirical accounts that make up the novel, Dupin feels himself able to synthesize them into a 'true narrative' which will not only accurately recount events but also be of universal interest:

my attitude here is not that of a man recording his personal experiences only, but of one who is the official mouthpiece and representative of the commune, and whose duty it is to render to government and to the human race a true narrative of the very wonderful facts to which every citizen of Semur can bear witness. In this capacity it has become my duty so to arrange and edit the different accounts of the mystery, as to present one coherent and trustworthy chronicle to the world. (p. 10)

As the novel progresses, we may feel 'coherent and trust-worthy' to be something of an overstatement, seeing that most of the witnesses who submit accounts to Dupin admit that their narratives cannot fully represent their experiences. At the beginning of his narration, when he is describing events prior to the arrival of the dead, Dupin finds no difference between those events and their narration: 'I have related them as they happened' (p. 10). But as his account progresses, he admits that his representation can never be equivalent to what he thinks of as the 'natural' events, a narrative position that proves as conditional as that of the narrator of *The Three Perils of Man* who hopes to get matters narrated 'in their proper places'.[22] Dupin writes:

The mysterious and wonderful then find their natural place in the course of affairs; but when a man thinks for himself, and has to take everything on his own responsibility, and make all the necessary explanations, there is often great difficulty. So many things will not fit into their places, they straggle like weary men on a march. One cannot put them together, or satisfy one's self. (pp. 67–8)

The need to make sense of experience by narrating it after it has happened recurs in 'The Open Door', a ghost story published two years after *A Beleaguered City*. The narrator of this story undergoes a similarly supernatural visitation in the form of a disembodied voice and can only come to terms with it by confronting it retrospectively. So reassuring is this process that the narrator sees his experience as doubly retrospective: first, he believes it not to be an immediate occurrence but a 'recollection' of one, and secondly (unlike Lecamus's more complex response) he finds his own explanation of that recollection to be 'satisfactory and composing':

> I suppose I got less alarmed as the thing went on. I began to recover the use of my senses—I seemed to explain it all to myself by saying that this had once happened, that it was a recollection of a real scene. Why there should have seemed something quite satisfactory and composing in this explanation I cannot tell, but so it was. (p. 141)

This story enacts the Oedipal stage in what seems at first to be a quite straightforward way. Colonel Mortimer, the narrator of 'The Open Door', and his family have taken a house in a village outside Edinburgh on their return from India. During a visit to London, the Colonel is summoned back home as his son Roland is dangerously ill, though with what, no one is quite sure. Whatever Roland is suffering from, it evidently has its roots in the Oedipal crisis. Roland claims to have heard a ghostly voice (which his father also hears in the extract above) in the ruins of an older house on the estate. This disembodied voice cries over and over again 'Oh, mother let me in!' (p. 123), a phrase which Roland himself repeats. Roland identifies strongly with the voice and knows he will not be well again until its 'owner' is helped. He is convinced that his father, his role model, will be able to take authoritative action on this score: when Mortimer asks his son what he wants him to do, Roland replies, 'I should know if I was you ... That is what I always said to myself—Father will know' (p. 127). And indeed, with the help of the local minister, Mortimer successfully exorcizes the ghost, which the minister believes to be that of a local boy named Willie.

Although the ghost has an independent existence, both father and son also recognize it as a part of Roland himself. Roland says 'think, papa, think, if it was me' (p. 127) and Colonel Mortimer does think so, acknowledging, 'I had to act the part of a father to Roland's ghost' (p. 128). Mortimer considers the whole process of dealing with the ghost to be vital for his son's passage into the adult world. If it remains unexorcized, Roland's continued existence is threatened and he will remain, with the ghost, in perpetual childhood. Rather than consciously resisting the exorcism of his Oedipal desires, Roland collaborates with his father in it. He is worried that he is behaving 'like a baby' and his father is anxious that his son is identifying too much with the supposedly feminine in the form of that well-known 'women's illness', 'a hysterical temperament'. The father is violently opposed to such a thing, which he considers to be 'all that men most hate and fear for their children' (p. 127). The ghostly voice, however, is not quite so happy to be exorcized and rebels violently against the father, who reports: 'I declare that it seemed to me as if I were pushed aside, put aside, by the owner of the voice as he paced up and down in his trouble' (p. 152).

Oliphant's story, however, does not accommodate itself quite so happily to the Law of the Father. If he wants to be like his father, as seems to be the case, Roland must submit to his Law, but this is not the only option offered by the novel. Willie's ghost *does* succeed in being let in by his mother, with the permission of a divine Father-figure. The moment before Willie's departure, the minister says, 'Lord, let that woman there draw him inower!' (p. 154), which seems to have the desired effect. Like *A Beleaguered City*, 'The Open Door' goes beyond a simple acquiescence in the social necessity of taboo, perhaps because the view that the fulfilment of desire is a tragedy for the male individual is based on a profound antipathy to the woman's body. Oliphant's stories raise the possibility that women's bodies might really be quite desirable and not something to be repressed by sons (in the case of mothers) or rejected by fathers (in the case of daughters).

In this story the repression of desire itself stands in a metaphoric relation to the action of writing on speech. The story suggests that, in one sense, the ghostly voice is exorcized by being written down. The two sides of this relationship are brought together immediately after Mortimer has told the whole story to Moncrieff, the clergyman who succeeds in banishing the ghost. Moncrieff says, 'I must write it down for the "Children's Record" ' (p. 148). Roland's story, subject to the imposed order of writing, will become instructional in the education of other children, whereas the oral Willie escapes to the subversive union with his mother.

Finally, I want to turn to the late story, 'The Library Window'. It is one of Oliphant's most complicated stories and, although it will bring this study to an end by returning to the ideological positioning of Scottish literacy, it does not offer any very portable conclusions. Published in 1896, the story looks back across a century of Scottish literature as well as picking up some of the ideas Oliphant had already explored in *A Beleaguered City*. 'The Library Window' is narrated by an unnamed girl who is spending the summer, without her parents, at her aunt's house in the Scottish town of St Rule's (modelled on St Andrews). Naturally solitary and isolated from her aunt's elderly friends she spends much of her time reading, seated next to a window which gives out on to the College Library opposite. One of the windows of the library occasions much discussion among Aunt Mary and her friends as to whether it is a real window, or painted on the side of the building, or a former window now bricked up. Only the narrator, it seems at first, has the ability to see through the library window, and she witnesses a man continually and busily covering paper with writing but never coming to the end of the page. Eventually the aunt admits to having seen this figure herself and tells the narrator that it is the ghost of 'a Scholar', now dead, who, because he 'liked his books more than any lady's love' (p. 328), ignored the advances of a particular woman and was (the narrator assumes) murdered by her brothers. The narrator is deeply shocked by this news and the next day is unexpectedly taken home by her mother in preparation for going abroad.

The interplay between female visionary and male ghost recalls a further way of managing death in the late nineteenth century, the seance. Spiritualism's *pièce de résistance*, 'materialization', was a phenomenon that reached a pinnacle of popularity in the 1870s and is thus equally important for *A Beleaguered City* and its exploration of the materiality of signs. But of particular significance for 'The Library Window' is the fact that, as Judith Walkowitz has shown, spiritualism put women in an ambiguous position. On the one hand, 'The séance reversed the usual sexual hierarchy of knowledge and power: it shifted attention away from men and focused it on the female medium, the center of spiritual knowledge and insight.' On the other hand, this occult power was often contained by its authorization by a masculine figure in the form of a male 'spirit guide': 'women could authoritatively "speak spirit" if they were controlled by others, notably men'.[23] It is this problematic status of women who are empowered within a patriarchal order that 'The Library Window' addresses.

The story confuses the roles that speech and writing had played in the earlier stories, as it also disrupts the psychology of gender. The narrator of 'The Library Window' is uniquely empowered by claiming access to *both* speech and writing; unlike Dr Mortimer or the residents of Semur, she can both hear and see: 'Aunt Mary always said I could do two or indeed three things at once—both read and listen, and see' (p. 291). The narrator has invaded the space reserved by Andrew Lang for male bookmen ('remote from the interruptions of servants, wife, and children')[24] by forging a study for herself (like Jane Eyre at the start of that novel) in 'the deep recess of the drawing-room window' (p. 289). From this space, she proceeds to look into a Langian masculine preserve—she is told that 'there are no women-servants in the Old Library' (p. 292)—and to challenge the patriarchal authority of representation, thus becoming a representative figure of the woman writer.[25] In this story the absent figure whose presence is summoned up by imagery is not the mother but the father of the narrator. Yet this apparent search for the substitute father is not an attempt to access the desired *otherness* (Freud's hypothesis of the daughter's frustrated seduction of the father) but a fascination with the *sameness* of a position which mirrors her own. The ghost is both male (the

---

[23] Judith Walkowitz, *City of Dreadful Delight: Narratives of Sexual Danger in Late-Victorian London* (London: Virago, 1992), 176, 177. It should be acknowledged, however, that many male spirit guides were figures from the margins of Victorian class and race (American Indians were particularly popular), and that some of the most famous and successful visitors from the spirit world were young women. See Alex Owen, *The Darkened Room: Women, Power and Spiritualism in Late Victorian England* (London: Virago, 1989).

[24] Andrew Lang, *The Library* (London: Macmillan, 1881), 34.

[25] There are a number of biographical parallels between the narrator and Oliphant herself, most notably the fact that both tell the story after returning from abroad a widow with children.

emblem of writing) and female in that he is a 'ghost writer', in the same position as 'Mrs Oliphant' and other nineteenth-century women who wrote under their husband's names or under male pseudonyms.

Even before the narrator sees the writing man, the ghostly library conjures up images of the narrator's father when she sees a writing-table: 'There was one just like it in my father's library at home. It was such a surprise to see it all so clearly that I closed my eyes, for the moment almost giddy, wondering how papa's desk could have come here' (p. 299).[26] The process of signification is not itself a given to which the narrator must submit, but something which takes place in the mind of the female narrator. The writing ghost himself seems locked into a pattern of endless writing (futilely seeking substitutes for the absent referent) as the narrator never sees him finisning a page. However, despite what seems like her control of writing, the female narrator faces the problem that to appropriate such authority for herself is to accept it as the dominant culturally determining force. Like the ghosts of *A Beleaguered City*, she seeks not to endorse the figurative but to resist it—a process which is played out both in a rejection of the sexuality which will define her gender and in a concomitant distrust of the signs which will deny her subjectivity. Thus the narrator telling her story is caught in a vicious circle—the power of language can be annexed by the writing woman, but it remains inscribed as a male authority.

Even as the narrator creates images for the absent father she denies their significance; her half-conscious identification of the ghost with her father is consciously denied as 'Papa' writes slowly and takes breaks whereas the ghost never stops writing (p. 307). The story seeks out the root of the narrator's dilemma. Among Aunt Mary's friends is the elderly Lady Carnbee who wears a large and rather sinister ring. This ring greatly impresses itself upon, and unnerves, the narrator who fears that 'it might clutch me with sharp claws and the lurking, dazzling creature

---

[26] There is an obvious connection here with Lily Briscoe's ability, in *To the Lighthouse*, to imagine a table when she is not there, which Margaret Homans reads as Woolf's mockery of the androcentric assumption of the absence of the object (*Bearing the Word*, 1–2).

bite—with a sting that would go to the heart' (p. 293). Her consternation at this phallic, penetrative object is not only an adolescent fear of sexuality itself: Lady Carnbee's ring is malevolent because the narrator is aware that it is a sign: 'I am certain that it stung me again—a sharp malignant prick, oh full of meaning!' (p. 308). 'Meaning' is exactly what the narrator does not want, because it enacts the separation of the sign from the desired experience itself and because, as here, such a process is culturally identified with the phallus.

In her search for a pre-gendered, 'matter-of-fact' self, the narrator recognizes that the patriarchal construction of meaning wipes out female subjectivity, so that, for women, to be figured in language is 'against the self': 'I was then young and very matter-of-fact. I had not found out that one may mean something, yet not half or a hundredth part of what one seems to mean: and even then probably hoping to be contradicted if it is anyhow against one's self' (p. 301).

At the end of the story, the narrator describes what seems to be her acquiescence in the symbolic order and its triangular relationships which replace her dyadic union with the male writing ghost. She is taken back to London, 'papa having settled to go abroad': 'At first I had a wild thought I would not go. But how can a girl say I will not, when her mother has come for her, and there is no reason, no reason in the world, to resist, and no right!' (p. 330). However, this change is not as absolute as it might seem. The narrator is telling (or writing) the story from a position in which she has married and had children and thus become socially identified as a woman. Yet in another sense she is still caught between the desire to be 'matter-of-fact' and the continuing creation of male substitutes. As an afterword, she recounts an incident in which she believes she again sees the ghost. Her husband has died and she returns from India, 'very sad' with her children. At the port she experiences an acute sense of loss and absence: 'There was nobody to welcome me,—for I was not expected: and very sad was I, without a face I knew: when all at once I saw him, and he waved his hand to me' (pp. 330–1). Yet despite her ability to call up the absent Father the narrator continues to deny the nature of signs and their phallic authority. When Aunt Mary tells her the story of the ghost's murder she says Lady Carnbee's ring was a 'token' between the scholar and his lover. At the end of the story, the narrator tells us that, after her death, Lady Carnbee left her the ring in her will. After informing the reader of this detail, she ends her story with: 'Yet I never knew what Aunt Mary meant when she said, "Yon ring was the token", nor what it could have to do with that strange window in the old College Library of St Rule's' (p. 331). Tokens, particularly phallic ones, remain a threat to the narrator's status *as* the narrator of her own story.

Finally, this story returns us to the ideological representation of speech and writing in nineteenth-century Scotland. The figure of the writing man reminds the narrator of Scott who, in Lockhart's *Life*, is famously glimpsed from a window as he writes at his desk. One of Lockhart's friends is unnerved by the sight of Scott's hand: 'I have been watching it, it fascinates my eye—it never stops—page after page is finished and thrown on that heap of MS. and still it goes on unwearied—and so it will be till candles are brought and God knows how long after that. It is the same every night.'[27] In the double synecdoche of the hand as writing itself and as the author of writing, the ghost/father-figure is characterized as Oliphant's literary father, fuelling the fear that all women might be ghost writers, writing only under the Name of the Father. Papa, who is 'a great writer, everybody says' (p. 307), stands in for Scott's 'vast, broad, manly genius' which Oliphant had earlier described as an adventuring force, colonizing Europe on behalf of Scotland: 'It is not Scottish character but Scotland herself that beams upon the world out of his tales—tales which one finds wherever one goes—books, perhaps more universally diffused in every European state and language than any other books in existence.'[28] Scott, as the icon of writing, joins the ranks of the bookmen whose productions emerge 'like a knight into the lists'.[29] But even from Scott's patriarchal writing, orality escapes, in disguise, into 'The Library Window'. The narrator comments on her reputation:

---

[27] *Life*, iii. 128–9.
[28] Magaret Oliphant, 'Scottish National Character', *BM* 87 (1860), 715–31 (p. 717).
[29] Margaret Oliphant, 'John Gibson Lockhart', *BM* 160 (1896), 607–25 (p. 607).

Everyone had said, since ever I learned to speak, that I was fantastic
and fanciful and dreamy . . . People don't know what they mean when
they say fantastic. It sounds like Madge Wildfire or something of that
sort. My mother thought I should always be busy, to keep nonsense out
of my head. But really I was not at all fond of nonsense. (p. 290)

For the narrator, as for Archie Weir, learning to speak is an
access of power. Here that power is associated with the Madge
Wildfire-like oral qualities of the irrational and the illegitimate,
but the narrator insists that such power is *not* 'nonsense' but a
valid means of female expression. The oral, then, in one of its
last nineteenth-century incarnations, is reclaimed as a resource
for the female author, and even as a voice which slips out of the
defining order of writing as a system of social and gendering
laws. Unlike the Romantic orality in which the speaker is alleged
to be fully present, Oliphant's female orality disrupts the
hegemonic ordering of identity, replacing it with voices whose
origins cannot be traced. At the end of 'The Open Door',
Colonel Mortimer, still unsure about the nature of the ghost,
surveys the possible explanations offered to him by the doctor:
'The miserable voice, the spirit in pain, he could think of as the
result of ventriloquism, or reverberation, or—anything you
please' (p. 159). And in the psychological territory which
Oliphant's supernatural stories inhabit, the voice *is* a kind of
ventriloquism. Willie's ghostly 'mother, let me in' emanates not
only from him, but also from Roland. In *A Beleaguered City*, the
speaking voice and the position from which it is heard are
divided between the same character. Dupin, during his exposure
to the dead, begins to recognize divisions in himself as he is
frightened by the sound of his own voice, and *A Beleaguered
City* is haunted throughout by such disembodied voices without
discernible origins. In the early stages of the novel, spoken
language has no origin because it comes from no individual
speaker. This is the first of the strange phenomena which
precede the arrival of the dead. There seems to be a limited
circulation of utterances which, although they are shared among
the characters, no single speaker can claim as his or her own.
Before the return of the dead, two independent speakers give
voice to what Dupin calls a 'remarkable repetition', repeating,
'it is enough to make the dead rise out of their graves' (pp. 6 and
7). Ventriloquism, then, acts as a kind of speaking which, like

the orphaned nature of writing, does not contain the presence of the speaker. Far from denoting the depersonalization of women under patriarchal subjectivity, Oliphant's ventriloquism challenges and disrupts that same masculinist security, reclaiming a female orality from the marginal space where it had resided for most of the century.

Bibliography

PRIMARY SOURCES

BLAIR, HUGH, *A Critical Dissertation on the Poems of Ossian, the Son of Fingal* (London: T. Becket and P. A. De Hondt, 1763).
—— *Lectures on Rhetoric and Belles Lettres* (2 vols., London: W. Strahan and T. Cadell, 1783).
BOSWELL, JAMES., *The Journal of a Tour to the Hebrides*, ed. Frederick A. Pottle and Charles H. Bennet (London: Heinemann, 1963).
DARLOW, T. H., *William Robertson Nicoll: His Life and Letters* (London: Hodder and Stoughton, 1925).
DICK, THOMAS, *On the Improvement of Society by the Diffusion of Knowledge* (Edinburgh: Waugh and Innes, 1833).
DUNCAN, HENRY, *The Young South Country Weaver; or, A Journey to Glasgow: A Tale for the Radicals*, 2nd edn. (Edinburgh: Waugh and Innes, 1821).
—— *The Cottage Fireside, or, The Parish Schoolmaster*, 6th edn. (Edinburgh: William Oliphant, 1862).
—— *et al., Tales of the Scottish Peasantry* (Edinburgh: William Oliphant, n.d.).
'Errors in the Education of the Lower Orders, a Fatal Cause of Corruption and Misery to the Higher', *Monthly Monitor and Philanthropic Museum*, 1 (1815), 121–30.
FERGUSON, ADAM, *An Essay on the History of Civil Society*, ed. Duncan Forbes (Edinburgh: Edinburgh University Press, 1966).
FIELDING, HENRY, *The History of Tom Jones, A Foundling*, ed. Fredson Bowers (2 vols., Oxford: Clarendon Press, 1974).
FREUD, SIGMUND, 'The Uncanny', in *The Standard Edition of the Complete Psychological Works of Sigmund Freud*, trans. and ed. James Strachey (24 vols., London: Hogarth Press and the Institute of Psychoanalysis, 1953–72), xvii. 217–56.
GEDDIE, JOHN, *The Balladists* (Edinburgh and London: Oliphant, Anderson and Ferrier, n.d.).
HOGG, JAMES, 'A Scots Mummy', *Blackwood's Edinburgh Magazine*, 14 (1823), 188–90.
—— 'On the Changes in the Habits, Amusements, and Condition of the Scottish Peasantry', *Quarterly Journal of Agriculture*, 3 (1831–2), 256–63.

HOGG, JAMES, *The Private Memoirs and Confessions of a Justified Sinner*, ed. John Carey (Oxford: Oxford University Press, 1969).

—— '*Memoirs of Author's Life*' *and* '*Familiar Anecdotes of Sir Walter Scott*', ed. Douglas S. Mack (Edinburgh and London: Scottish Academic Press, 1972).

—— *The Brownie of Bodsbeck*, ed. Douglas Mack (Edinburgh and London: Scottish Academic Press, 1976).

—— *Selected Stories and Sketches*, ed. Douglas S. Mack (Edinburgh: Scottish Academic Press, 1982).

—— *Tales of Love and Mystery*, ed. David Groves (Edinburgh: Canongate, 1985).

—— *The Three Perils of Man: War, Women and Witchcraft*, ed. Douglas Gifford, 2nd edn. (Edinburgh: Scottish Academic Press, 1989).

JAMES, HENRY, *Letters*, ed. Leon Edel, iv, *1895–1916* (Cambridge, Mass. and London: Harvard University Press, 1984).

[JOHNS, B. G.], 'The Literature of the Streets', *Edinburgh Review*, 165 (1887), 40–65.

JOHNSON, SAMUEL, *A Journey to the Western Islands of Scotland*, ed. Mary Lascelles (New Haven and London: Yale University Press, 1971).

KERRIGAN, CATHERINE (ed.), *An Anthology of Scottish Women Poets* (Edinburgh: Edinburgh University Press, 1991).

LANG, ANDREW, *The Library* (London: Macmillan, 1881).

—— *Custom and Myth* (London: Longman's, Green and Co., 1884).

—— *Books and Bookmen* (London: Longman's, Green and Co., 1887).

—— 'Realism and Romance', *Contemporary Review*, 52 (1887), 683–93.

—— *Essays in Little* (London: Henry and Co., 1891).

—— *The Book of Dreams and Ghosts* (London: Longman's, Green and Co., 1897).

—— 'History as She Ought to be Wrote', *Blackwood's Edinburgh Magazine*, 166 (1899), 266–74.

—— 'Notes on Ballad Origins', *Folklore*, 14 (1903), 147–61.

—— *Adventures Among Books* (London: Longman's, Green and Co. 1905).

—— *The Clyde Mystery: A Study in Forgeries and Folklore* (Glasgow: James MacLehose and Sons, 1905).

—— *Sir Walter Scott and the 'Border Minstrelsy'* (London: Longman's, Green and Co., 1910).

LEONARD, TOM, *Intimate Voices* (Newcastle upon Tyne: Galloping Dog Press, 1984).

[LEWIS, GEORGE], *Scotland A Half-Educated Nation Both in the*

Quantity and Quality of her Educational Institutions (Glasgow: William Collins, 1834).

LOCKHART, J. G., 'Lives of Uneducated Poets', *Quarterly Review*, 44 (1831), 52–82.

—— *Memoirs of the Life of Sir Walter Scott, Bart* (7 vols., Edinburgh: Robert Cadell, 1837).

MAIXNER, PAUL (ed.), *Robert Louis Stevenson: The Critical Heritage* (London: Routledge and Kegan Paul, 1981).

'Memorial for the Parish-schoolmasters in Scotland', *Scots Magazine*, 46 (1784), 1–4.

[MILL, J. S.]., 'The Claims of Labour: An Essay on the Duties of Employers to the Employed', *Edinburgh Review*, 81 (1845), 498–525.

[MOSELEY, HENRY], 'Church and State Education', *Edinburgh Review*, 92 (1850), 94–136.

MOTHERWELL, WILLIAM, *Minstrelsy: Ancient and Modern* (Glasgow, John Wylie, 1827).

OLIPHANT, MARGARET, 'The Byways of Literature: Reading for the Million', *Blackwood's Edinburgh Magazine*, 84 (1858), 200–16.

—— 'Scottish National Character', *Blackwood's Edinburgh Magazine*, 87 (1860), 715–31.

—— 'Scotland and her Accusers', *Blackwood's Edinburgh Magazine*, 90 (1861), 267–83.

—— 'John Gibson Lockhart', *Blackwood's Edinburgh Magazine*, 160 (1896), 607–25.

—— *The Autobiography and Letters of Mrs Margaret Oliphant* (Leicester: Leicester University Press, 1974).

—— *A Beleaguered City and Other Stories*, ed. Merryn Williams (Oxford: Oxford University Press, 1988).

—— *The Autobiography of Margaret Oliphant*, ed. Elisabeth Jay (Oxford: Oxford University Press, 1990).

'On the influence of the diffusion of knowledge upon the happiness of the lower ranks of society', *Edinburgh Magazine and Literary Miscellany*, 4 (1819), 121–9.

'On the Modern Education of the Middling Classes', *Edinburgh Magazine and Literary Miscellany*, 4 (1819), 314–18.

ORWELL, GEORGE, *Burmese Days* (London: Secker and Warburg, 1986).

PAINE, TOM, *Rights of Man*, ed. Henry Collins (Harmondsworth: Penguin, 1984).

REID, THOMAS, *An Inquiry into the Human Mind on the Principles of Common Sense* (Edinburgh: A. Kincaid and J. Bell, 1764).

ROUSSEAU, JEAN-JACQUES, *Essay on the Origin of Languages*, trans. John H. Moran (New York: Frederick Ungar, 1966).

SCOTT, WALTER, *The Poetical Works of Sir Walter Scott, Bart.* (12 vols., Edinburgh: Robert Cadell, 1833–4).

—— *The Miscellaneous Prose Works of Sir Walter Scott, Bart*, ed. J. G. Lockhart (30 vols., Edinburgh: Adam and Charles Black, 1869–71).

—— *Waverley Novels*, Border Edition, ed. Andrew Lang (24 vols., London: Charles C. Nimmo, 1898–9.

—— *The Letters of Sir Walter Scott*, ed. H. J. C. Grierson (12 vols., London, 1932–7.

—— *Old Mortality*, ed. Angus Calder (Harmondsworth: Penguin, 1975).

—— *The Heart of Midlothian*, ed. Claire Lamont (Oxford: Oxford University Press, 1982).

—— *Redgauntlet*, ed. Kathryn Sutherland (Oxford: Oxford University Press, 1985).

—— *'The Two Drovers' and Other Stories*, ed. Graham Tulloch (Oxford: Oxford University Press, 1987).

[SOUTHEY, ROBERT], Review of 'Landt's Description of the Feroe Islands', *Quarterly Review*, 4 (1810), 333–42.

—— Review of 'Bell and Lancaster's Systems of Education', *Quarterly Review*, 6 (1811), 264–304.

STERNE, LAURENCE, *The Life and Opinions of Tristram Shandy, Gentleman*, ed. Ian Campbell Ross (Oxford: Oxford University Press, 1983).

STEVENSON, ROBERT LOUIS, *Memories and Portraits* (London: Chatto and Windus, 1887).

—— *The Merry Men and Other Tales and Fables* (London: Chatto and Windus, 1887).

—— *R. L. S.: Stevenson's Letters to Charles Baxter*, ed. DeLancey Ferguson and Marshall Waingrow (New Haven: Yale University Press, 1956).

—— *The Ebb-Tide*, in *Dr Jekyll and Mr Hyde and Other Stories*, ed. Jenni Calder (Harmondsworth: Penguin, 1979).

—— *The Master of Ballantrae*, ed. Emma Letley (Oxford: Oxford University Press, 1983).

—— *'Dr Jekyll and Mr Hyde' and 'Weir of Hermiston'*, ed. Emma Letley (Oxford: Oxford University Press, 1987).

—— *Selected Essays and Poems*, ed. Claire Harman (London: Dent, 1992).

STOW, DAVID, *The Training System* (New Edition, Glasgow: Blackie and Sons, 1840).

The Tavern Sages: Selections from the 'Noctes Ambrosianae', ed. J. H. Alexander (Aberdeen: Association for Scottish Literary Studies, 1992).

TYLOR, E. B., *Primitive Culture: Researches, into the Development of Mythology, Philosophy, Religion, Art, and Custom* (2 vols., London: John Murray, 1871).

VEITCH, JOHN, *The History and Poetry of the Scottish Border: Their Main Features and Relations* (Glasgow: James Maclehose, 1878).

[WILSON, JOHN], 'On the Effects of Knowledge upon Society', *Blackwood's Edinburgh Magazine*, 4 (1818–19), 80–4.

—— 'On the Revival of a Taste for our Ancient Literature', *Blackwood's Edinburgh Magazine*, 4 (1818–19), 264–6.

—— 'Burns and the Ettrick Shepherd', *Blackwood's Edinburgh Magazine*, 4 (1818–19), 521–9.

SECONDARY TEXTS

ALEXANDER, J. H., 'Hogg in the *Noctes Ambrosianae*', *Studies in Hogg and his World*, 4 (1993), 37–47.

ANDERSON, CAROL, 'The Powers of Naming: Language, Identity and Betrayal in *The Heart of Midlothian*', in *Scott in Carnival*, ed. J. H. Alexander and David Hewitt (Aberdeen: Association for Scottish Literary Studies, 1993), 189–201.

ANDERSON, PATRICIA, *The Printed Image and the Transformation of Popular Culture 1790–1860* (Oxford: Clarendon Press, 1991).

ANDERSON, R. D., *Education and Opportunity in Victorian Scotland* (Oxford: Clarendon Press, 1983).

ARIÈS, PHILIPPE, *The Hour of Our Death*, trans. Helen Weaver (Harmondsworth: Penguin, 1983).

AUSTIN, J. L., *How to Do Things with Words* (Oxford: Clarendon Press, 1962).

BASHAM, DIANA, *The Trial of Woman: Feminism and the Occult Sciences in Victorian Literature and Society* (Basingstoke: Macmillan, 1992).

BASKER, JAMES G., 'Scotticisms and the Problem of Cultural Identity in Eighteenth-Century Britain', in *Sociability and Society in Eighteenth-Century Scotland*, ed. John Dwyer and Richard B. Sher (Edinburgh: Mercat Press, 1993), 81–95.

BAUMAN, RICHARD, *Story, Performance, and Event: Contextual Studies of Oral Narrative* (Cambridge: Cambridge University Press, 1986).

—— (ed.), *Verbal Art as Performance*, 2nd edn. (Prospect Heights, Ill.: Waveland Press, 1984).

BENJAMIN, WALTER, *Illuminations*, trans. Harry Zohn, ed. Hannah Arendt (London: Fontana, 1973).

BENJAMIN, WALTER, *One-Way Street and Other Writings*, trans. Edmund Jephcott and Kingsley Shorter (London: Verso, 1985).

BRATHWAITE, EDWARD KAMAU, *The History of the Voice: The Development of Nation Language in Anglophone Caribbean Poetry* (London and Port of Spain: New Beacon Books, 1984).

BRISTOW, JOSEPH, *Empire Boys: Adventures in a Man's World* (London: Harper Collins, 1991).

BROOKS, PETER, *Reading For the Plot: Design and Intention in Narrative* (Oxford: Clarendon Press, 1984).

—— 'The Tale vs. The Novel', in *Why the Novel Matters: A Postmodern Perplex*, ed. Mark Spilka and Caroline McCracken-Flesher (1977; repr. Bloomington and Indianapolis: Indiana University Press, 1990), 303–10.

BROWN, MARY ELLEN, *Burns and Tradition* (Urbana and Chicago: University of Illinois Press, 1984).

BUCHAN, DAVID, *The Ballad and the Folk* (London: Routledge and Kegan Paul, 1972).

—— 'The Expressive Culture of Nineteenth-Century Farm Servants', in *Farm Servants and Labour in Lowland Scotland, 1770–1914*, ed. T. M. Devine (Edinburgh: John Donald, 1984), 226–42.

CALDER, JENNI (ed.), *Stevenson and Victorian Scotland* (Edinburgh: Edinburgh University Press, 1981).

—— *The Enterprising Scot: Scottish Adventure and Achievement* (Edinburgh: Royal Museum of Scotland, 1986).

CAMPBELL, IAN (ed.), *Nineteenth-Century Scottish Fiction* (Manchester: Manchester University Press, 1979).

CASTLE, TERRY, 'The Spectralization of the Other in *The Mysteries of Udolpho*', in *The New Eighteenth Century*, ed. Felicity Nussbaum and Laura Brown (London and New York: Methuen, 1987), 231–53.

CHANDLER, JAMES, *Wordsworth's Second Nature: A Study of the Poetry and Politics* (Chicago and London: University of Chicago Press, 1984).

CHATMAN, SEYMOUR, *Story and Discourse* (Ithaca, NY: Cornell University Press, 1978).

COCKSHUT, A. O. J., *The Achievement of Walter Scott* (London: Collins, 1969).

CONNOR, STEVEN, *Theory and Cultural Value* (Oxford and Cambridge, Mass.: Blackwell, 1992).

CONRAD, JOSEPH, *'Heart of Darkness' and Other Tales*, ed. Cedric Watts (Oxford: Oxford University Press, 1990).

COOK-GUMPERZ, JENNY (ed.), *The Social Construction of Literacy* (London: Cambridge University Press, 1986).

COONEY, SEAMUS, 'Scott and Progress: The Tragedy of "The Highland Widow" ', *Studies in Short Fiction*, 11 (1974), 11–16.

COUTURIER, MAURICE, *Textual Communication: A Print-Based Theory of the Novel* (London and New York: Routledge, 1991).

COWAN, EDWARD J. (ed.), *The People's Past* (Edinburgh: Polygon, 1991).

CRAWFORD, ROBERT, 'Pater's *Renaissance*, Andrew Lang, and Anthropological Romanticism', *ELH* 53 (1986), 849–79.

—— *Devolving English Literature* (Oxford: Clarendon Press, 1992).

CRISCUOLA, MARGARET M., 'Constancy and Change: The Process of History in Scott's *Redgauntlet*', *Studies in Scottish Literature*, 10 (1985), 123–36.

CULLER, JONATHAN, *Structuralist Poetics: Structuralism, Linguistics and the Study of Literature* (London: Routledge, 1975).

CULLINAN, MARY, 'History and Language in Scott's Redgauntlet', *Studies in English Literature*, 18 (1978), 695–75.

DAICHES, DAVID, *Literature and Gentility in Scotland* (Edinburgh: Edinburgh University Press, 1982).

DAVIE, GEORGE E., *The Democratic Intellect: Scotland and her Universities in the Nineteenth Century* (Edinburgh: Edinburgh University Press, 1961).

DAVIES, LEITH, ' "Origins of the Specious": James Macpherson's Ossian and the Forging of the British Empire', *The Eighteenth Century: Theory and Interpretation*, 34 (1993), 132–50.

DE GROOT, H. B., 'The Imperilled Reader in *The Three Perils of Man*', *Studies in Hogg and his World*, 1 (1990), 114–25.

—— 'History and Fiction: The Case of *Redgauntlet*', in *Scott in Carnival*, ed. J. H. Alexander and David Hewitt (Aberdeen: Association for Scottish Literary Studies, 1993), 358–69.

DERRIDA, JACQUES, *Of Grammatology*, trans. Gayatri Chakravorty Spivak (Baltimore and London: Johns Hopkins University Press, 1976).

—— *Dissemination*, trans. Barbara Johnson (London: Athlone Press, 1981).

—— 'Signature Event Context', in *Margins of Philosophy*, trans. Alan Bass (Brighton: Harvester Press, 1982).

DONALDSON, WILLIAM, *Popular Literature in Victorian Scotland: Language, Fiction and the Press* (Aberdeen: Aberdeen University Press, 1986).

DUNCAN, IAN, *Modern Romance and Transformations of the Novel: The Gothic, Scott, Dickens* (Cambridge: Cambridge University Press, 1992).

EIGNER, EDWIN M., *Robert Louis Stevenson and Romantic Tradition* (Princeton: Princeton University Press, 1966).

Elam, Diana, *Romancing the Postmodern* (London and New York: Routledge, 1992).

Enos, Richard Leo (ed.), *Oral and Written Communication: Historical Approaches* (Newbury Park, Calif.: Sage Publications, 1990).

Ermarth, Elizabeth Deeds, *Realism and Consensus in the English Novel* (Princeton: Princeton University Press, 1983).

Favret, Mary A., and Watson, Nicola J. (eds.), *At the Limits of Romanticism: Essays in Cultural, Feminist, and Materialist Criticism* (Bloomington and Indianapolis: Indiana University Press, 1994).

Ferris, Ina, 'The Reader in the Rhetoric of Realism: Scott, Thackeray and Eliot', in *Scott and his Influence*, ed. J. H. Alexander and David Hewitt (Aberdeen: Association for Scottish Literary Studies, 1983), pp. 382–92.

—— 'Story-telling and the Subversion of Literary Form in Walter Scott's Fiction', *Genre*, 18 (1985), 23–35.

—— *The Achievement of Literary Authority: Gender, History and the Waverley Novels* (Ithaca, NY and London: Cornell University Press, 1991).

Finnegan, Ruth, *Literacy and Orality: Studies in the Technology of Communication* (Oxford: Blackwell, 1988).

—— *Oral Poetry: Its Nature, Significance and Social Context*, 2nd edn. (1977; repr. Bloomington and Indianapolis: Indiana University Press, 1992).

Fish, Stanley, 'How to Do Things with Austin and Searle: Speech-Theory and Literary Criticism', in *Is There a Text in this Class?* (Cambridge, Mass.: Harvard University Press, 1980), 197–245.

—— 'With the Compliments of the Author: Reflections on Austin and Derrida', in *Doing What Comes Naturally: Change, Rhetoric, and the Practice of Theory in Literary and Legal Studies* (Oxford: Clarendon Press, 1989), 37–67.

Frye, Northrop, *The Secular Scripture: A Study of the Structure of the Romance* (Cambridge, Mass.: Harvard University Press, 1976).

Garside, Peter, '*Old Mortality*'s Silent Minority', *Scottish Literary Journal*, 7/1 (1980), 127–44.

—— 'Popular Fiction and National Tale: Hidden Origins of Scott's *Waverley*', *Nineteenth-Century Literature*, 46 (1991–2), 30–53.

—— 'Three Perils in Publishing: Hogg and the Popular Novel', *Studies in Hogg and his World*, 2 (1991), 45–63.

Gaston, Patricia S., *Prefacing the Waverley Prefaces: A Reading of*

Sir Walter Scott's Prefaces to the Waverley Novels (New York: Peter Lang, 1991).

GIFFORD, DOUGLAS, *James Hogg* (Edinburgh: The Ramsay Head Press, 1976).

—— (ed.), *The History of Scottish Literature*, iii, *The Nineteenth Century* (Aberdeen: Aberdeen University Press, 1988).

GODZICH, WLAD, *The Culture of Literacy* (Cambridge, Mass.: Harvard University Press, 1994).

GOOD, GRAHAM, 'Re-reading Robert Louis Stevenson', *Dalhousie Review*, 62 (1982), 44–59.

GOODY, JACK, *The Interface Between the Written and the Oral* (Cambridge: Cambridge University Press, 1987).

GRAFF, HARVEY J., *The Literacy Myth: Literacy and Social Structure in the Nineteenth Century City* (New York and London: Academic Press, 1979).

GREEN, ROGER LANCELYN, *Andrew Lang: A Critical Biography* (Leicester: Edmund Ward, 1946).

GREENSLADE, WILLIAM, 'Fitness and the Fin de Siècle', in *Fin de Siècle/Fin du Globe: Fears and Fantasies of the Late Nineteenth Century*, ed. John Stokes (Basingstoke: Macmillan, 1992), 37–51.

GROSS, JOHN, *The Rise and Fall of the Man of Letters: English Literary Life Since 1800* (1969; repr. Harmondsworth: Penguin, 1991).

GROVES, DAVID, *James Hogg: The Growth of a Writer* (Edinburgh: Scottish Academic Press, 1988).

HART, FRANCIS RUSSELL, *The Scottish Novel: From Smollett to Spark* (Cambridge, Mass.: Harvard University Press, 1978).

HAVELOCK, ERIC A., *The Muse Learns to Write: Reflections on Orality and Literacy from Antiquity to the Present* (New Haven and London: Yale University Press, 1986).

HILLIER, ROBERT I., 'Folklore and Oral Tradition in Stevenson's South Seas Narrative Poems and Short Stories', *Scottish Literary Journal*, 14/2 (1987), 32–47.

HOMANS, MARGARET, *Bearing the Word: Language and Female Experience in Nineteenth-Century Women's Writing* (Chicago and London: University of Chicago Press, 1986).

HOUSTON, R. A., *Scottish Literacy and the Scottish Identity: Illiteracy and Society in Scotland and Northern England, 1600–1800* (Cambridge: Cambridge University Press, 1985).

HUGHES, GILLIAN, 'The Importance of the Periodical Environment in Hogg's Work for Chambers's Edinburgh Journal', in *Papers Given at the First Conference of the James Hogg Society*, ed. Gillian Hughes (Stirling: James Hogg Society, 1983), 40–8.

HUGHES, GILLIAN, 'The Spy and Literary Edinburgh', *Scottish Literary Journal*, 10/1 (1983), 42–53.

HUMES, WALTER M., and PATERSON, HAMISH M., (eds.), *Scottish Culture and Scottish Education 1800–1980* (Edinburgh: John Donald, 1983).

HUNTER, LYNETTE, 'A Rhetoric of Mass Communication: Collective or Corporate Public Discourse', in *Oral and Written Communication: Historical Approaches* ed. Richard Leo Enos (Newbury Park, Calif.: Sage Publications, 1990), 216–61.

HUTCHINSON, CHRIS, 'The Act of Narration: A Critical Survey of Some Speech-Act Theories of Discourse', *Journal of Literary Semantics*, 13 (1984), 3–35.

JACOBUS, MARY, 'The Art of Managing Books: Romantic Prose and the Writing of the Past', in *Romanticism and Language*, ed. Arden Reed (London: Methuen, 1984), 215–46.

JOHNSON, EDGAR, *Sir Walter Scott: The Great Unknown* (2 vols., London: Hamish Hamilton, 1970).

JORDAN, FRANK, 'Chrystal Croftangry: Scott's Last and Best Mask', *Scottish Literary Journal*, 7/1 (1980), 185–92.

KEATING, PETER, *The Haunted Study: A Social History of the English Novel 1875–1914* (London: Secker and Warburg, 1989).

KELLY, GARY, 'The Limits of Genre and the Institution of Literature: Romanticism between Fact and Fiction', in *Romantic Revolutions: Criticism and Theory*, ed. Kenneth R. Johnson *et al.* (Bloomington and Indianapolis: Indiana University Press, 1990), 158–75.

KERR, JAMES, *Fiction Against History: Scott as Storyteller* (Cambridge: Cambridge University Press, 1989).

KESTNER, JOSEPH, 'Linguistic Transmission in Scott: *Waverley, Old Mortality, Rob Roy*, and *Redgauntlet*', *Wordsworth Circle*, 8 (1977), 333–48.

KIDD, COLIN, *Subverting Scotland's Past: Scottish Whig Historians and the Creation of an Anglo-British Identity, 1689–c.1830* (Cambridge: Cambridge University Press, 1993).

KIELY, ROBERT, *Robert Louis Stevenson and the Fiction of Adventure* (Cambridge, Mass.: Harvard University Press, 1964).

KILROY, JAMES F., 'Narrative Techniques in *The Master of Ballantrae*', *Studies in Scottish Literature*, 5 (1967–8), 98–106.

KLANCHER, JON, *The Making of English Reading Audiences, 1790–1832* (Madison: University of Wisconsin Press, 1987).

KOESTENBAUM, WAYNE, *Double Talk: The Erotics of Male Literary Collaboration* (New York and London: Routledge, 1989).

KRISTEVA, JULIA, *Powers of Horror: An Essay on Abjection*, trans. Leon S. Roudiez (New York: Columbia University Press, 1982).

Lamont, Claire, 'Scott as Story-Teller: *The Bride of Lammermoor*', *Scottish Literary Journal*, 7/1 (1980), 113–26.

LASCELLES, MARY, *The Story-Teller Retrieves the Past: Historical Fiction and Fictitious History in the Art of Scott, Stevenson, Kipling and Some Others* (Oxford: Clarendon Press, 1980).

LETLEY, EMMA, *From John Galt to Douglas Brown: Nineteenth-Century Fiction and Scots Language* (Edinburgh: Scottish Academic Press, 1988).

LÉVY-BRUHL, LUCIEN, *Primitive Mentality*, trans. Lillian A. Clare (New York: Macmillan, 1923).

LOGUE, KENNETH J., *Popular Disturbances in Scotland 1780–1815* (Edinburgh: John Donald, 1979).

LORD, ALBERT, *The Singer of Tales* (Cambridge: Cambridge University Press, 1960).

LUMSDEN, ALISON, 'Postmodern Thought and the Fiction of R. L. Stevenson', in *Of Lion and of Unicorn: Essays on Anglo-Scottish Relations in Honour of Professor John MacQueen*, ed. R. D. S. Jack and Kevin McGinley (Edinburgh: Quadriga Publishing, 1993), 115–38.

LURIA, A. R., *Cognitive Development: Its Cultural and Social Foundations*, trans. Martin Lopez-Morillas and Lynn Solotaroff, ed. Michael Cole (Cambridge, Mass.: Harvard University Press, 1976).

LYON, JOHN, 'Half-Written Tales: Kipling and Conrad', in *Kipling Considered*, ed. Phillip Mallett (Basingstoke: Macmillan, 1989), 115–34.

McCRACKEN-FLESHER, CAROLINE, 'Thinking Nationally/Writing Colonially? Scott, Stevenson, and England', *Novel*, 24 (1991), 296–318.

MacGILLIVRAY, ALLAN, 'Exile and Empire', in *The History of Scottish Literature*, iii, *The Nineteenth Century*, ed. Douglas Gifford (Aberdeen: Aberdeen University Press, 1988, 411–27).

MACK, DOUGLAS, 'Hogg, Lockhart, and Familiar Anecdotes of Sir Walter Scott', *Scottish Literary Journal*, 10/1 (1983), 5–13.

—— 'James Hogg's Second Thoughts on *The Three Perils of Man*', *Studies in Scottish Literature*, 21 (1986), 167–75.

MACLEAN, MARIE, *Narrative as Performance: The Baudelairean Experiment* (London and New York: Routledge, 1988).

McLUHAN, MARSHALL, *The Gutenberg Galaxy: The Making of Typographical Man* (Toronto: University of Toronto Press, 1962).

—— *Counterblast* (London: Rapp and Whiting, 1970).

MACQUEEN, JOHN, *The Rise of the Historical Novel* (Edinburgh: Scottish Academic Press, 1989).

MANNING, SUSAN, 'Scott and Hawthorn: The Making of A

National Literary Tradition', in *Scott and his Influence*, ed. J. H. Alexander and David Hewitt (Aberdeen: Association for Scottish Literary Studies, 1983), 421–31.

—— *The Puritan-Provincial Vision: Scottish and American Literature in the Nineteenth Century* (Cambridge: Cambridge University Press, 1990).

MAYER, ROBERT, 'The Internal Machinery Displayed: *The Heart of Midlothian* and Scott's Apparatus for the Waverley Novels', *Clio*, 17 (1987), 1–20.

MERGENTHAL, SILVIA, *James Hogg: Selbstbilt und Bild: Zur Rezeption des 'Ettrick Shepherd'* (Frankfurt am Main: Peter Lang, 1990).

MILLGATE, JANE, *Walter Scott: The Making of the Novelist* (Edinburgh: Edinburgh University Press, 1984).

—— *Scott's Last Edition: A Study in Publishing History* (Edinburgh: Edinburgh University Press, 1987).

—— 'Making it New: Scott, Constable, Ballantyne, and the Publication of *Ivanhoe*', *Studies in English Literature 1500–1900*, 34 (1994), 795–811.

MITCHELL, W. J. T., 'Visible Language: Blake's Wond'rous Art of Writing', in *Romanticism and Contemporary Criticism*, ed. Morris Eaves and Michael Fischer (Ithaca, NY and London: Cornell University Press, 1986).

MURPHY, PETER T., *Poetry as an Occupation and an Art in Britain, 1760–1830* (Cambridge: Cambridge University Press, 1993).

NICOLAISEN, W. F. H., 'Scott and the Folk Tradition', in *Sir Walter Scott: The Long-Forgotten Melody*, ed. Alan Bold (London: Vision, 1983), 127–42.

OLSON, DAVID R., *The World on Paper: The Cognitive Implications of Writing and Reading* (Cambridge, Cambridge University Press, 1994).

——, TORRANCE, NANCY, AND HILDYARD, ANGELA (eds.), *Literacy, Language and Learning: The Nature and Consequences of Reading and Writing* (Cambridge: Cambridge University Press, 1985).

ONG, WALTER J., *Orality and Literacy: The Technologizing of the Word* (London and New York: Methuen, 1982).

ORR, MARILYN, 'Voices and Text: Scott the Storyteller, Scott the Novelist', *Scottish Literary Journal*, 16/2 (1989), 41–59.

OWEN, ALEX, *The Darkened Room: Women, Power and Spiritualism in Late Victorian England* (London: Virago, 1989).

PATTISON, ROBERT, *On Literacy: The Politics of the Word from Homer to the Age of Rock* (Oxford: Oxford University Press, 1982).

PETREY, SANDY, *Speech Acts and Literary Theory* (New York and London: Routledge, 1990).

Pittock, Murray G. H., *The Invention of Scotland: The Stuart Myth and Scottish Identity, 1638 to the Present* (Edinburgh: Edinburgh University Press, 1991).

Politi, Jina, 'Narrative and Historical Transformations in *The Bride of Lammermoor*', *Scottish Literary Journal*, 15/1 (1988), 70–81.

Radcliffe, David Hill, 'Ossian and the Genus of Culture', *Studies in Romanticism*, 31 (1992), 213–32.

Rajan, Tilottama, *The Supplement of Reading: Figures of Understanding in Romantic Theory and Practice* (Ithaca, NY and London: Cornell University Press, 1990).

Redekop, Magdalen, 'Trials, Dreams and Endings in the Tales of James Hogg', in *Papers Given at the Second James Hogg Society Conference*, ed. Gillian Hughes (Aberdeen: Association for Scottish Literary Studies, 1988), 32–41.

Robertson, Fiona, *Legitimate Histories: Scott, Gothic, and the Authorities of Fiction* (Oxford: Clarendon Press, 1994).

Saunders, Laurance James, *Scottish Democracy 1815–1840: The Social and Intellectual Background* (Edinburgh and London: Oliver and Boyd, 1950).

Scribner, Sylvia, and Cole, Michael, *The Psychology of Literacy* (Cambridge, Mass.: Harvard University Press, 1981).

Searle, John, *Expression and Meaning: Studies in the Theory of Speech Acts* (Cambridge: Cambridge University Press, 1979).

Shattock, Joanne, *Politics and Reviewers: The 'Edinburgh' and the 'Quarterly' in the Early Victorian Age* (London: Leicester University Press, 1989).

Shaw, Harry E., *The Forms of Historical Fiction: Sir Walter Scott and his Successors* (Ithaca, NY: Cornell University Press, 1983).

Shepherd, W. G., 'Fat Flesh: The Poetic Theme of *The Three Perils of Man*', *Studies in Hogg and his World*, 3 (1992), 1–9.

Sher, Richard B., *Church and University in the Scottish Enlightenment: The Moderate Literati of Edinburgh* (Edinburgh: Edinburgh University Press, 1985).

—— 'Percy, Shaw and the Ferguson "Cheat": National Prejudice in the Ossian Wars', in *Ossian Revisited*, ed. Howard Gaskill (Edinburgh: Edinburgh University Press, 1991), 207–45.

Shuman, Amy, *Storytelling Rights: The Uses of Oral and Written Texts by Urban Adolescents* (Cambridge: Cambridge University Press, 1986).

Simpson, Kenneth, 'Author and Narrator in *Weir of Hermiston*', in *Robert Louis Stevenson*, ed. Andrew Noble (London: Vision, 1983), 202–27.

—— *The Protean Scot: The Crisis of Identity in Eighteenth Century Scottish Literature* (Aberdeen: Aberdeen University Press, 1988).

SMOUT, T. C., *A History of the Scottish People, 1560–1830* (London: Collins, 1969).

—— *A Century of the Scottish People, 1830–1950* (London: Collins, 1986).

STAFFORD, FIONA, *The Sublime Savage: A Study of James Macpherson and the Poems of Ossian* (Edinburgh: Edinburgh University Press, 1988).

STOCK, BRIAN, *Listening for the Text: On the Uses of the Past* (Baltimore and London: Johns Hopkins University Press, 1990).

STONE, LAWRENCE, 'Literacy and Education in England, 1649–1900', *Past and Present*, 42 (1969), 69–139.

STRAWHORN, JOHN, 'Burns and the Bardie Clan', *Scottish Literary Journal*, 8/2 (1981), 5–23.

STREET, BRIAN V., *The Savage in Literature: Representations of 'Primitive' Society in English Fiction 1858–1920* (London and Boston: Routledge and Kegan Paul, 1975).

—— *Literacy in Theory and Practice* (Cambridge: Cambridge University Press, 1984).

SUTHERLAND, KATHRYN, 'Fictional Economies: Adam Smith, Walter Scott and the Nineteenth-Century Novel', *ELH* 54 (1987), 97–127.

TANNEN, DEBORAH (ed.), *Spoken and Written Language: Exploring Orality and Literacy* (Norwood, NJ: Ablex, 1982).

THOMPSON, JON, 'Sir Walter Scott and Madge Widfire: Strategies of Containment', *Literature and History*, 13 (1987), 188–99.

TRODD, ANTHEA, *Domestic Crime in the Victorian Novel* (London: Macmillan, 1989).

TULLOCH, GRAHAM, 'Imagery in "The Highland Widow"', *Studies in Scottish Literature*, 21 (1986), 147–57.

VEEDER, WILLIAM, and HIRSCH, GORDON (eds.), *'Dr Jekyll and Mr Hyde' After One Hundred Years* (Chicago and London: Chicago University Press, 1988).

VINCENT, DAVID, 'The Decline of the Oral Tradition in Popular Culture', in *Popular Culture and Custom in Nineteenth-Century England*, ed. Robert D. Storch (London and Canberra: Croom Helm, 1982), 20–47.

—— *Literacy and Popular Culture, England 1750–1914* (Cambridge: Cambridge University Press, 1989).

WALKOWITZ, JUDITH, *City of Dreadful Delight: Narratives of Sexual Danger in Late-Victorian London* (London: Virago, 1992).

WASWO, RICHARD, 'Story as Historiography in the Waverley Novels', *ELH* 47 (1980), 304–30.

WHITMORE, DANIEL, 'Bibliolatry and the Rule of the Word: A Study of Scott's *Old Mortality*', *Philological Quarterly*, 65 (1986), 243–62.

WILLIAMS, MERRYN, *Margaret Oliphant: A Critical Biography* (Basingstoke: Macmillan, 1986).

—— 'The Scottish Stories of Margaret Oliphant', in *The Literature of Place*, ed. Norman Page and Peter Preston (Basingstoke: Macmillan, 1993), 76–86.

WILSON, W. E., 'The Making of the "Minstrelsy": Scott and Shortreed in Liddesdale', *Cornhill Magazine*, 73 (1932), 266–83.

WILT, JUDITH, *Secret Leaves: The Novels of Walter Scott* (Chicago: University of Chicago Press, 1985).

WRIGHT, DAVID F., *The Bible in Scottish Life and Literature* (Edinburgh: Saint Andrew Press, 1988).

ZENINGER, PETER, 'The Ballad Spirit and the Modern Mind: Narrative Perspective in Stevenson's *Weir of Hermiston*', in *Studies in Scottish Literature: Nineteenth Century*, ed. Horst W. Drescher and Joachim Schwend (Frankfurt am Main: Peter Lang, 1987), 233–51.

Index